READING

the

Vampire

Slayer

THE NEW, UPDATED, UNOFFICIAL GUIDE

TO BUFFY AND ANGEL

revised and expanded second edition

EDITED BY
ROZ KAVENEY

TAURISPARKE
PAPERBACKS

*This is for Paule, again
and for Michael and Elizabeth*

Published in this revised and updated edition in 2004
by Tauris Parke Paperbacks, an imprint of I.B. Tauris & Co Ltd
6 Salem Road, London W2 4BU
175 Fifth Avenue, New York NY 10010
www.ibtauris.com

In the United States of America and in Canada distributed by
Palgrave Macmillan, a division of St Martin's Press
175 Fifth Avenue, New York NY 10010

First published in 2001 by Tauris Parke Paperbacks

ISBN 1 86064 984 X

A full CIP record for this book is available from the British Library
A full CIP record for this book is available from the Library of Congress

Library of Congress catalog card: available

Cover design by Graham Seamon
Typeset in Perpetua by Steve Tribe, Andover
Printed and bound in Great Britain by MPG Books Ltd, Bodmin

contents

acknowledgements

First of all, I have to thank all those with whom I have watched the shows, especially Paule. Tapes were lent to me or made for me by Grahame Kent, Oliver Morton and Nancy Hynes, Anna Chen and Charles Shaar Murray, Rob Hansen and Avedon Carol – Charles also explained *Star Trek* to me. All of my friends have been endlessly tolerant of my obsession with *Buffy* and *Angel* over the last three years – and I thank them all for this. Ian Shuttleworth, Marcus Rowlands and Chris Jordan gave me considerable technical support in watching the later seasons.

I want especially to thank Lisa Brown, with whom I was originally going to collaborate on this book and who had to drop out because of ill health; she suggested a number of contributors to me and acted as liaison with them. She and her partner Polly Richards have been a part of my intellectual support system on this project, along with all those mentioned above and the following – Tanja Kinkel, Farah Mendlesohn, Mary Gentle, Alex Stewart and the Battistas' gang. The late Lorna Sage encouraged me to write the book; Kate More made me explain large parts of the *Buffy* mythos to her; John Clute read a draft of my chapter and told me what I had failed to tell him.

Not everyone with whom I discuss the shows shares my high opinion of the later seasons. I owe many of my own insights to the articulacy with which they have put forward opinions from which I fundamentally dissent.

The Buffy Studies Conference, 'Blood Text and Fears' at UEA, was a wonderful occasion, for which the entire community of *Buffy* scholars owes thanks to everyone at UEA, most particularly Catherine Fuller, Scott Mackenzie, Carol O'Sullivan and Claire Thomson. The conference was also a chance to meet Rhonda Wilcox and David Lavery, whose *Fighting the Forces: What's at Stake in Buffy the Vampire Slayer* is an invaluable intellectual resource, as is their online journal *Slayage* (www.slayage.tv/Buffy).

My thanks and apologies are particularly due to Anne Millard Daugherty, Esther Saxey, Brian Wall, Dave West, Steve Wilson and Michael Zryd whose essays were so integral a part of the first edition of this book and which it was a real wrench to sacrifice to the dictates of updating.

The writers and staff of Mutant Enemy were particularly helpful during my visit to their studio. Jane Espenson and Steven S. DeKnight were especially helpful – see the interviews in the present volume – but Rebecca Rand Kirshner and Drew Goddard also said many illuminating things.

Philippa Brewster and Susan Lawson have been a joy to work with, as have all at I.B. Tauris.

Online, I have to thank the cix Buffy conferences, the late great Buffylist, JossBtVS, Joss's Stakehouse, BRAXS, the Buffista message board and IreUK_BAfans. In the Buffy and Angel slash communities, I have in particular to thank Dymphna, Dolores, Faithtastic, Jennyo, Kitsune, Lar and Te, but more generally the community associated with the UCSL list and chatroom – I would not have understood slash and fan fiction without you.

I want also to thank Jennifer Godwin for running the defunct BuffyNewsWire, Rayne for Buffylist and the now defunct Shooting Script Site, the team behind slayage.com and Little Willow for her smooth moderation of the JossBtVS list, all of whom have been personally helpful.

My thanks are also due to the DSA PR Agency, the 20th Century Fox London office, the United Talent Agency in LA, Pauline Montgomery and the committee of the Nocturnal3K Convention.

Resources

The online resources for researching matters related to *Buffy* and *Angel* are too plentiful to list; a few indispensable ones are listed below.

www.slayage.com is an almost unbelievably helpful site and updates service for casting, associative films, spoilers, picture galleries and so on.

Thanks to a cease and desist notice from 20th Century Fox, there is no longer a readily available online US source for scripts. Scripts for the first and second seasons are now available in book form from Pocket Books.

The episode guides Buffyguide.com (www.buffyguide.com) and The Screening Room, Home of the Angelguide (www.sanctuary. digitalspace.net/screening/screeningrm.html) are excellent sources of quotage and pop culture references.

Contributors

Roz Kaveney is a freelance literary journalist and publisher's advisory reader.

Justine Larbalestier is ARC Research Fellow in the Department of English at the University of Sydney.

Zoe-Jane Playdon is Head of Education at Kent, Surrey and Sussex Department of Postgraduate Medical and Dental Education, University of London.

Karen Sayer is Head of History at Trinity and All Saints College, University of Leeds.

Ian Shuttleworth reviews theatre for the *Financial Times*.

Jennifer Stoy is a doctoral candidate at UCLA, Santa Barbara.

Boyd Tonkin is Literary Editor of *The Independent*.

the regular, recurring or otherwise significant characters of

BUFFY and ANGEL

The Summers Family

Buffy Anne Summers, a Vampire Slayer, (S1–3) schoolgirl, (S4–5) student, (S6) burger flipper and (S7) school counsellor, daughter of **Joyce Summers**, a gallery owner, divorced from **Hank Summers**, a neglectful father.

Dawn Summers, (S5–7) schoolgirl, apparently Buffy's younger sister and Joyce and Hank's child, actually the Key, a mystical pattern of energy given human form and memories.

(S5–6) The **Buffybot**, a copy.

Sunnydale High School

1. Faculty

(S1) **Principal Flutie**, eaten by pupils and replaced by (S1–3) **Principal Snyder**, eaten by the Mayor at the end of Season Three.

Rupert Giles, known when young and wild as Ripper, (S1–3) school librarian and Buffy's watcher, (S2) in love with **Jenny Calendar**, (S1–2) computer teacher and technopagan, actually Janna, agent of the Kalderash tribe.

Various doomed teachers.

(S7) **Principal Robin Wood** of the rebuilt Sunnydale High.

2. Pupils

(S1–3) **Willow Rosenberg**, a computer nerd (later a witch) in love with **Xander Harris**, who is in love with Buffy.

Oz (Daniel Osbourne), a guitarist in Dingoes Ate My Baby and a werewolf, (S2–4) in love with Willow.

Cordelia Chase, cheerleader and queen bitch, (S2–3) girlfriend of Xander. Later (*Angel* all seasons) part of Angel Investigations.

Harmony Kendall, one of Cordelia's courtiers, latterly (S4/AS2) a vampire and girlfriend of Spike.

Jonathan Levinson, a shy unpopular short boy.

Devon, lead singer of Dingoes Ate My Baby.

Amy Madison, (S1–3) aspiring cheerleader, (S3–6) a rat, and a witch.

Larry, football captain and in the closet.

Tucker, a demonologist.

Various Cordettes, members of the swim team, stoners and variously doomed others.

(S7) **Cassie**, a doomed girl.

Amanda, a potential Slayer.

Various friends of Dawn.

The City of Sunnydale

Mayor Richard P. Wilkins the Third (also the First and the Second).

Deputy Mayor **Allan Finch**, a henchman.

Willie the Snitch, a bar owner.

Various doomed proprietors of the Magic Shop.

Rupert Giles, (S4) unemployed, (S5) proprietor of the Magic Shop, (S6–7) sleeping partner in the Magic Shop.

Xander Harris, (S4) salesman, ice-cream truck driver etc, (S5 onwards) builder, carpenter, foreman, site manager.

Various builders.

Slayers and The Watcher's Council

Kendra, (S2) a Vampire Slayer.

Faith, (S3–7) another Vampire Slayer.

Wesley Wyndham-Price, (S3) a Watcher, (*Angel* all seasons) part of or associated with Angel Investigations.

Quentin Travers, a senior Watcher.

Gwendolen Post, (S3) a renegade Watcher.

Various scholars and hit-men working for the Council.

The **First Slayer**, an avatar.

A Chinese Slayer.

Nikki Wood, a Slayer in 1970s New York.

(S7) Various **Potential Slayers**, including: Kennedy, Chloe, Eve, a Southerner Molly, a cockney Violet, Rona, Annabelle and Chao-An, another Chinese Slayer.

Sunnydale University and the Initiative

(S4) **Maggie Walsh**, head of the Psychology deparment, actually head of the covert Government research facility the Initiative, commanding officer of, and in love with, **Riley**, a teaching assistant and commando, in love with Buffy, commander of **Graham** and **Forrest**, posthumously in the service of **Adam**, an experiment.

Kathy, a roommate.

Parker Abrams, a seducer.

Willow Rosenberg, (S4 onwards) a student and Buffy's roommate

Tara McLay, a witch, (S4–6) in love with Willow.

Sunday, a cool vampire.

The Troika, aka the Geeks etc.

Warren Mears, a robot builder; **Jonathan Levinson**; **Andrew**, Tucker's brother.

April, Warren's robot girlfriend.

Katrina, Warren's human girlfriend.

Robots

Moloch, an incarnation.

Ted, a paterfamilias.

April.

The **Buffybot**.

Vampires and other supernatural entities connected with Sunnydale

(S1) **The Master** (of the Order of Aurelius), an ancient vampire whose acolytes include **Luke**, (S2) **Absalom**, (S1–2) **Colin**, the Anointed One, and **Darla**, the sire and lover of **Angelus** (formerly **Liam** and latterly **Angel** after regaining his soul, losing it and getting it back), in love with Buffy, sire of (S2, S5, AS2) **Drusilla**, sire of (S2 onwards) **Spike** (formerly **William**, a minor Victorian poet) and of Darla, staked by Angel (S1), resurrected as human by Wolfram and Hart (AS1), resired by Drusilla (AS2).

Dalton, a scholarly vampire in the service of Spike and Drusilla.

(AS3–4) **Connor**, Darla's more-or-less human son by Angel.

(S3) **Kakistos** (another ancient vampire).

Mr Trick, an African-American, computer-literate vampire, latterly in the service of the Mayor.

Machida, a snake demon.

Lurconis, another big snake.

Ethan Rayne, a sorcerer, Ripper's fellow-member in the demon-raising cult of Eyghon.

Whistler, a demon in the service of the Powers.

(S3 onwards) **D'Hoffryn**, master of vengeance demons.

Anyanka, patron demon of wronged women, latterly (S3) reduced to humanity as **Anya**, (S4–7) lover of **Xander**, redemonized briefly after he jilts her.

(S6–7) **Halfrek**, another vengeance demon.

(S5) **Glory**, a Hellgoddess imprisoned in the form of **Ben**, an intern at Sunnydale Hospital, and served by **Jinx**, **Dreg** and other minions.

(S6) The **Hellions**, a demon motor-cycle gang.

(S3, S7) **The First Evil**.

Various Harbingers in the service of the First Evil.

Caleb, a spoiled minister.

Los Angeles

1. Humans

(AS1–2) **Kate Lockley**, a policewoman.

Gunn, a vampire hunter, latterly (AS2–4) part of Angel Investigations.

(AS1) **Alana**, his sister.

Various members of his crew.

Fred, (AS2) a missing librarian, latterly (AS3–4) part of Angel Investigations.

(AS1–2) **David Nabbit**, a millionaire client and sponsor of Angel Investigations.

(AS4) **Gwen**, a mutant burglar.

2. Wolfram and Hart

Holland Manners, (AS1–2) head of Special Projects, boss of: **Lindsey McDonald**, latterly (AS2) in love with Darla; and **Lilah Morgan**, latterly (AS3–4) sexual partner of Wesley and (AS4) **Linwood**'s replacement; and (AS1) **Lee Manners**.

(AS2) **Nathan**, Holland's boss.

(AS3–4) **Gavin Park**, Lilah's rival.

(AS3–4) **Linwood**, Holland's replacement.

Files and Records

Holtz, an eighteenth-century vampire-hunter in the service of **Sahjhan**.

Justine, a vampire-hunter.

Various members of Holtz's gang.

3. Demons

(AS1) **Doyle**, a half-breed Brakken demon in the service of the **Powers That Be**, and part of Angel Investigations.

(AS2–3) **Merle**, a demon stoolpigeon.

(AS2) The **Host** – **Lorne** – a demon karaoke-club owner, the Pylaean also known as Krevlornswath of the Deathwok Clan, latterly (AS3–4) part of Angel Investigations.

The **Oracles**.

Sahjhan, a demon at an angle to time and space.

Skip, allegedly a servant of the Powers.

Jasmine, a goddess.

The **Beast**, a minion.

Pylaea

Landok, Lorne's cousin.

Numfar, Lorne's other cousin.

Lorne's mother.

Seth, a priest.

The **Groosalug** ('Groo') – a hero.

Various priests, demons, enslaved humans, free humans and members of Cordelia's entourage.

The Scooby Gang

Season One – **Buffy, Giles, Willow, Xander**.

Seasons Two and Three – **Buffy, Giles, Willow, Xander, Oz, Cordelia**.

Season Four – **Buffy, Giles, Willow, Xander, Oz** (prior to his departure), **Riley, Anya**.

Season Five – **Buffy, Giles, Willow, Xander, Riley** (prior to his departure), **Anya, Tara** and (effectively) **Spike**.

Season Six – **Buffy, Willow, Xander, Anya, Tara, Spike, Dawn** and (occasionally) **Giles**.

Season Seven – **Buffy, Willow, Xander, Anya, Spike, Dawn, Giles,** various Potential Slayers, **Principal Wood, Faith** and **Andrew.**

Angel Investigations

Angel, Doyle (until his death), **Cordelia, Wesley, Gunn, Fred, Connor** and **Lorne.**

The Alternate Universe of the Wish

1. White Hats

Giles, Oz, Larry, Nancy.

2. Vampires

The Master, Xander, Willow.

she saved the world. a lot

an introduction to the themes and structures of BUFFY and ANGEL

roz kaveney

I had never quite been seduced by a television show before.

There were British television drama series I liked, of course. Howard Schuman's *Rock Follies* had snappy one-liners and a few good songs. *Gangsters*, starting from the premise of multi-racial gang-warfare in 1970s Birmingham, kept inventively absurd twists and turns of the plot coming right up to the moment that the hero was killed by a Vietnamese martial artist who looked like W.C. Fields. *The Avengers*, in its Diana Rigg heyday, had visual style and sex appeal and a refusal to take itself entirely seriously.

Of American shows, *Twin Peaks* and *Babylon 5* both created their own worlds and endlessly recomplicated them; *Twin Peaks* also had weird music and an inventive lewdness in its writing. *The X-Files* had a great visual style, largely appropriated from Demme's *Silence of the Lambs*, and a central couple with a chemistry all the more intense for not being specifically sexual. *Due South*, though excessively cute, had a classy soundtrack that introduced me to some terrific blues bands and jazz singers like Holly Cole. *My So-Called Life* managed in its single season to say wonderful, passionate, real things about teen angst and mid-life crisis.

None of these ever became obsessions, because none of them did everything that I wanted a show to do.

Buffy the Vampire Slayer, though, had just about everything I wanted. Its central conceit – a bunch of high-school kids who fight supernatural evils that often map metaphorically over teenage preoccupations – was not automatically promising, but the comedy and the nightmarish horror kept brilliantly wrong-footing each other. There was romantic chemistry, both overt and subtextual, that scorched the screen. The show constantly tinkered with its own premises – important characters matured, died or became evil; our sense of how the supernatural order works is endlessly complicated. The writing was snappy – high-school bitches and centenarian vampires alike got lines like 'What is your childhood trauma?' or 'I'm love's bitch, but at least I'm man enough to admit it'. The fight scenes were some of the most energetic and kinetic on television; the show's directors acquired visual flair as they went. As the show continued, it became apparent that its use of foreshadowing and echo across seasons indicated a real commitment to, and respect for, the intelligence of its viewers – the finale of the seventh season, the show's ending, is full of references back that are none of them merely self-indulgences. As a critic, I found it just full enough of ambiguities and moments where poetic sense pre-empted literal sense that I could spend happy hours thinking them through – as will be apparent in some of what follows. And it had great live indie bands and a hyper-Romantic orchestral score. The spin-off show, *Angel*, was more of the same with extra noir and a more passionately perverse sexiness.

And I was not alone in my obsession: pre-teen fans buy posters of the shows, and middle-aged writers and intellectuals discuss it over dinner. The vast internet fandom includes both discussions – of spoilers, pedantic trivia and the shows' philosophical implications – and a large amount of fan fiction, much of it erotica that draws on the shows' polymorphously perverse subtext, and it is dominated by undergraduates and post-graduate students. Typically, people watch a few episodes and then go back to the beginning, watching videotapes in order to pick up the complex storylines.

I was lucky enough to start watching at the beginning and experience the conviction that this was something special slowly and as a personal discovery. I had written about revisionist fantasy,[1] fantasy that plays with standard genre tropes and makes different readings of them stand both for extra-textual real-world concerns and as a source of delight, so I knew pretty much from the start what I was watching. Sitting with friends watching and re-watching the shows on video made it clear that they were complex texts, the conceptual and verbal wit of the surface, the sheer loopy romanticism of the emotional plots and visceral excitement of the action plots, the range of cultural references, high and pop, sustaining deep readings of the shows' underlying implied discussion of feminism, religion, politics and so on. The amount of offence they caused to the Religious Right, oddly more for their sexual libertarianism than for their inventively heretical treatment of theology, was also a point in their favour.

One crucial factor for me was the impressive performances of the large central stock company – by the fourth season, the shows' principal creato, Joss Whedon, could trust them with a script, 'Hush' (4.10), in which for half an hour or more they never uttered a word – fairy-tale monsters, the Gentlemen, having stolen the voices of everyone in town. Later, in 'Once More With Feeling' (6.7), he obliged them to perform in a musical and most of them managed to turn themselves into song-and-dance performers for the occasion. It is also worth remarking that, even for a Hollywood series, the cast are for the most part staggeringly beautiful.

Above and beyond all this, though, there was, particularly from the second season of *Buffy* onwards, a sense of the shows as not merely sharp individual episodes. Joss Whedon, the shows' creator and writer and director of many of its finest episodes, gradually built a stable of writers around him who fitted in with, and contributed to, his evolving vision; interviews indicate that the core writers have come to see the show as a collective enterprise with Whedon as its benign dictator. Perhaps because of this working method, the show developed its particular strengths, its complex clustering of characters and the solid formalized architecture of its seasons.

Definitions

Briefly, then, *Buffy* is a show which ran for seven years; it generated one successful spin-off, *Angel*, which has run for four years and has been commissioned for a fifth. It may yet generate further spin-offs; two that have been mentioned but not yet come to fruition are one dealing with Buffy's mentor and Watcher, Giles, and the other an animated recap and expansion of the show's first year. For a while, a spin-off dealing with the other Slayer, Faith, was in negotiation as an immediate successor to *Buffy*, but this fell through, apparently because the actress, Eliza Dushku, was unhappy with the proposed show's picaresque format.

Buffy is the Chosen One, a teenage Californian called, upon the death of her predecessor, to cull vampires[2] and combat a variety of supernatural evils that congregate at the Hellmouth in Sunnydale. In the course of the show's seven years, she has built up an impressive group of friends and allies, protected her class at Sunnydale High, averted six or more apocalypses and coped with a variety of personal traumas, including, at the end of Seasons One and Five, her self-sacrificing deaths and her return from Heaven at the start of Season Six. Finally, and satisfyingly, she changes the rules of her situation and shares the Slayer power with all young women capable of it.

Angel takes a selection of *Buffy* characters – Buffy's lover, Angel, the vampire cursed with a soul, a conscience and the memory of the atrocities he committed when he did not have them; Wesley, the Watcher who replaced Giles and badly failed both Buffy and her dark shadow, the rogue Slayer, Faith, through cowardice and prissiness; Cordelia, queen bitch of Sunnydale High – and puts them to work fighting evil in Los Angeles and elsewhere. Most of the good characters in *Angel* have something to atone for; though *Buffy* has its fair share of moral ambiguity, *Angel* is so noir that almost everything takes place in shades of grey. By Season Four, that sense of moral ambiguity has extended not merely to the central characters – they have been badly betrayed by their supposed supernatural employers, the Powers That Be, and have entered into a pragmatic alliance with their nemesis, the evil law firm of Wolfram and Hart.

Both shows take place in something like real time – the first three seasons of *Buffy* were closely tied to the rhythms of the American high-school year, and latterly Buffy and her friends Willow and Tara attend UC Sunnydale. The human characters have accordingly aged in something unusually close to real time for an American television show that is not formally a soap opera.

Character Clusters

In most genre series, the relationships between the central core of characters are predetermined by status structures within an organization; the characters of the various *Star Trek* series are officers of Star Fleet, say, while Mulder and Scully are Special Agents of the FBI and have roles in a hierarchy standardly represented by Skinner as their immediate boss, but ultimately determined by an elaborate and corrupt system. Though her original relationship with Giles, her Watcher, is supposed to operate within a hierarchical structure laid down by the Watcher's Council, Buffy's relationships are for the most part determined by emotional structures – Giles is eventually sacked by the Council for developing 'a father's love' for her.

These emotional structures have more in common with soap opera relationships than with most genre series – an original core of characters, which eventually becomes known as the Scooby gang,[3] forms in the first episode around a mixture of affinity, attraction and mutual protection against both supernatural evil and high school. Giles is an adult but, as a rather stuffy Englishman adrift in Southern California, is fairly vulnerable; Willow and

Xander have already attained pariah-hood as bright geek and the class clown who hangs out with her. Buffy passes the test of coolness imposed on her by Cordelia, but chooses to hang out with Willow and Xander and Giles instead of joining Cordelia's coterie. Gradually, most especially in 'Out of Mind, Out of Sight' (1.11), Cordelia reveals the angst and loneliness that lies behind her pursuit of popularity.

There is a strong element of family in all this – Buffy's mother, Joyce, may be the queen of denial about her daughter's nocturnal activities, but, compared to Xander and Willow's respectively abusive and neglectful parents, she is a paragon. When she dies in 'The Body' (5.16), it is clear that all of the younger Scoobies, not just Buffy and her sister Dawn, have lost a parent – the thousand-year old ex-demon Anya is as affected as any. Giles, of course, has lost a friend and – briefly and in extraordinary circumstances – lover; in 'Forever' (5.17), he drinks to Joyce's memory by himself and listens to the Cream track they once listened to together.

The original quartet of Buffy, Giles, Willow and Xander acquires Angel, Jenny, Oz and Cordelia as partners, all of whom are important for a time and then depart – Angel and Cordelia to become in their turn the core of a new group in a spin-off series. Joining up with the Scoobies demands the sacrifice of what they were before – Angel definitively breaks with his past by staking Darla, his vampire lover and sire; Cordelia quarrels, ultimately irrevocably, with her clique of snobbish Valley girls; loving Giles places Jenny in a conflict of interests between the Scoobies and her gypsy clan.

In the latter part of *Buffy* Season Three, Cordelia continues to help the Scoobies, but is endlessly malignant in her verbal treatment of them; Xander finds out about her poverty and uses his savings to buy her a Prom dress – this moment of grace and her equally graceful acceptance is a surprisingly touching closure. At the end of Season Three, she fights uncomplicatedly by their side, shares the moment of peace after the destruction of the Mayor and departs for LA, hardly ever to speak to them again.

Oz is the exception here – his existing relationship with his band remains the same – but becoming a werewolf and being put down a year are serious enough disruptions to his life, even if not caused by his tie-up with the Scoobies. It is perhaps significant that, of the four, he is the one least caught up in hierarchies – his group Dingoes Ate My Baby does not even have roadies. Vampirism, as we see it in the first series, is very precisely seen as a hierarchy in which the Master's dominance is endlessly enforced by terrible and counter-productive punishments of those who fail him; the Cordettes are seen by those they victimize socially as almost equally terrifying, like the KGB 'if they cared a lot about shoes'.

In due course, in Season Four, Buffy is involved with Riley, Xander with Anya and Willow with Tara; Giles's relationship with the rather shadowy Olivia never really amounts to much. Significantly, all three are refugees from hierarchy of one sort or another – Riley from the Initiative, Anya from the demon dimension ruled callously by D'Hoffryn and Tara from a dysfunctional family whose males rule by lies. Riley leaves Buffy and the show halfway through Season Five; after developing a fixation on illicit 'suckjobs' from vampire whores, he returns to the Army. In a far more gradual process, the vampire Spike becomes the Scoobies' reluctant ally and Buffy's lover and friend.

The core group in *Angel* is slightly different, since what unites them is in large part exile, penance and redemption. Angel has no family, because he is an immortal and because he killed them; he has left Sunnydale in order to reduce the risk posed by his relationship with Buffy – the perfect happiness caused by their one night of love broke his curse and returned him to evil.

Cordelia's family lost their money shortly after her traumatic break-up with Xander and she is aware of a need to atone for her earlier snobbery and callousness; she is also exiled by her desire to succeed as an actress and her almost complete lack of talent. Doyle failed in his marriage and allowed a group of his demon kin to be massacred by the Scourge; he bequeaths to Cordelia his role as Angel's link to the Powers That Be and the blinding headaches that go with the visions.

Of the later additions that follow Doyle's death, Wesley is belatedly growing up out of his earlier persona as effete cowardly fop and coming to terms with his abusive treatment by his father, a senior Watcher; Gunn has fought vampires all his life to protect his sister, only to have to stake her when she is captured and turned. Physicist Fred has normal and loving parents, but was shanghaied away from normality to enslavement in a demon dimension, leaving her with shaky sanity. The high camp, demon club-owner Lorne is a refugee from a dimension full of noisy warriors like his family; when Angel Investigations gets his club destroyed for the third time, he settles into their hotel base, the Hyperion, as babysitter and therapist. This dark disturbed group nonetheless becomes a family of sorts, with Angel first serving as the parent who cooks breakfast and then as the bad father who neglects his family for other loyalties.

When Angel acquires a literal family, in the shape of Connor, his son by Darla, it disrupts the group. Angel briefly diverts the group's attention from their mission to making money for the infant's college fund. More importantly, Wesley defects from the group in an attempt to save Connor from his prophesied fate – death at Angel's hands. When Connor returns, it is as an adult who has been reared in a demon dimension by Angel's worst enemy – he is incapable of trusting Angel and his need to find a place in the world leads him to terrible actions. In the end, Angel has to rearrange reality so that Connor has an entirely different life with an entirely normal family and history – the cost is that he will never know his son again. At the beginning of Season Four, the trapped Angel dreams of Connor and Angel Investigations as a family who are together in a way they will never again be; at the end of the season, he watches as Connor toasts his new family.

The affair between Wesley and Lilah Morgan, Wolfram and Hart's most effective persecutor of Angel, complicates matters still further; the charming but irredeemable Lilah is not part of the family even when, in 'Calvary' (A4.12), she takes refuge with them. Yet, by the end of the season, she has become the crucial figure in their new relationship with the firm. It remains to be seen how this, and the presence of the resurrected Spike, will play out the theme of family in Season Five.

The group of evil vampires we have come to know best were also, in their way, a family – and another one in which Angel is seen as untrustworthy patriarch. If this seems almost too human a trait, it is part of the package of human pleasures that Angelus and Darla chose, along with each other, when they walked away from the Master and his ascetic Order of Aurelius in 'Darla' (A2.7). Their objective in driving Drusilla mad and turning her was pure malice, but their relationship with the resulting vampire Drusilla is a blend of (highly incestuous) parental love, sadomasochism, amused tolerance and genuine affection. When Drusilla in her turn sires Spike, the older generation find him entirely infuriating; Spike's relationship to them is a mixture of mockery, hatred and adulation – when he belatedly finds out, in 'School Hard' (2.3), that Angel has become ensouled, his disillusionment is bitter.[4] Just as Drusilla is both Darla's grandchild and her mother, Spike is her child, her lover and her brother; vampire families, after all, are demonic.

Spike's subsequent status as a quasi-Scooby and Buffy's suitor could thus be explained without the assumption that he is necessarily originally engaged in any process of redemption.[5] As we saw in a poignant moment in 'Pangs' (4.8), when he stared in at a vampire feast like a Dickens orphan, Spike needs a family to belong to. Buffy has enough darkness in her that he finds her attractive; when he talks of family and friends as keeping her from her death wish, in 'Fool For Love' (5.7), the occasionally suicidal and often foolhardy Spike is also talking about himself.

Significantly, his other major relationship is with Harmony, a vampire, formerly Cordelia's disloyal lieutenant and an abject failure at forming her own gang. His tragedy, and that of Darla and Drusilla, is that they are capable of passionate love, but not of the broader emotional register that goes with it on a quotidian level. Even when

Spike endeavours to change for love of Buffy, and because the chip planted in his head by government surgeons prevents him harming humans, his obsessive love is so caught up with violence that their first sexual encounter grows out of a vicious fight.

This group of vampires serves as one of the major focuses of the show's revisionist treatment of fantasy themes – the other principal ones being the figures of the Slayers themselves, and of the group of variously empowered humans that surround them, and the various one-off monsters and season villains. Spike and Angel, the latter posing as his earlier evil self, make jokes about Anne Rice vampires with tortured consciences – ironically given what later happens to both of them.

There is a neat joke across the series about the social construction versus essentialism debate – the Master is evil because he regards it as his ascetic religious duty to be so, the younger Darla and Angelus out of a selfish aristocratic hedonism, Spike purely because he is a predator. The precise form evil takes recapitulates medievalism, the *ancien régime* and cut-throat capitalism.

Just as these three groups exist partly in opposition to each other, their memberships partly overlapping, so the relationships between individual characters are made even more complex by a set of shadow-double relationships. Characters are alternate versions of each other – Buffy and Cordelia (Buffy before her powers), Buffy and Faith (Buffy without family and friends) – or recapitulate aspects of each other's careers – Angel and Faith. Angel and Spike are not only related through their ties to Drusilla and Buffy, but also by being respectively dark and blond and by being originally called Liam and William. One of the reasons why the poet William becomes the streetfighter Spike is because the roisterer Liam has become the moody sadistic aesthete Angelus, and the role of family intellectual is taken.[6]

Similarly, in *Angel*, Cordelia is compared and contrasted with Lilah – 'I was you. Only with better shoes' – and Darla, both in their emotional entanglements and in their relationship with death, damnation and salvation. The musical themes associated with the African-American Gunn in the heavily composed score are closely related to those motifs associated with Angel.

The regular use of doppelganger plots – Willow and her evil twin in 'Doppelgangland' (3.16), the two Xanders in 'The Replacement' (5.3), the Faith/Buffy body switch in 'Who Are You?' (4.16), Spike's acquisition of a Buffy robot for sexual purposes in 'Intervention' (5.18) – is only one special case of the ways in which these patterns of doubling and opposition are used to enhance the show's exploration of moral ambiguity, especially in the context of the show's almost obsessional reflexivity. One example will serve here – in the aftermath of Buffy's sleeping with Angel in 'Innocence' (2.14), he experiences agony and turns into Angelus, whereas in the aftermath of sleeping with Darla in 'Reprise' (A2.15), he experiences a similar agony but does not; both women, deeply confused by the behaviour of the man they love, utter the same line: 'Was I… was it… not good?'

Joss Whedon has said, partly in response to erotic fan fiction, much of it dealing with imagined lesbian and gay relationships between the characters: 'All the relationships on the show are sort of romantic (Hence the BYO Subtext principle).' Other shows, such as those in the *Star Trek* franchise, have carefully avoided the implication that characters not formally in a relationship are attracted to each other; *Buffy* and *Angel* have consistently implied both heterosexual and homosexual relationships outside the show's official canon.

In a dream, in 'Restless' (4.22), Willow writes out Sappho's invocation to the goddess on Tara's back, foreshadowing the eventual estrangement of these two lovers. Xander flirts with every woman on the show and has, at one time or another, homosexual panic about every male in it – his reaction to the vast underground military base under Sunnydale when Buffy takes him there is: 'I totally get it – can I have sex with Riley too?' Darla, necking with the ambivalently villainous lawyer Lindsey, says: 'It's not me you want to screw, it's him [Angel].' When Cordelia threatens Lilah, the femme fatale gives her a sultry look and says: 'Are you trying to turn me on?' And so on – it is almost easier to list character pairings in the show where there is no sexual chemistry than those where there is.

All of the large core central characters have personal story arcs that develop consistently across time. Buffy becomes steadily more self-centred – a habit of sacrificing yourself to save the world is not necessarily good for the character – before having to take care of her sister, and believing herself always to have had a sister, changes her. Willow loses her shyness and blossoms, losing the edge of resentment that, in 'Something Blue' (4.9), had made her powers dangerous. In Season Five, the fight with Glory forces her to become so powerful that her power becomes explicitly amoral – unlike the less powerful, more focused Tara, she is not interested in limits. The unacademic Xander gradually acquires a sense of his own worth. Envy and (by strong implication) unrequited and unspoken lust for Buffy drive Faith to evil for a time. Cordelia gets so many moral lessons, particularly once she takes over from Doyle as Angel's personal clairvoyant, that it is tempting to suppose that the Powers take an especial interest in her. And indeed one of them does – a distinctly predatory one.

Characters who do not fall into the central clusters, or the hierarchies which oppose them, are nonetheless often given a complex life of their own. The vampire wannabe Chanterelle in 'Lie To Me' (2.7) is just as drippy when seen as the feckless street-person Lily in 'Anne' (3.1) but grows into Anne, the savvy hard-bitten social activist of 'Blood Money' (A2.12) and 'The Thin Dead Line' (A2.14). Jonathan starts as an unnamed Sunnydale High student, evolves into a comic presence, becomes a central figure in one episode, 'Earshot' (3.18), and entirely dominates another show, even taking over the title credits, 'Superstar' (4.17). In Season Six, he becomes one of the threesome of villains who add to the misery of Buffy's adult life before becoming a figure of real pathos in Season Seven and dying after a charming speech about repentance. This is partly a matter of the writers responding to actors' performances and developing characters that work, partly the shows' fascination with human and inhuman personality.

Season Structure

Most American TV drama series, especially those with strong genre elements, have an anthology format – characters apart from the regular cast hardly ever recur and the stories concerning them do not have to be told in any particular order. For purely practical and pragmatic reasons, any overall story arc takes a back seat to ensuring that there are strong guest star episodes at the time of contract renewals – the November and February sweeps. An important commercial objective has traditionally been to run for enough seasons that syndication and endless reruns are possible; release on VHS and DVD has only become a commercial objective comparatively recently.

Star Trek: Voyager or *The X-Files* have rather stronger story arcs – the attempt by the Voyager to return from the far reaches of the galaxy to its home in the Alpha Quadrant in spite of its enemies; Mulder and Scully's gradual uncovering of the conspiracy between government and aliens crops up at regular intervals in the course of a season. Nonetheless, the major premises of both produce single-episode structures as a matter of course – *Voyager* finds a world or region of space that poses a threat or has a problem, and resolves the issue; Mulder and Scully investigate a case, discover something bizarre and deal with it. Individual episodes only occasionally have long-term continuity consequences, except for season endings, which may well culminate in a cliffhanger.

Babylon 5, particularly in its later seasons with the Shadow War and the overthrow of the Earth dictatorship, had a very strong story arc indeed, with some elements that ran throughout the five seasons; quite minor story elements occasionally turned out to be significant. Unfortunately, the decision, subsequently revoked, to end with the fourth season meant that a number of these storylines had their climaxes somewhat rushed. New storylines – the Drakh virus for example – which lacked some of the same mythic force, had to be invented for the eventual fifth season and the abortive spin-off series, *Crusade*, and were left hanging when the latter was cancelled.

Buffy the Vampire Slayer and *Angel* get much of their strength as series from their stronger than usual season construction. The seven seasons of *Buffy the Vampire Slayer* share a structural pattern as coherent as the statement, development, second statement, recapitulations and coda of sonata form. The extent to which each episode is crucial to this pattern varies: those which deal with a one-off monster or other menace generally include some elements from the main story arc, and from the romantic and other character-driven subplots. The seven seasons are self-contained in terms of their central plots; the story arcs that continue from season to season being for the most part those dealing in character development.

Buffy Season Openings

In the first four season premieres, Buffy's status as the Slayer is affirmed or reaffirmed by her arrival in or return to Sunnydale. In 'Welcome to the Hellmouth' (1.1), she arrives at Sunnydale High determined to live down the events of her life in LA (which both are and are not those of the film *Buffy The Vampire Slayer*).[7] In 'When She Was Bad' (2.1), she comes back from an extended stay with her father, Hank, in LA. In 'Anne', she is working under an assumed name as a waitress in an unnamed metropolis and only returns to Sunnydale at the episode's end. In 'The Freshman' (4.1), she arrives at UC Sunnydale and finds herself a fish out of water.

In each of these episodes, Buffy has to reaffirm her self and her Slayerhood. In 'Welcome to the Hellmouth', for example, she is appalled to discover that Giles, the School Librarian at Sunnydale High is her new Watcher and that Sunnydale is even more infested with the supernatural than LA was, but resists the idea of taking up Slayerhood again. It is only when her new friends Willow, Xander and Jesse come under threat from Darla, Luke and the other servants of the Master that she fully recommits herself to the fight.

As a series, as well as season, premiere, 'Welcome to the Hellmouth' is a virtuoso introduction of the core of central characters – Giles, Xander and Willow, and to a lesser extent Angel and Cordelia, in her role as comic foil rather than the more interesting character she subsequently becomes. Indeed, one shocking piece of trickery is the introduction of Jesse along with the others as if he were important and not to be first turned and then dusted in the following episode. Importantly for the world of Buffy as a whole, though not for Season One, one of the two first characters we meet is Darla, who allows a male pick-up to tempt her inside Sunnydale High and then despatches him; the show announces in its first minutes that this is not a show where, as would be the stock assumption in slasher movies, a cute blonde with loose morals is necessarily going to be a victim.[8]

In 'When She Was Bad', Buffy is still recovering from the trauma of her death at the hands of the Master in 'Prophesy Girl' (1.12) and behaves, as Willow says, 'like a complete b-i-t-c-h', using Xander to make Angel jealous and failing to understand until it is almost too late that her friends are in mortal danger. Here, it is not her vocation as Slayer, but her particular strength as Slayer – loyalty to friends and family – that she has neglected; as the vampire Spike points out in 'Fool For Love', it is her commitments that have so far muffled the death wish she shares with earlier Slayers.

'Anne' takes place in the aftermath of 'Becoming Part Two' (2.22), when Buffy was expelled from school and home and had to send Angel to Hell to save the world from the demon Acathla; traumatized by this, she runs away to LA and works, under her second name, as a waitress. The street-person, Lily, whom Buffy knew and saved in Lily's earlier incarnation as vampire-wannabe Chanterelle in 'Lie To Me', recognizes the Slayer and gets her involved with the disappearance of her boyfriend. When the demonic social worker Ken abducts them to a Hell where they are specifically condemned to anonymity, Buffy reclaims her name and calling and frees the slaves, iconically seizing a hammer and a sickle-shaped axe.[9]

After her return to Sunnydale, however, it takes the whole of the next episode – 'Dead Man's Party' (3.2) – before she is entirely at her ease with her mother and her friends and it is only at the end of 'Faith, Hope and Trick' (3.3) that she tells Giles and Willow exactly what happened between her and Angelus/Angel and lets go of the sorrow she has been repressing. She goes back to Angel's mansion and leaves the claddagh ring – an Irish token of friendship – he gave her there. It is never entirely clear whether his return from Hell is triggered by this act of renunciation, by the emotional resignation of which it is the trigger, by her earlier harrowing of Hell or merely happens at this point for the inscrutable reasons of the Powers That Be.

'The Freshman' sees Buffy and Willow arrive at UC Sunnydale, where Buffy is at sea. She is 'off her game' and fighting 'like a girl', sure signs of supernatural skulduggery – we find in the following episode 'Living Conditions' (4.2) that her roommate Kathy has been stealing her soul. The super-cool campus bitch vampire Sunday mocks Buffy's clothes and hair; it is when her mockery extends to smashing the parasol given to Buffy by Sunnydale High students as Class Protector in 'The Prom' (3.20) that Buffy summons the will to fight back and win.

The partial exception is 'Buffy vs. Dracula' (5.1), in which a relaxed summer on the local beach and in the arms of her boyfriend Riley Finn, only marginally punctuated by rising from their bed to go out and kill some routine vampires, is broken by a change in the weather and the arrival of the Count himself. Here the return is to the seriousness of her vocation – she realizes that she needs to understand the darker aspects of being a Slayer, 'What you are, what you are to become' (the cryptic remark made to her in turn by the dream version of Tara and by Dracula) and persuades Giles to return to his original status as her Watcher at a point where he is considering leaving Sunnydale for good. At its end, the episode also introduces Buffy's younger sister Dawn; earlier explicit statements that Buffy is an only child and the 'flashy Gypsy tricks' of Dracula indicate that all is not entirely as it seems.

At the start of Season Six – 'Bargaining Parts One and Two' (6.1, 6.2) – Buffy is dead and in her grave and we see, as we did in 'Anne', the Scoobies trying to take her place, rather more effectively now given their own greater skills and the assistance of Spike and a rebuilt Buffybot. All they can do, though, is manage a holding action with disasters mundane and supernatural constantly averted – the Buffybot's genial cluelessness is something that may go down well at PTA meetings, but she has to be kept from conversations with Buffy's father and eventually malfunctions in front of a vampire who guesses the truth.

All of the Scoobies have their own private worries. Giles feels he no longer has a purpose now his Slayer is dead, and leaves in the course of 'Bargaining Part One', while Xander is already having second thoughts about his engagement to Anya, which he is still keeping a secret. Willow is getting more caught up in magic – she directs vampire hunts by telepathy to an extent that Xander for one finds intrusive. Her eventual spell to resurrect Buffy involves some actions – the sacrifice of a fawn – that she knows to be sufficiently morally equivocal that she avoids telling her friends, and most of all her lover Tara, about them. Spike is obsessed with his failure to save Buffy: later, in 'After Life' (6.3) when she asks how long she was gone, he can tell her to the day and spent every night going over his failure – 'Every night I saved you'. He cannot bear to look at the Buffybot he had created and which now acts as a constant rebuke. Meanwhile, Dawn's loneliness takes the form of secretly cuddling this image of her dead sister while it recharges.

The Buffybot's failure brings demon bikers to raid Sunnydale – they interrupt Willow's spell and Buffy returns to life inside her coffin at the end of 'Bargaining Part One'. In a stunning reversal, she has to crawl out of her grave as if she were a vampire and is so traumatized that she remains mute for much of the episode, wandering around a burning Sunnydale as if it were Hell. She saves her friends from the demons and climbs back up the tower from which she made her death plunge – this particular recapitulation of something we saw earlier has a sublime feeling of the utterly wrong about it. Dawn follows her and puts herself in peril on the rickety structure in order to force Buffy to save her rather than kill herself – in 'The Gift' (5.22), of course, she saved Dawn by killing herself. This sense of wrongness pervades the whole episode and much of the season – it is with a dull thud of recognition, not surprise, that we discover at the end of 'After Life', that Willow has mistakenly dragged Buffy back, not from the Hell dimension she feared, but from Heaven.

'Lessons', the opening episode of Season Seven, is much more like the earlier season's openers in its lightness of tone, as Buffy teaches Dawn the fundamentals of Slayage and helps her survive a zombie attack in the basement of the rebuilt Sunnydale High. In England, the chastened and repentant Willow is being instructed in a gentler magic by Giles and his friends in the coven. Yet there is a darker side to the episode – a girl is chased and killed in Istanbul, Halfrek warns Anya that D'Hoffryn is unhappy with her productivity in the vengeance business and Spike's new soul is clearly driving him mad. Finally, in the basement, he is taunted by something that changes into previous villains – Warren, Glory, Adam, the Mayor, Drusilla, the Master – and then into Buffy herself. Something bad is coming and, in the end, the false Buffy says, it is all about power.

'It's all about power' – this is a line we have heard several times. Buffy uses it when teaching Dawn, as she has earlier used it when mocking the Watcher's Council in 'Checkpoint' (5.12). Dark Willow uses it to mock Buffy when they fight in 'Two To Go' (6.21) – and now it comes from what is not in fact Buffy's mouth yet again. Interestingly, the opening titles for Season Seven end with a shot of this evil false Buffy, as Season Six's end with the more benign fake of the Buffybot, where earlier seasons' titles ended with the doomed Buffy of 'Prophecy Girl' or the heroic Buffy of 'Anne'. In these two last seasons, we are told, all old certainties are up for grabs and things are not always what they seem. And when we get to the end of Season Seven, to 'Chosen' (7.22), power and the wisdom to use it properly is indeed what the entire season, and each of the previous ones, has been about.

Big Bads and Emotional Traumas

Early in each of the first five seasons, we get what appears to be a conclusive statement about the nature of the conflict and adversary Buffy is going to be involved with as the season's major story arc; then, at about the halfway mark, there is some radical revision of the rules of that conflict. In each season, and particularly in its second half, there is also a more abstract enemy to be dealt with – an emotional atmosphere that pervades and enhances the storyline. These plot twists often coincide with the February sweeps or precede them by few enough episodes to have raised the emotional temperature to fever pitch in time for them. Seasons Six and Seven honour this pattern more complexly while breaching them in detail.

Season One

In 'Never Kill a Boy on the First Date' (1.5), the Master, deprived of his massive aide, Luke, by Buffy in 'The Harvest' (1.2), creates the Anointed One; Buffy and Giles fail to realize that the Anointed One is not the crazed fundamentalist they kill in the local crematorium, but a small child; in 'Angel' (1.7), we discover that the mysterious ally to whom Buffy has already started to feel herself attracted, is himself a vampire, albeit one with a soul who is struggling with his past – his old vampire lover Darla – and his vampiric urges to side with Good.

'Angel' is also the point at which the series starts to explore the areas of moral ambiguity that have become its hallmark. Season One is about letting go of the illusions of childhood, the sense that the world is a safe place in which one's actions have no serious consequences. Cordelia starts her long journey out of entirely narcissistic solipsism when one of the victims of her sharp tongue turns on her violently in 'Out of Mind, Out of Sight'. In 'Prophesy Girl', Xander realizes that not only can he not have Buffy, he cannot expect Willow to date him as his fallback. Childhood fears become deadly in 'Nightmares' (1.10) and Buffy has to come to terms with the strong possibility that what she has had of her life may be all there is – 'I'm sixteen years old. And I don't want to die': acceptance of the fact of death is a definitive end of childhood illusions. Significantly, it is her rejected suitor Xander, not her idealized beloved Angel, who confounds prophesy by bringing her back from death with CPR (and by doing so, incidentally, changing destiny – see the demon Whistler's remarks in 'Becoming Part Two'); life is as it is, not as we might wish it to be.[10]

Season Two

The arrival in Sunnydale of Spike and Drusilla in 'School Hard' and their irritated despatch of 'The Annoying One' indicate that a different kind of evil has come to Sunnydale; where the Master was concerned with bringing about mayhem and Apocalypse as a religious duty, Spike does so out of pure pragmatism, Drusilla out of insane whim – 'From now on,' Spike says, 'there's going to be a lot less ritual and a lot more fun.' No audience could be seduced by the Nosferatu-like Master, but the bleached blond punk Spike and Gothish Drusilla brought evil in the show its own glamour, though not as much as we find in the second half of the season when, after taking Buffy's virginity in 'Surprise' (2.13), Angel loses his soul in 'Innocence' (2.14) and reverts to being the charming murderous monster Angelus. Where Spike's determination to kill Buffy is purely a matter of self-preservation, Angelus hates her because she is what his ensouled self loved. He determines to destroy her a little at a time, just as he did Drusilla in the days when she was still human, eventually deciding to destroy the world primarily as a piece of spite against her.

Angelus is not only dangerous in and of himself; he is the principal representative of the menace posed by love gone rancid, a theme variously picked up in 'Bewitched, Bothered and Bewildered' (2.16), where Xander ill-advisedly casts a love spell which affects every female in Sunnydale, human and otherwise, except for Cordelia whom it was meant for, in 'Passion' (2.17) and in 'I Only Have Eyes

For You' (2.19), where Buffy and Angelus find themselves possessed by the ghosts of another pair of doomed lovers.

Buffy is torn between her love for what Angel was and her duty to destroy what he has become, but is not the only representative in Season Two of the conflict of love and duty. The technopagan computer teacher Jenny Calendar's possession by the highly sexualized and androgynous demon Eyghon in 'The Dark Age' (2.8) causes what ought to have been a temporary rift between her and Giles. (Both this episode and the earlier 'Halloween' (2.6) also reveal an intense, possibly sexual, past friendship between Giles in his rebellious 'Ripper' phase and the evil sorcerer Ethan Rayne.) By the time Jenny is ready to forgive Giles, other issues have supervened.

Jenny is torn between her love for Giles and her real identity as Janna Kalderash, one of the clan who cursed Angelus and were in large measure destroyed for doing so; her uncle appears to remind her of her duty. She tries ineffectually to prevent Angel and Buffy consummating their love, but cannot bring herself to tell the truth and warn them that the curse will be annulled if Angel knows that one true moment of happiness. Jenny's particular story arc ends with her attempt to reconcile love and duty by recasting the curse – Angelus finds out and kills her, but her research eventually helps destroy him when Willow finds the crucial computer disc he failed to destroy.

The conflict of love and duty has its satanic parody among the vampires; as early as 'Innocence', Spike and Drusilla were warned by the reassembled demon the Judge that their affection for each other was human and therefore, from a demonic perspective, corrupt. Even an ensouled Angel, captured and tortured in 'What's My Line? Part Two' (2.10), teased Spike about his failure to give the sadomasochistic Drusilla everything she needs; Angelus, who drove Drusilla mad with his atrocities and then sired her, renews their relationship because he can, and as a way of tormenting both Spike and Buffy. Spike retaliates, in 'Becoming Part Two' by betraying Angelus and Drusilla, by trading the life of his sire and lover Drusilla for Giles.

Buffy's reaction is a little unfair given the way her own sense of duty has got muddled by her relationship with Angel: 'The whole world could be sucked into Hell and you need my help 'cause your girlfriend's a big ho? Let me take this opportunity to not care.' Spike follows his heart, proving that a vampire can have one, but loses Drusilla by doing so, as we hear from him in 'Lover's Walk' (3.8) and see in 'Fool For Love'. Buffy follows the path of duty and breaks hers.

Season Three

We have known ever since 'School Hard' that Principal Snyder was well aware of the nature of Sunnydale, and that he and other parts of the town's power structure – including at least some of the police – are consciously involved in covering up the depredations of, for example, vampires. Gradually we become aware of the importance to all of this of the unseen Mayor, of whom Snyder is clearly frightened in 'I Only Have Eyes For You' and rings in 'Becoming Part Two' with the news that he has found a pretext for expelling Buffy.

When Mr Trick arrives in town in 'Faith, Hope and Trick' and forms an alliance with the Mayor in 'Homecoming' (3.5), the pattern of Season Three appears to be emerging but, in spite of some impressively sassy dialogue and his computer skills, Mr Trick never quite acquires the impact needed by a major Buffy villain, partly because every scene that contains them both is stolen by the effortless folksy charisma of Harry Groener as the Mayor.

The season's major twist was delayed until February and 'Consequences' (3.15), when Faith, after saving Buffy by staking Mr Trick, goes to the Mayor and offers to take Trick's place as the Mayor's hitman. Though Faith's motives are never made explicit, the extent to which her betrayal is motivated not only by Buffy's ability to combine skill as a Slayer with having a life, but also by unrequited desire for Buffy is indicated in 'Consequences' by clear echoes of Angel in 'Surprise' – the attempt to leave town on a freighter, the fight against overwhelming odds on the docks.

The theme of betrayal had been established earlier, by her friends' hostile reactions to Buffy's long absence in 'Dead Man's Party', by her secrecy about Angel's return from Hell in 'Revelations' (3.7) and by their decision to help Cordelia's campaign for Homecoming Queen in 'Homecoming', as well as by the flirtation between Xander and Willow that starts during 'Homecoming' and reaches its culmination in 'Lover's Walk'. Gwendolen Post, the disgraced Watcher turned black magician, betrays both her calling and Faith, whose appointed replacement Watcher she has claimed to be, in 'Revelations'.

Similarly, in 'Gingerbread' (3.11), Buffy's mother Joyce tries to kill her under the influence of a demon, while in 'Helpless' (3.12) Giles obeys the orders of the Watcher's Council to subject Buffy to a potentially fatal test and is in turn himself betrayed by the Council. In 'Doppelgangland', another February sweeps episode, Sunnydale is visited by an alternate world's vampire Willow and in 'Enemies' (3.17) Angel appears to lose his soul again and become the ally of Faith and the Mayor.

Even evil is betrayed – by what was least evil about it. Buffy sacrifices herself to save Angel, giving him her Slayer's blood to save his life from Faith's poison and in her resulting swoon learns, in a dream, from Faith, whom she has earlier fought and put in a coma, that the Mayor has an area of vulnerability – his paternal love for Faith. When he turns into a dragonish demon, Buffy taunts him with the knife with which she stabbed Faith and tricks him into chasing her into Sunnydale High, which Giles and she then blow up.

Season Four

By the time she leaves Sunnydale High, Buffy has grown from being the new girl in town to being the Class Protector, who has given her year at Sunnydale High the school's lowest known death rate; at university, in 'The Freshman', the parasol that she was given as Class Protector is broken by the cool vampire on campus, Sunday. Buffy has to struggle to find a role, making serious mistakes like sleeping with the sleazy Parker Abrams in 'The Harsh Light of Day' (4.3).

She begins to fall for the corn-fed teaching assistant Riley Finn and is impressed by her intense Psychology teacher Doctor Maggie Walsh; at the same time, she becomes aware of the presence on campus of mysterious commandos.

In 'The Initiative' (4.7), we learn that Riley is the commandos' leader and Maggie Walsh his untrustworthy superior, and that she is engaged in scientific experiments on vampires and demons; after Buffy finds this out at the end of 'Hush', she becomes, for a while, steadily infatuated with the high-tech demon-fighting of the Initiative and estranged from her real friends.

When Maggie Walsh makes an attempt on Buffy's life in 'The I in Team' (4.13) and is herself butchered by her Frankensteinian creation Adam, the season moves into a new phase, in which the physical opponent is Adam and his attempt to conquer the world for cyborgs that blend demon, human and demon parts. It is significant that Riley, one of Buffy's principal allies, has in fact already undergone treatment with surgery and drugs, secretly intended as a preliminary to making him over into Adam's image. Adam does succeed in altering Forrest, one of Riley's friends, into a monster like himself, in 'Primeval' (4.21).

The emotional theme of Season Four is estrangement, estrangement from one's friends and from one's true nature, of which one's friends are part. Adam is the most estranged of all; he has almost no memory of who he was in his earlier life, though he is partially aware of his human past:

Adam	Scout's honour
Spike	You were a boy scout?
Adam	Parts of me

'New Moon Rising' (4.19)

Forrest's transformation into a monster is an outward sign of his murderous jealousy of Buffy who has come between him and his friend Riley. The chip placed in Spike's head by the Initiative estranges him from his true nature as a predator on humans and leaves him, from 'Doomed' (4.11) onwards, as a predator on vampires and demons.

Spike is at this point incapable of loyalty, sometimes supporting the Scoobies out of self-interest, as in 'Doomed', and sometimes betraying them – as in 'The Yoko Factor' (4.20) – by exploiting his knowledge of their weaknesses to drive a wedge between them. When he does finally save Giles, Willow and Xander, in 'Primeval', after Adam has betrayed him, it is a purely pragmatic decision; challenged by Xander with the suggestion that he has only acted to save himself from being staked, he merely asks 'Did it work?' His alienation is total – hunted by the Initiative and by other demons, with only the Scoobies, whom he hates, to turn to.

When Faith awakes from her coma and briefly exchanges bodies with Buffy, she could not be more estranged from who she is; the body-switch episode is even called 'Who Are You?' Tara realizes the truth by sensing the unnaturalness of Faith's presence. And yet, from this brief total estrangement from her body, Faith rediscovers her true nature as Slayer and her redemption begins, to be continued in various episodes of *Angel*, a show where redemption is a more central theme.

When she is first in Buffy's body, she takes a bath that is clearly a form of perverse lovemaking, before pulling faces in a mirror and endlessly and mockingly repeating what she sees as Buffy's mantra, 'Because it's wrong', a phrase she also uses when sexually teasing Spike. She has to be prompted by Willow to kill a vampire in the Bronze; the fact that his victim thanks her starts a process of reconnection to obligation. Seducing Riley does not work out for her either; his lovemaking leaves her confused and sad. When Riley's fellow-commando Forrest, who dislikes Buffy, calls her 'Killer', Faith claims the title of 'Slayer'; about to board a plane to Mexico in Buffy's body, she goes back to save a church congregation from Adam's vampire – and this time, when she says 'because it's wrong', she means it.

In the two episodes of *Angel* that continue her personal arc, Faith, unable to live with her conscience, tries to drive Angel to destroy her by threatening him, beating Cordelia and torturing Wesley. Able to identify with her, he persuades her that death is too easy a redemption and she chooses the harder path of sustained self-sacrifice, giving herself up to human justice.

The question of following one's true nature arises in the story arcs concerning Oz and Willow. In 'Wild at Heart' (4.6), Oz meets the werewolf (and rock singer) Veruca, who tempts him to her life of wild and murderous abandon, reminding him that the wolf is with him all the time; as the wolf, he kills her to save Willow, but then becomes a threat to Willow himself. Willow explores her nature as witch, and through this meets Tara. By the time Oz returns with his lycanthropy under control, Willow has made her own decisions about her true nature – 'New Moon Rising' – a decision which Faith and Spike understand considerably more rapidly than her friends. It is significant of the liberal atmosphere of the shows that Willow's love affair with Tara is quite specifically not seen as any sort of break with the natural order – needless to say, this is one of the many issues for which the show has been denounced by Christian believers.

The only way in which Buffy and the others can destroy Adam is by becoming closer than they have ever been, not only bridging the rift Spike has created between them, but also literally melding, in 'Primeval', into a single warrior with Giles's knowledge, Willow's supernatural abilities, Xander's good-heartedness and Buffy's prowess. Adam's belief that magic is simply a matter of temporary glamours and delusions, welcome influxes of the chaotic – 'Superstar' – is a misconception: some magics make true things, like the positive force of friendship, more true.

The dreams in 'Restless', as well as being an opportunity for the First Slayer to punish them for drawing on her power, bring the four central characters of the show face to face with the dilemmas at the heart of their situations. Willow is confronted with issues around her identity and sexuality; Xander with his failure to find a productive adult role; Giles with the contradiction between his parental relationship with Buffy and his need for self-expression; and Buffy with deep questions about the nature of her Slayer powers. Buffy needs them to keep her human; they need her to keep them alive.

Their dreams, like those Buffy shares with Faith, foreshadow bits of the future. Faith's remark 'counting down from 7-3-0' foreshadows Buffy's death in the Season Five finale, exactly 730 days after the Season Three finale, 'Graduation Day Part Two' (3.22); and the child Willow's book report in 'Restless' – *The Lion, the Witch and the Wardrobe* is after all a story of redemptive sacrifice, followed, it should be noted, by resurrection.[11] Enough details from the four dreams crop up in the next three seasons that it is possible to suspect that sometimes their recurrences were happy inventions rather than part of a long game. Evidence for this comes in the presence of the mysterious Cheese Man, who appears in all four dreams and in Andrew and Jonathan's shared dream in Season Seven; Whedon has specifically said that the Cheese Man has no meaning, and this is presumably the point about his reappearance.

Season Five

Season Five starts with a master of trickery and illusion in Dracula, and is full of illusion thereafter. Not only the characters, but also the audience assume that one or other of the two Xanders in 'The Replacement' must be evil, rather than just a representative of different strengths and weaknesses; when both Xanders laughingly reference the parallel episode of *Star Trek* – 'Kill us both, Spock' – it is an acknowledgement that they and we have been misled by a stock trope of popular culture: not every double is a shadow double. Buffy's assumption in 'No Place Like Home' (5.5) that Joyce's illness is the result of magic, rather than a physical problem with medical answers, is similarly an illusion: there are some enemies that the Slayer cannot fight.

Love is real, but particular relationships may be delusions: from 'The Replacement' onwards, with his almost casual remark that 'She doesn't love me', we are served notice that Buffy's affair with Riley is doomed. Riley's jealous assumption that he needs to be closer to evil for Buffy to love him leads him to brief murderous liaisons with vampire women; the fact that the first of these we see him kill is someone we earlier saw killed as a human makes our feelings considerably more ambivalent.[12] Ironically, his eventual departure from Sunnydale in 'Into the Woods' (5.10) is precipitated by an entirely wrong belief that Buffy has chosen to ignore his ultimatum; she simply arrives at the helicopter landing-pad too late to beg him not to go.

Buffy's brief attraction to Ben the intern is based on her assumption that someone charming and apparently good might be a suitable replacement – Ben is in fact the male aspect of her divine enemy Glory. In 'I Was Made to Love You' (5.15), April is noticed as attractive by Xander, Spike and Willow, but she is simply a machine designed for love; it is a long conversation with the dying April that reminds Buffy that she does not need a lover to be complete. Her use of Spike in Season Six confirms rather than contradicts this insight; her last conversation with Angel in 'Chosen', in which she compares herself to cookie dough, not yet ready, reaffirms it.

Spike in Season Five is perhaps the most deluded of all, from his sudden awakening from a dream of sex with Buffy in 'Out of My Mind' (5.4) to his untrustworthy account of his earlier life in 'Fool For Love'[13] and his near-demented behaviour in 'Crush' (5.14), where his offer to stake Drusilla to prove his love for Buffy entirely alienates her. Spike's memory of love as a human and his century of obsession with Drusilla confuse him hopelessly about what love is. His fetishistic stealing of Buffy's underwear and sweaters, his persuading Harmony to dress up as Buffy for sex games, his commissioning of the Buffybot – these ensure his rejection, perhaps all the more so because there is a genuine, if perverse, sexual chemistry between them.

And yet, there is a connection between Spike and all three Summers women. Joyce made him cups of tea, and his mourning for her is genuine. He endures torture to near-destruction to protect

Dawn from Glory, and to protect Buffy from killing grief were anything to happen to Dawn. When Dawn explores Sunnydale by night, in search of her identity and then in search of ways of resurrecting her mother, he becomes her guardian. When Buffy dies, he weeps; earlier that same night, he says to her: 'I'm a monster, but you treated me like a man. And that's...' The tailing into silence is one of the most moving moments in one of Whedon's most powerfully upsetting scripts. When Buffy poses as the Buffybot to find out whether Spike has betrayed her, she sees him stripped of his attitudes and his bravado; she does not love him, but she forgives him and kisses him, as a friend. He has made love to her double for days, but instantly knows, and is content with, the real thing. (Similarly, their passionately sadomasochistic relationship in Season Six culminates in, and is contrasted with, their nights of chaste bed-sharing love in Season Seven.)

The answer to illusion and delusion is making fine distinctions, knowing what the truth is. Dawn is not, in literal fact, Buffy's younger sister – she is a superstructure of personality and humanity created by monks as a way to hide a supernatural Key from Glory. But it doesn't matter – she is Buffy's sister in memory and affection; she is the family of Buffy's heart, and, after Joyce's death at the end of 'I Was Made to Love You', all the literal family Buffy has left. It is significant that, in 'Family' (5.6), Dawn is as quick as Buffy to defend Tara's right to be regarded as part of the extended family of the Scooby gang and defended by them against Tara's oppressive birth family. (It is also a significant piece of ambiguity that the question of Tara's true nature is clarified by Spike, who hits her in order to prove her humanity by having it hurt him – a character highly deluded about his own concerns can nonetheless be a truth-teller in other areas.) Dawn is, as the monk tells Buffy, an innocent; the Scoobies embrace their changed memories even after the truth is revealed, as, very precisely, they could not and did not when they discovered Jonathan's entirely selfish deceit in 'Superstar'.

Storytelling is also trickery. Various of the side issues of the series – the troll in 'Triangle' (5.11), the Buffybot, the link to herself that Glory's mindsuck produces even in Tara – turn out to be desperately relevant to the final conflict, just as the demon Doc turns out to be tragically more to do with Glory's plans than anyone guessed.

Family is a major preoccupation of Season Five and is portrayed as crucial to identity – we have Tara's dysfunctional family based on the practice of deceit as a way of continuing the oppression of women as opposed to the loose family of the heart that the Scoobies have become as they have grown into adults, a family that helps Willow care for Tara after Glory sucks out her sanity. We have the corrupt family of sensuality into which Spike was born as a vampire.[14] His preparedness to kill Drusilla to prove his love for Buffy is a renunciation of Drusilla as his sire as well as his lover.

The relationship between Glory and Ben, originally presented as sister and brother, but later revealed to be divine prisoner and mortal prison, and the fact that Ben has to keep Glory's dress in his locker to change into when changing persona is perhaps a sacrilegious joke at the expense of the Christian doctrine of the incarnation. Gradually they merge – identity and illusion are crucial to the nature of the series villain. Buffy beats Glory back into Ben, and Giles kills him to save the world, just as Ben was prepared to sacrifice the world to remain incarnate in a small corner of Glory.

Buffy's certainty that the monks wrought their illusion well is something on which, at the end she is prepared to gamble her life, guessing that the created sisterhood between her and Dawn is so solidly built that she can be the blood sacrifice which might save the world. Some people have criticized the finale as illogical, but this is only so if you assume that all portrayal of magic has to play by Frazer's rules of similarity and contagion. The sacrifice of innocent blood is charm enough in itself – which innocent blood is almost beside the point. Buffy sacrificed Angel to save the world; she will not kill her sister.

The Prime Slayer tells her that her gift is death, and she chooses to interpret that unselfishly, by dying rather than killing. Everyone has been keen to tell her that the Slayer is a killer, from Dracula to Spike – 'Death is your art. You make it with your hands everyday' – but, as when everyone from Glory to the Council told her she was powerless, or when Ken and his demons told her she was no one, or when Angelus told her that she had nothing left, Buffy refuses to be told.

Season Six

In a panel discussion at the Academy of Television Arts, Joss Whedon claimed that Season Six was the season without a controlling metaphor, but did so with a cheeriness that indicated that this was Joss the Trickster at work. In fact, this most controversial of seasons – fans either love or hate it – had a very strong metaphor at its heart, which was simply, and radically for a show that had previously concerned itself with adolescence and the transition out of it, that sometimes growing up feels like leaving Heaven. At a mythical level, Willow's 'rescue' of Buffy has left her bereft; at a mundane one, coming back from the dead has forced her to deal with questions like paying her debts and making a living. Joyce's death has had consequences – her medical bills ate up her life insurance.

Because Season Six is a season about adulthood, it is a season in which process is as important as sudden surprises, although there are various such surprises, from Buffy and Spike's first kiss at the end of 'Once More With Feeling' to Willow's de-ratting of Amy in 'Smashed' (6.9) and the return of Riley, with his new wife, in 'As You Were' (6.14). What these surprises contribute to the storyline, though, is not sudden reversal so much as amplification of what we already know to be going on – Willow's slide into amorality, Buffy's depression, Warren's murderous misogyny and so on. Even the great plot turns – Tara's death for example – are in retrospect less surprising than they were at the time – sooner or later Warren was going to kill another woman.

Buffy's position is dire – protecting Dawn means that she has to ensure she holds her family together, even if it means working shifts in a hamburger restaurant – 'Doublemeat Palace' (6.12) – that leaves her hair stinking of used fat. Her emotional numbness estranges her from her friends, particularly when, in 'Once More With Feeling', they learn what they did to her and cope less than well with the guilt. Buffy sings, in her pain, that 'I want to feel'; she finds that sex with Spike is a convenient way of giving herself the desired package of self-hatred and sensation as well as a camaraderie that will always be partial.

The profound wrongness she feels about what she is doing is demonstrated in 'Smashed', where their first sexual encounter starts as a fight and demolishes a house; Spike tells her, and she believes him, that he can now hit her because 'she came back wrong'. There is an element of irresponsibility here: she wants to believe that she is not choosing, choosing quite explicitly rough sex involving handcuffs, and is disappointed when Tara attributes the failure of Spike's chip to recognize her as human as a trivial consequence of her return from the grave.

Adulthood is all about consequences; the villains of most of the season are three coevals of the Scoobies who refuse to grow up and think that they can live in a world without consequences, or at least a world in which consequences can be passed on to other people. These are the Little Bad with the most banal of backstories – one day Warren Mears looks round at his friends Jonathan and Andrew and says 'You guys want to team up and take over Sunnydale?' Their respective areas of expertise – Warren's flair for comic-book weird science, like robots and invisibility rays, Jonathan's not inconsiderable skills at magic and Andrew's abilities as a summoner of demons[15] – make them capable of progressively more dangerous pranks, which only turn entirely sour in 'Dead Things' (6.13), when Warren brainwashes, rapes and murders his ex-girlfriend, Katrina.

Sex and sexuality comprise one of the areas in which the trio refuse to grow up. Warren has a deeply embedded misogyny, first manifested in his building of April and further demonstrated by his reduction of Katrina to a hypnotized sex slave; the other two are guilty here as well, but less profoundly so. When, in 'Seeing Red' (6.19), he briefly achieves the superpowers he always wanted, he uses them like a bully; when Buffy smashes the magic spheres that have empowered him, this castration renders him maniacally murderous. And he finally learns too late that actions have consequences.

Andrew has his own issues – as early as 'Life Serial' (6.5), Warren is teasing him about his defensive homophobia – 'You know what that says about you'. By the end of the season it is clear to everyone except perhaps him that he has a sexual crush on Warren – when Buffy finds documents in the Troika's abandoned lair, Xander decodes them as love poetry, in Klingon, and is typically tactful about whose love poetry they are to whom. Typically of the show's liberalism, and this plays out over Season Seven, Andrew's dangerous immaturity lies in his not accepting his sexual ambivalence.

Of the three, Jonathan is the character with whom we have most history – and it is tempting to see his involvement with the other two as a poor substitute for his never quite explicit wish to be fully a Scooby – after all, in narrative terms, it was he who first spotted Adam's area of vulnerability. He is the least committed of the three and the one unhappiest with Warren's blithe acceptance of the need to harm or kill Buffy if their plans are to succeed. A crucial part of Warren's corruption of Andrew is his persuasion of him that Jonathan has to be betrayed; briefly in jail, Jonathan allows Andrew to persuade him in turn that the betrayal was not serious. The geeks are stuck in a perpetual adolescence where no sin or betrayal is permanent or serious.

The other point about the geeks is that they have consumed vast quantities of popular media, but taken nothing more from them than a collector's obsession with trivia and spin-off action figures. In this, they are explicitly contrasted with Xander, whose obsession with the same material leads to his applying what he has learned from it: in 'Flooded' (6.4), Anya suggests that Buffy start charging for her services and claims that Spiderman does – Xander confirms that this is not the case, preferring truth to his beloved. Unlike the other two, Warren is at least logical in his perception that villainy means murderousness – Jonathan and Andrew aspire only to the prankster aspects of comic-book villainy, which is to say that they fail to read comics with due care and attention. In a show which is itself part of popular culture, the portrayal of those who would consume it keenly is here subtle and nuanced.

On the one hand, the Troika are 'little men', whose ineffectiveness is used by the psychiatrist in Buffy's toxic delusions in 'Normal Again' (6.17) as evidence that Buffy is returning from the grand madness of hallucinated Slayerhood to the pettier concerns of 'reality'. Of course, his claim to represent reality is a fraud, and one created by the Troika's actions. Much of the time, their role in her life is as the last straw – they make bad situations worse. They are a vehicle through which truth comes to light, something they share with the song-and-dance demon Sweet in 'Once More With Feeling'. Their attempt to convince Buffy that she killed Katrina brings to a head the abusive violence of her relationship with Spike; their system of spy cameras allows Buffy and Xander to witness Anya and Spike's bout of revenge sex in 'Entropy' (6.18).

On the other hand, Warren does as much damage as any of the previous Big Bads, killing Tara, nearly killing Buffy and precipitating Willow's vengeful embrace of her dark side. Again, in this he is the last straw; the problematic nature of Willow's magic is a theme that goes back to Season Two, when Giles first warned her that she was opening doors in herself best left closed. Tara's touchy-feely Wicca can seem a little mawkish, but Willow has a hacker's attitude to magic which at times becomes dangerous in its sheer absurdity. The first of their quarrels about magic is precipitated, in 'All the Way' (6.6), by Willow's suggestion that she shift everyone else in the Bronze into another dimension for a moment in order to find Dawn in the crowd. Tara at least recognizes that magic has to be ethical; Willow will use it for good purposes, but increasingly uses it for trivial ones as well. She is in love with power, but also in love with the exercise of skill. This was always true of Willow, even before she discovered magical ability when, in Season One, she broke regularly through the firewalls of local and national computers.

Where Season Six makes one of its worst stumbles is in tying this down to the limited status of a metaphor about addiction – it is far more interesting as a metaphor for creativity and its amorality, and my guess is that the writers found this too close to home. The episode in which addiction is specifically referenced – 'Wrecked' (6.10) – is the show's weakest since Season Four, partly because of the crude embodiment of this message in a magic crack house and the warlock dealer Rack. For several episodes, Willow goes through withdrawal and, faced with temptations to use magic, just says no. This is particularly spurious, since the show's internal logic always dictated that eventually she would return to sorcery when the story needed her to. Addiction would always have been referenced by Willow's abuse of power; that reference is weakened by tying it down.

Tara's murder by Warren at the end of 'Seeing Red' is one of the most upsetting moments in the show's seven seasons. Some fans, who saw her as an iconic lesbian role model as much as a character, were so angry that they threatened to boycott the show. Their argument is, briefly, that in a heteronormative society, the default setting in heterosexist writing is to punish lesbianism with suicide and/or madness and that the show compromised with this cliché. But this is nonsense – Tara is murdered by Warren, who is not even shooting at her, and Willow's madness is an excess of legitimate grief. The show references the cliché and subverts it, proving that it is possible for a queer character to die in popular culture without that death being the surrogate vengeance of the straight world.

What is peculiarly upsetting about the death is that it comes just at the point when the two characters have reconciled. Tara, who left Willow when she discovered Willow tampering with her memory to dispose of quarrels, is supportive of her on occasions when, as in 'Older and Far Away' (6.15), Willow refuses to use magic even to save herself and her friends, and eventually decides that she cannot stay away any longer:

> There's so much to work through. Trust has to build again, on both sides... you have to learn if you're even the same people you were, if you can fit in each other's lives, it's a long and important process and can we just skip it? Can you just be kissing me now?

Of the three major pairings in Season Six, it is Tara and Willow who come closest, in the end, to acting like adults in their handling of forgiveness. The test of adulthood Willow then faces, and fails, is continuing to act like an adult in the face of grief.

Even inside the show, characters disagree about Willow's vengeance. The demon Anya and the adolescent Dawn are both sympathetic to the idea that Warren needs to die. Willow assumes Buffy and Xander's acquiescence to the extent that she heals Buffy's possibly mortal wound in order to have her at her side when she confronts Warren and is disappointed when they want nothing to do with murder. The scenes of Willow's vendetta in 'Villains' (6.20) are chilling: she summons the Magic Shop's books of dark magic which flutter to her like doves and plunges her hands into them so that their formulae and cantrips crawl up her arms and face turning her eyes and hair black. She is unstoppable – Warren tries a robot double, various spells, and even hitting her with an axe and she shrugs everything he does aside, trapping him in hobbling vines with a gesture.

By this time, she has ditched Buffy and Xander, who were shocked by her casual demolition of the robot. She tortures Warren bodily, by moving the bullet she took from Buffy slowly around his innards, and mentally, by showing him the vengeful ghost of the dead Katrina. Finally, echoing that earlier evil Willow, the vampire of 'Doppel-gangland', with a casual 'Bored now', she tears his skin off and burns him alive. The extent to which she has lost herself and her normal rationality is evinced by the way she turns to Buffy, Xander and Anya, as they arrive too late, with the pregnantly elided remark 'One down...'.

Vengeance against Warren has a certain wild justice; to carry that vengeance to his abandoned friends, who are in jail at the time of Tara's death, is clearly wrong. In 'Two To Go', Willow has entirely lost any sense of limits. Yet, though she claims to have lost herself entirely – 'Willow's a junkie' is a line that would have been more effective and upsetting without the extended magic equals drugs subplot earlier in the season – her spite and malice make her say things about Buffy and Dawn that Willow must, at some dark level, have always thought. Prevented by Anya from using magic to strike Jonathan and Andrew down, she makes herself superstrong and fights Buffy as an equal or superior, any sidekick or adolescent's fantasy.

At her moment of triumph – 'And there's no one in the world with the power to stop me now' – she is sandbagged temporarily by Giles, who returns with a bolt of green energy and the quiet remark 'I'd like to test that theory'. Earlier in the season, in 'Flooded', when Giles confronted Willow about the dangerous resurrection of Buffy and called her a rank amateur, she warned him of her power and that he had better not piss her off – the confrontation that ensues is one which Giles ultimately loses and, it turns out, has planned to lose. Willow drains herself fighting him and leeches magic away from him, magic that eventually calms her. The difference between Giles and Willow is not between a witch and an informed layman, it is between two adult people who know magic, one of whom knows its dangers of old and normally abstains.

Before that, though, her grief takes the form of trying to end the world, its pain and her own. Suicide is, it needs to be pointed out, often an adolescent act. Throughout the season, Buffy has been trying to kill herself, either literally, by jumping off Glory's tower a second time and by dancing herself into spontaneous combustion, or metaphorically, by accepting a reality in which she is mad but loved by Joyce over one in which she has friends and adult responsibilities. Evil Willow points out to both Buffy and Dawn that their constant moaning about their lives means they are ill-equipped to talk her out of universal destruction – and she has a point.

Xander confronts her armed with nothing save the history of their friendship and his unconditional love; she lashes out at him with energies that could destroy the world and only manages to tear his cheek and his shirt. This profoundly sentimental scene with its religious content – a carpenter, on a hill, saves the world through love – works because his appeal to her is based on continuity:

> First day of kindergarten you cried 'cause you broke the yellow crayon and you were too afraid to tell anyone. You've come pretty far, ending the world, not a *terrific* notion but the thing is, yeah. I love you. I loved crayon-breaky Willow and I love scary veiny Willow. So if I'm going out, it's here. You wanna kill the world you start with me. I've earned that.

He stands and he takes all the pain she hits him with and eventually she collapses in his arms and cries. This is the first point since Tara's death when she has cried; her eyes have gone red and black; she has assaulted gods and killed humans and summoned demons, but she has not cried. Tears are a part of adult sorrow, which is why pseudo-adult traditional masculinity suppresses them, because tears can be dried and sorrow moved on from.

Xander saves the world by telling Willow the exact truth about his feelings – earlier in the season, Xander has betrayed his own best self by remaining silent. In their scene in 'Once More With Feeling', Xander and Anya sing aloud about the problems of their forthcoming marriage – 'I'll never tell' – but neither of them confronts the possibility that there are too many issues in both their lives for a proposal in the heat of apocalypse to be desirably binding; their cheerful song includes an uncharacteristic discord on the lying phrase 'coz there's nothing to tell'. (This is explicit in the script directions, and not merely a vocal failure by untrained singers.) Xander fears that adulthood may sour him into a vicious drunk like his father and cannot vocalize those fears – his longing for a happy ending causes him to summon Sweet, thinking that singing and dancing come without a price in dead people. Anya loves him, but also wants a husband as an accessory to a bourgeois lifestyle. The deceiving visions that precipitate his jilting her at the altar work because they express real fears; moral responsibility, though, is shared between them. Anya, after all, has explicitly foreseen what will happen in their song: 'I've read this tale/ There's wedding then betrayal'.

Both are capable of murderous anger – Anya returns to demonhood in order to get vengeance on Xander and he goes after Spike with an axe when Anya gets her entirely human vengeance by having sex with Spike. The circle of vengeance continues when Spike, beaten rather than killed by Xander, deliberately lets slip during one of Xander's tirades to Anya that he was 'good enough for Buffy', and causes Xander yet more emotional pain. Buffy has never told her close friends about the affair with Spike – Tara is calm and sweet about it, Willow and Dawn surprisingly calm when they find out, while Giles giggles and guffaws in a way that punctures Buffy's dramatic revelation. She was always worried about Xander's reaction – and was right to worry. He in turn passes his anger on by telling Dawn about Spike's attempted rape of Buffy, destroying Dawn's actually quite accurate sense of Spike as her own protector.

This is a season in which revenge is a worryingly present theme, yet is seen as something from which the truely adult person refrains. Dawn constantly acts up, in an adolescent attempt to get attention from her preoccupied sister: stealing from her friends; accidentally summoning Anya's colleague Halfrek; inadvertently dating a vampire. With the exception of Giles and Tara, the adults fail to set her a good example.

The fact that, for once, it is not Buffy who saves the world means that she has to spend the finale in a hole in the ground learning to appreciate her sister, whom she has always tried to keep away from Slayage, and who nonetheless proves surprisingly competent in a fight to the death. 'You think I don't watch you,' Dawn says, after niftily somersaulting past a monster to retrieve her sword and skewer him. In 'The Gift', Buffy told Dawn 'The hardest thing in this world is to live in it', a statement which Dawn reprised to Buffy in 'Once More With Feeling', but which neither of them has honoured properly until this last moment when they climb together out of the grave to which Willow has consigned them into the sunlight of a new day.

This is not, however, how the season ends – it ends with Spike. For several episodes, the writers have consistently misled us about his trip to Africa – he asks the demon who subjects him to trials to 'Give me what I want. Make me what I was... so Buffy can get what she deserves'. We have been allowed to believe that what Spike is after is the removal of his chip so that he can be evil again, but what we are seeing is yet another of the mixed messages that Spike and Buffy's relationship has consisted of. In fact, he wants his soul back.

Many critics and fans have complained that the Spike storyline dominates the latter seasons of *Buffy* and that this is in some sense a betrayal of the show's original mission statement – that the turn to interest in the infinitely cool Spike is a betrayal of the geeks and teen outcasts in whom the show originally made us invest our emotions. This is a fallacy. Just as the show gradually demonstrated the inner cool of, say, Xander, so part of Spike's way to salvation, as for Cordelia's previously, is acknowledging his own inner vulnerabilities.

One of the best things about Season Six is its exploration of the paradoxes of love. Spike, who is fundamentally evil, is tormented by love for Buffy, who is a champion of Good, who abuses and exploits him shamelessly as a temporary fix for her anomie. Even pain is better than blankness; she sings 'I want to feel – my skin should crack and peel – I want the fire back'. When she does break with him, in 'As You Were', she stops treating him as a convenience and addresses him by his original human name, William. In 'The Gift', he said: 'I'm a monster, but you treat me like a man, and that's...' Where he had earlier mocked Riley that 'she needs a little monster in her man', here she acknowledges his human history, but breaks with him.

Spike finds himself the recipient of all Buffy's bad erotic past, including those bits of it she never lets herself think about. Her vicious beating of him in 'Dead Things' is surely precipitated by the echo of 'Bad Girls' (3.14) back in Season Three; he does for her what she would not do for Faith, and dumps Katrina's body in the river. She, in turn, is caught up in his past with Drusilla – Spike never particularly enjoyed Drusilla's taste for sadomasochism ('I'm not one for the pre-show,' he says as she drips holy water onto Angel in 'What's My Line? Part Two') and only after she leaves him does he decide that he lives in her world of eroticized pain:

> I want Dru back, I just have to be the man I was. The man she loved. I'm gonna do what I shoulda done in the first place. I'll find her, wherever she is… and I'll tie her up and torture her until she likes me again.

Now, with Buffy, he takes her on trips to the dark side. Even before they become lovers, he sweeps her off to the demon bar where he plays poker for kittens – 'Life Serial' – and gets her involved in frightening off his loan shark, in 'Tabula Rasa' (6.8). Later, they play games with handcuffs – he loves her, but does not trust that love by itself and so estranges her from her sense of self. More importantly perhaps, note the echo of 'I just have to be the man I was' in 'Make me what I was'.

But before the trip to Africa comes the most heinous of Spike's acts in Season Six, or indeed, on screen, ever. Dumped by Buffy and clear from her reaction to his sex with Anya that she has some feelings left for him, he turns up in her bathroom to plead for another chance and ends up attempting rape. He is a monster who wants to be treated as a man – and he ends up committing a peculiarly human crime against the woman he loves. 'Ask me now, why I could never love you,' Buffy says after fighting him off, and it is hard to say which of them feels the most damaged and betrayed by his actions.

The harshest paradox of all about this is that he finally accepts what he has never before understood, that the chip preventing him from killing is no substitute for his lack of moral centre. His bluster leads us to suppose he plans vengeance but this is just another of his mixed messages. In 'Once More With Feeling', he sang 'I hope she fries. I'm free if that bitch dies. I'd better help her out… First I'll kill her then I'll save her', before stopping her deathdance with a plea: 'You have to go on living. So one of us is living.' (Significantly, his singing of 'living' echoes Buffy's earlier minor-key singing of 'heaven'.) He talks again of Buffy as a bitch, but when he talks of what she deserves, it turns out to be him, with a soul. Some commentators have disliked the rape scene to the extent of regarding it as making Spike irredeemable – his attempt to make any future such crime impossible regains our sympathy, especially when it proves, in the short term, a tragic mistake in the following season. Spike is already over a century old, but he too has a lot of growing up to do.

Season Six upset many viewers because it told them more explicitly than ever before that these admirable and exemplary characters were nonetheless all of them seriously flawed. It was a season in which all the Scoobies have to accept unpalatable truths about themselves – even Giles is torn between his loyalty and his feeling that he is preventing Buffy accepting adult responsibility. It was also a season in which one or two very weak episodes – 'Wrecked', 'As You Were' – raised the possibility that the tour-de-force musical episode had leached creative energy from elsewhere. Those hostile to the season represented the chastened aspect of the characters as a thinning out of the show's charm.

To which the response has to be what the writers discussed as the season's mission statement: 'Oh, grow up.' It was a season in which a number of the writers were at the top of their game – Steve DeKnight, for example, wrote the extraordinarily good 'Dead Things' under extreme pressure in a weekend – and the actors were stretched as never before. Inevitably too, it was the gloomily satisfying prelude to the show's last season, like going through shadows to earn sunlight at the end. All of the characters, Buffy especially, have been on a Night Journey, and her journey ends with Dawn – with whom she starts the next season, teaching her to slay.

Season Seven

It became known for certain, about halfway through the writing of Season Seven, that it would be the last season of *Buffy*, though it was always fairly likely. Joss Whedon returned to full-time work on the show at about this point after concentrating on *Firefly*, his new space opera show, up to the point of that show's unexpected cancellation, and radically revised much of *Buffy*'s planned arc – according to Jane Espenson, in an interview, he arrived in the office and wiped clean the whiteboard with the rest of the plot arc on it. Accordingly, there are some loose ends in this season, though fewer than some critics have claimed, and one or two plot points – such as the Beljoxa's Eye business – which were either never explicitly made or never clearly resolved.

In the end, though, Season Seven ended up being one of the most satisfactory and enjoyable seasons of the show, partly because of a finale which simultaneously wrapped up the show's themes in a satisfactory way and was in other respects an open slingshot ending – the imaginations of the audience are allowed to play endlessly on the futures of these characters and this world and the consequences of Buffy's final decision. That decision becomes retrospectively the entire point of the show's seven seasons – if, as seems likely, it was a late improvisation by Whedon, it is as much a master stroke display of his genius as anything else he has ever done.

As finally conceived, then, Season Seven is a season in which the prevailing theme is the getting of wisdom – its first episode is called 'Lessons' and that is what Buffy and the others get constantly throughout the season. Retroactively, in the biggest retcon of a show obsessed with re-imagining itself, all seven seasons are re-envisaged as educating Buffy to the point where she makes the right decision. In Season Seven, Buffy learns, for example, that she should follow her heart and her instinct, but that she cannot always demand unconditional acceptance from her followers, who temporarily reject her in 'Empty Places' (7.19); she also learns to become a leader and teacher in her turn, finding herself responsible for a house full of Potential Slayers.

Willow finally learns limits and restraints, because the magic with which she is now imbued is capable of responding destructively to her subconscious fears and guilt: 'I've been in a place where I kinda should be restrained. I've been controlling myself and if I get out of control… if I let myself go, I could just… go' – Touched' (7.20). She also learns a certain acceptance, working through her grief for the dead Tara and finding a new lover, the oldest of the Potential Slayers, Kennedy, who could not be more unlike Tara in her brattishness and sexual pushiness.

Xander and Anya work through their hostility to fondness and sexual friendship – her death is tragic because it cuts short her rehumanization; Xander's maiming by Caleb – he loses an eye – is a piece of spite by evil, but it is also the traditional symbolic price of hard-gained wisdom. Maiming also makes its victims liminal, partaking of two states at once, since one part of them is dead and the rest alive. Xander thus joins his friends in liminality – Buffy has returned from death and Willow from Evil. Our first sight of Giles in Season Seven, on his way to teach Willow, has him on horseback – can this be an allusion to the centaurs, who traditionally act as the instructors of heroes and are also liminal, caught between animal and human?

Anya, Spike, Faith and Andrew all achieve measures of redemption; Dawn spectacularly becomes an adult, rather younger than her sister and friends. If, of the show's standard characters, Giles is given short measure in this last season and mostly functions as a plot device, it is because in a show that is about the getting of wisdom, the character who has always been the mentor is necessarily going to be less important than his various pupils.

Generally, this is somewhat less than usual a season about Buffy's relationship with her friends, partly because by now it can usually be taken as a given – except when, briefly, she exceeds her authority as their leader and they tell her so. Nonetheless, there is a wonderful moment just before the final battle when, after the rest of their companions have been sent to their posts, the original four Scoobies have a moment in which they echo their original relationship – Buffy, Willow and Xander babbling about going to the Mall and Giles feigning irritation at being ignored, ending, as the trio stroll off without him, with a deliberate echo of 'The Harvest': 'The Earth is definitely doomed.'

The early episodes take us back to a rebuilt Sunnydale High, as is appropriate to a season whose theme is education, and the first episodes indicate things that Buffy and the others still need to know. 'Same Time, Same Place' (7.3), for example, demonstrates that Buffy and Xander have not entirely got over Willow's behaviour in Season Six: when someone is found flayed, they suspect her, and the estrangement is signalled further by her inability to see them, or they her. But the episode also re-establishes the bond between them: Buffy lends Willow healing power in one of the tenderest moments between them in all seven years. In 'Help' (7.4), Buffy tries and fails to save Cassie, a precognitive girl who is one of her clients as school counsellor. She rescues Cassie from sacrifice and a boobytrap, but a heart attack fulfils the girl's prediction; Buffy could not save her, but her attempts meant that Cassie died knowing friends cared for her. The comedy 'Him' (7.6), in which all four female leads are bewitched by a football player's magic jacket, indicate how crucial female solidarity is, in a season in which Buffy becomes general of an army of young girls.

Several of the season's 'sidebar' episodes take particular characters on a journey of self-discovery and renewal. Anya, in 'Selfless' (7.5), revisits her entire past as human and vengeance demon, and discovers how little she has ever invested in her own identity rather than roles. As a Swedish peasant, she obsessed with the unfaithful lover she turned into a troll and bred the rabbits of which she became phobic. As a vengeance demon, she not only tried to trigger the Russian Revolution – believing Communism to be the panacea she later and equally laughably identified as capitalism – but achieved only the failure of 1905. Human again, she invested her identity in marriage to Xander, irrespective of whether this would work. Anxious to please D'Hoffryn, she butchers fraternity boys, and finds Buffy on her trail. It is Willow, whom she has never liked, who saves her and D'Hoffryn, whom she trusted, that kills her remaining demon friend Halfrek to cause her pain.

Willow's guilt is manifested in 'The Killer Inside Me' (7.13) in a progressive transformation into Warren – Tanja Kinkel has pointed out the parallels between Willow and Warren (geekiness, lack of limits, preparedness to brainwash lovers) – and she is only saved by Kennedy's love. Significantly, the wilful, brattish know-it-all Kennedy also has to accept the power of magic, which she earlier mocked, to do the right fairy-tale thing and free Willow with a kiss.

For a moment, it seems as if Dawn is to join Buffy in the family business: in 'Potential' (7.12), a locator spell seems to indicate that she is another Potential. In fact, however, the Sunnydale Potential is another of Buffy's counselling clients, the gawky Amanda. Dawn has to reconcile herself to being ordinary – Xander consoles her in a moving speech – and she throws herself into research, acquiring new languages at a jokily terrifying speed.

The most remarkable of all the secondary character arcs is possibly that of Andrew, who starts his season as a killer and ends up a reluctant heroic survivor; he is at the same time an embodiment of the show's interest in redemption and a hilarious parody of it, who at one point struts round Sunnydale in a leather coat and boots that he has copied from Spike and on another talks of his 'epic quest for redemption'. In an extension of Season Six's running comment on his consumption of popular media and blindness to their folk morality, he is persuaded by the *Star Wars* references of what he takes to be Warren's ghost to kill Jonathan so that his blood might open the Hellmouth. Just before this shocking death, in 'Conversations With Dead People' (7.7), Jonathan has a little aria of a speech in which he talks of missing home and old friends – he is genuinely touching here.

Andrew is not very good at evil – Jonathan does not have enough blood to open the Seal, he muffs sacrificing a pig with the remark '*Babe in the City* was way overrated', and is caught by Willow buying blood at the butcher. For much of the season, he is the Scoobies' prisoner, often tied to a chair as Spike was in Season Four, and gradually earning their trust. He becomes the male friend Xander has lacked since Oz, and develops something of a crush. In 'Storyteller' (7.16), he tries to make a video diary of life with Buffy and the Potentials; this is one of Jane Espenson's funniest ever episodes, as well as a clear signal of the importance of story and modes of storytelling as one of the ways in which moral instruction is conveyed. Buffy takes him to the Seal and confronts him with the sordid truth of his betrayal and murder of Jonathan instead of various comforting and self-serving scenarios; faced with what he thinks is execution, Andrew weeps for himself and his friend and his tears close what his blood would not have.

From then on, he accepts his probable death and struggles manfully through the final conflict, making an abortive Oscar acceptance-style speech about the privilege of dying with the Scoobies and Potentials, fighting 'like Jerry Lewis with a sword' and entirely amazed and saddened to have survived when Anya did not:

Andrew   She was incredible. She died saving my life.

Xander puts a hand on Andrew's shoulder.

Xander   *(welling up)* That's my girl. Always doing the stupid thing.

Redemption is about acceptance of death and atonement, rather than necessarily dying, or doing so permanently; this is one of several unjoky ways in which Andrew parallels Spike.

It is a season which introduces an unusually large group of new characters, and has to sketch them in very lightly and not always with entire success. Principal Wood has considerable style in spite of the handicap of being forced to appear morally ambiguous until well into the season – like Giles, on his escape from certain death at the hands of a Bringer, Wood is set up in early episodes as a possible Bad, a false teacher, but is only a red herring. The various Potentials have few individual characteristics, and how much we are aware of each depends as much on the performances as anything else. Inyari Limoni is not frightened to pick up the brattishness and sexual predation of Kennedy without concern for audience disapproval – she is annoying and that is part of the point, since she is the AntiTara. Felicia Day turns the shy scaredy-cat Violet into a three-dimensional character with very few lines. On the other hand, the cockney Molly is played by an actress whose accent is several shades more laughable than Drusilla at her most stylized. In spite of some shaky moments, we end up caring just about enough about the Potentials that their jeopardy and need for instruction is an important plot issue.

This is a season with a particularly amorphous Big Bad, whose identity is kept from the characters until 'Never Leave Me' (7.9) but was guessed by most long-term watchers of the show from its first appearance in 'Lessons'. On its first appearance in 'Amends' (3.10), back in Season Three, we learned that the First Evil could take on the shapes and personas of anyone who had died and that its prime method was to use these impersonations to drive people to madness, despair or becoming its cat's-paws, and that it was served by blind, hooded agents, the Harbingers or Bringers. As we gradually also learn, the First has ambitions: its objective is to wipe out the Slayer line as a principle obstacle in its attempt to overrun the world with ancient vampires and achieve physical form when the dead outnumber the living. This is as ambitious a scheme as any *Buffy* villain has had – no one can accuse what is at risk in Season Seven of being an anticlamax.

The season has no formal Little Bad, its place being taken first by the intermittently brainwashed Spike, whom the First has hypnotized so that a trigger, the song 'Early One Morning', will bypass his repentant soul and his chip and send him out killing and turning randomly selected passers-by. Subsequently – and parodically – the incompetent Andrew fulfils the role, as, later, does the hideous, terrifying and at first apparently invulnerable first Ubervamp, the Turok Han. When the Ubervamp first appears, in 'Never Leave Me', the First mocks Spike, whom it has had abducted from Buffy's house, contrasting the Ubervamp's bestial appearance and utter savagery with Spike's beauty and passivity: 'Do you want to see what a real vampire looks like?'

It helps the First torture the captive Spike, whose blood opened the Seal and raised it; it dismembers a Potential who runs from it; it beats Buffy as badly as she has ever been hurt. And yet, in 'Showtime' (7.11), it falls victim to one of Buffy's most decisive object lessons. She leads it into a killing zone she has chosen, blinds it and garrottes it with wire until its head comes off. One of the problems with Buffy's inspirational speeches, of which she becomes so fond this season that even Andrew is allowed to mock her for them, is that she, like any good storyteller, is so much more effective when she shows rather than tells.

Angelus once remarked of Buffy that 'To kill this girl, you have to love her'. The First Evil is particularly equipped to hurt Buffy because it can adopt her shape and speech patterns, as it can Spike's. It is the culmination, among other things, of the show's obsession with shadows and doubles and impersonation – in a real sense, Buffy is fighting a dark self that knows all of her weaknesses. 'We are betrayed by what is false within,' George Meredith said of tragedy, and the First Evil is also the culmination of all those morally equivocal characters in the *Buffy*verse who tell the truth for reasons other than its own sake.

One of the reasons why Spike is so vulnerable to it is that he is entirely caught up in the paradoxes of his nature. When he was cursed with his soul, Angel went to pieces just as spectacularly as the Spike of the early episodes of Season Seven has over his. And the First knows things about Spike which no one else does – the mystery of the meaning of the song 'Early One Morning', with which Spike can be triggered into murderousness, is a satisfying one which takes from 'Sleeper' (7.8) to 'Lies My Parents Told Me' (7.17) to resolve.

The First is a liar. It appears to Spike sometimes as himself, sometimes as Buffy and sometimes as Drusilla and, in each shape, it tells him that he is worthless and will be killed if he does not come over to its side. Everyone, including Spike, thinks he is a liability who should be killed – Buffy is as obstinate in this as on so much else because she knows what she feels about Spike. She may or may not love him, but he has 'a place in my heart'.

The knowledge that she will come and save him keeps him sane and righteous during extended torture, and his loyalty to her becomes unquestioning. When the others exclude her, he rebukes them, and fights Faith. The chaste night he spends with Buffy in 'Touched' replaces, as the best night of his life, the night on which he killed his first Slayer and, according to scriptwriter Doug Petrie, possessed Drusilla for the first time. Because the First has no wisdom, it completely fails to understand this most complex of relationships.

In one of the season's most glaring paradoxes, however, it is hatred, not love, which helps free Spike from his partial enthralling by the First, and it is one of several examples of the First overreaching. Robin Wood, the new Principal, and Buffy's new ally, is the son of the New York Slayer whom Spike killed and whose coat he still wears as a trophy; the First appears to Wood as his mother and tells him this. What ensues is an alliance of the vengeful Wood and Giles, who believes Spike to be too dangerous a fellow-combatant with the trigger unresolved; Giles keeps Buffy away while Wood asks Spike back to his house, plays the triggering tune and proceeds to brutalize him.

This confrontation forces Spike to confront the truth – which is that he vampirized his dying human mother (whose favourite song the trigger was) and staked her when her demonic self flirted with, mocked and rejected him. All along, a crucial unacknowledged part of Spike has been his mother issues – the scene is perhaps the most unorthodox Freudian breakthrough in literature. Spike not only bites Wood, short of killing him, in return for the beating; he suggests with some justice that Wood has never got over the fact that his mother put her mission ahead of him. Adding insult to injury, Spike says 'My mother loved me', and this certainty makes him no longer vulnerable to the First.

(It has to be added that the scene between them, in which Wood strips down to a singlet and straps on a leather studded arm-piece to punish Spike, has a steamy level of subtext which is one of several moments in Season Seven where the writers tease the show's large group of slash fan writers. In 'Beneath You' (7.2), a rescued damsel says, exasperatedly, of the Scoobies: 'Is there anyone here who haven't slept together?' and the much slashed Spike and Xander look at each other nervously. In 'Chosen', even Buffy acknowledges mild slash fantasies about Angel and Spike: 'One of these days, I'm just gonna put you two in a room and let you rassle it out. There could maybe be oil of some kind involved.')

The First drives Chloe, one of the Potentials, to despair and suicide and tries to do the same to Willow, in 'Conversations With Dead People', impersonating the dead precognitive Cassie and claiming to bring a message from Tara – originally this was scripted as the First impersonating Tara herself, but Amber Benson declined to return, arguing that it would be too upsetting for viewers still grieving for her character. It appears to Dawn as Joyce, telling her that she cannot rely on Buffy – there was some dispute among fans about whether 'Joyce' was the First or not, but we have the direct statement of script writer Jane Espenson that no ambiguity was ever intended.

The First appears to Faith as the Mayor and touches her on her biggest area of vulnerability: 'Deep down, you've always wanted Buffy to accept you – to love you, even. Why do you think that is?' ('Touched'). Perhaps partly because of the possibility of a Faith-centred spin-off, the Faith of Season Seven and *Angel* Season Four is generally coded as heterosexual and becomes the lover of Principal Robin Wood (though note that his combination of butchness and androgyny is not limited to his name), but her feelings for Buffy are still the core issue on which the First can hurt her.

Yet the First has a weakness itself, which is that people can get past the vulnerabilities which give it power over them. Faith and Buffy talk through their differences and rediscover their original friendship as the Chosen Two:

> *Buffy*   But you're right. I mean, I guess everyone's alone, but… Being a Slayer. There's a burden we can't share.
>
> *Faith*   And no one else can feel it. *(Beat)* Thank god we're hot chicks with superpowers.
>
> *Buffy*   *(agreeing)* Takes the edge off.
>
> 'End of Days' (7.21)

This renewal of trust is credible because it does not happen at first, and Faith does not expect it immediately. She takes the Potentials and Dawn to the Bronze, where they are attacked by possessed cops; Buffy misunderstands the situation – regarding it as a return by Faith to her old 'Bad Girls' ways – and beats her. When this precipitates Buffy's brief deposition as leader, though, she accepts that Faith did not plot this and the conversation on the porch that follows is a display of grace on both sides. In the final battle, when Buffy is wounded, she passes the Scythe to Faith without a second thought, with a cry of 'Hold the Line'. In the show's final moments, Faith is given a rank in Buffy's heart equal to that of Dawn and Willow.

All previous *Buffy* villains have overreached, and the First is no exception, even though it knows them and their failures from the inside of its masks. Its hunger for the power to be made flesh and inflict pain and mayhem directly – 'I envy them [the various lovers in 'Touched']… I want to feel. I want to put my hands around an innocent neck and feel it crack. I want to bite off a young girl's face and feel the skin and gristle slither down my throat' – leads it to invest too much of its power in possessing its principal minion Caleb and to be robbed of some power when Buffy slices him in two.

(It is never sufficiently explicit that it had similarly possessed the first of the primordial Ubervamps to appear – but the above speech implies something of the sort. Caleb, unlike the Ubervamps, is not equipped to bite off faces. When something taking Buffy's shape echoes her song 'I want to feel' from 'Once More With Feeling', and the emotions which led to her affair with Spike, while also explicitly linking its envy for human sexuality with its desire for mayhem, we are entitled to assume that the echo also refers to the First's relationship with its vampire. The First is explicitly a parodic shadow of Buffy, and the Ubervamp – 'Do you want to see what a real vampire looks like' of Spike. This perhaps explains why subsequent Ubervamps are easier to kill.)

It is interesting to speculate whether the First's fleshly embodiment would have been Caleb had *Firefly* not been cancelled, putting Joss Whedon under a sense of obligation to his lead actor Nathan Fillion. (Similar considerations apply to another *Firefly* star, Gina Torres, who was cast as Jasmine, the finally unmasked Big Bad of *Angel* Season Four.) Rumours had the First become corporeal in Buffy's own shape, or that of the Master. As it is, Caleb is an effective embodiment of several horror clichés on which *Buffy* had not previously worked its spin – a *Night of the Hunter*-style Southern preacher turned maniac, whose misogynist rants use theological language with the precision of true blasphemy, a serial killer who uses the First's powers of impersonation to revisit favourite earlier murders. The First tends to appear to him as Buffy, creating a perverse chemistry entirely distinguished from Caleb's mocking hatred of the real Buffy. He is the formidable enemy Buffy kills most brutally of all her killings in seven seasons, in part because of that misogyny – she guts him, castrates him and slices him in half. (This is perhaps also the show's dream revenge on all the fundamentalists who tried to ban it through consumer boycotts of advertisers.)

Like all fictional villains, the First cannot shut up – Buffy says to it 'Since you're incorporeal and basically powerless, you could call yourself "The Taunter". Strikes fear...' One of the ironies of Season

Seven is that it is from her worst enemy that Buffy learns most. The Master taught her that prophesy can be confounded if you cheat – she died on cue, but came back to life. Angelus taunted her that she had nothing left and what had she got, but she simply said 'Me' and defeated him. The Mayor taught her that evil is weakened by its vestige of humanity, Adam that her friends were her strength, Glory that selfless sacrifice was the answer to someone who destroys worlds for their own needs, the geeks that being an adult was important. The First taunts her with the mission statement that has always been the core of the show and its inevitable corollary:

> 'Into every generation, a Slayer is born. One girl in all the world. She alone will have the strength and skill to fight the...' Well there's that word again. What you are. How you'll die. Alone.

Buffy has no snappy comeback, and the First comments on this mockingly, not realizing that it should have cause for concern. It knows her, but it does not understand her or her history. It has unwittingly brought Buffy to a quiet moment of thought where she makes the most momentous decision of seven years.

Joss Whedon has always discussed the core of the show as a metaphor for female empowerment and has to have been aware of the criticism that a sole Slayer is a problematic image because it lacks any hint of full solidarity with other women. In the course of the Seasons, Buffy has survived longer than other Slayers because of family and friends and a radical scepticism about authority, which I refer to in my account of Season Five as refusing to be told. Faced with an army of nearly unstoppable Ubervamps, she is helpless even with help from Willow, Faith and Spike, while the others – Xander, Dawn, Giles and so on – are mere cannon fodder.

In 'Get It Done' (7.15), she travels in time and space to confront the first Watchers, the Shadow Men who imbued the First Slayer with a demon and who offer to give her more demonic power than is her birthright as Slayer; she senses that this is the wrong answer for her and refuses. Later, she is told by their rival, the last woman Guardian, that the Scythe is also her birthright, the blade which killed the last pure demon on Earth – Buffy knows from her feelings on pulling it from the stone that the Scythe has a purity to its power and it is this side of her birthright that she chooses.

So she simply tears up the rulebook:

> What if you could have that power? Now. All of you. In every generation one Slayer is born because a bunch of guys that died thousands of years ago made up that rule. They were powerful men. *(Points to Willow)* This woman is more powerful than all of them combined. So I say we change the rules. I say my power should be our power. Tomorrow Willow will use the essence of this scythe, that contains the energy and history of so many Slayers, to change our destiny. From now on, every girl in the world who might be a Slayer will be a Slayer. Every girl who could have the power will have the power. Who can stand up will stand up. Every one of you, and girls we've never known, and generations to come... they will have strength they never dreamed of, and more than that, they will have each other. Slayers.

Willow casts her spell and all over the world we see young girls – most of them younger than the already heavily depleted age group of the Potentials we know – called and empowered. A tiny American girl playing baseball feels the power, looks at the pitcher and smiles – it is a very American moment and a sublime one. In the cavern where the suddenly empowered new Slayers await charging hordes of Ubervamps, the previously shy and timorous Violet says with confidence, 'These guys are dust.'

What follows is a deliberately cinematic battle sequence, which owes something to Spielberg and much to Peter Jackson's *Lord of the Rings*. In a typical Whedon bait and switch, it is the Potential we have perhaps liked most, Amanda – who the night before played

Dungeons and Dragons with Giles, Andrew and Xander – who dies. Buffy, apparently mortally wounded in the side in the course of the climactic battle in 'Chosen', is taunted by it in her own shape and voice and simply snaps at it: 'I want you… to get out of my face.'

Critics have complained at the way in which the First instantly vanishes, and Buffy is suddenly and miraculously healed of her wound. But Buffy is, among other things, by now the last leader of an abandoned Sunnydale (the Fisher King of a Waste Land?) and her mystic weapon, the so-called Scythe, has been explicitly compared in the scripts' stage directions to the Grail; it is also Excalibur. (Technically, of course, in many versions of the mythos, trying to reconcile disparate sources, the sword in the stone is not Excalibur, which is given to Arthur by the Lady in the Lake. Buffy gets the Scythe from the stone, but is then retroactively gifted it by the woman Guardian. The Scythe is Excalibur, for heaven's sake.)

We are by now deep in the realm of the mythic and for Buffy to expel the First with a simple verbal formula, like the one with which Eschenbach and Wagner's Parsifal heals Amfortas, that refuses its power to play on her weaknesses through impersonation, and to be healed thereby, has the resonance that comes from the material it is using. (Less elevatedly, the phrase is also a homage to one of the other masterpieces of episodic television, *Babylon 5*, whose also rather Arthurian protagonist John Sheridan tells the demonic Shadows and angelic Vorlons to 'Get the Hell out of our galaxy.' Also, Joss Whedon was a viewer of late-1980s *Doctor Who* – in which, in the midst of an explicit crossover with the Arthurian legends (the Doctor as Merlin), the Brigadier orders a similar primeval force to get off his planet.)

To consider it another way, the First's last temptation is to a combination of pride and despair. Buffy has ensured that her individual death does not matter and the imminent activation of Spike's talisman will ensure her victory. When it announces its own triumph, the First is telling the last of its many lies. And Buffy refuses to be told.

In this most desperate of fights, Spike's role is not, as one might expect, to be all-out fist and fangs, but to stand still in the middle of the battle waiting. Angel brings a talisman to Sunnydale – one given to him by the revived Lilah for her own, doubtless sinister, purposes – and Buffy insists that he leave, that Spike be her champion in this last battle. When she hands the talisman to him, their pose is that of a knight, a courtly lover receiving a token from his lady; just before turning Spike, in 'Darla', Drusilla talked of finding the bravest, truest knight in all the land, and this is one part of what Spike in the end becomes. Spike, who in Giles's Season Four dream posed in melodramatic black and white in, among other things, a Crucifixion pose, finds himself pinned by sunlight bursting from within him to destroy the Ubervamps and their dark world. Buffy and her Slayers have bought him a charm for this sacrificial magic to work – in the end, this time it is Spike who saves the world.

Buffy has, after all, died for the world twice already – she has always been not only one who saves people, but also one who inspires them to save others. She is the Messiah who teaches others to join her in Messiah-hood, including this redeemed murderous rapist vampire whom the rules say she should have killed long ago. He is as important to her as her other friends by now and she has to let him go.

She clasps his hand as it catches fire – before she kissed him in 'Once More With Feeling' she reprised her song 'I touch the fire and it freezes me' – and tells him that she loves him; he refuses to believe her and thanks her for saying so. In a sense, both of them are right – it is perhaps significant that neither the show's writers nor its cast seem to agree on a definitive interpretation of Buffy's feelings, save what she says to Angel early in 'Chosen', which is that she is cookie dough, not yet baked into a final form where it would be possible for her to make decisions. In some areas, wisdom consists of knowing that you are not yet ready.

Spike sends Buffy away, out of the collapsing building and, with a gleeful cry of 'I wanna see how it ends', turns to dust and ashes. His awfulness as a human poet was exemplified by his search for the word 'effulgent' and he goes to his doom glowing. His sacrifice is entirely voluntary and understood by him as total – Spike, unlike the rest of us, does not know that he will return in *Angel* Season Five, so that return in no way diminishes his sacrifice.

What follows is charming and brief. Joss Whedon has always said, and we thought he was joking, that the show would end with Sunnydale collapsing into the Hellmouth, and it does. One of the signs so regularly knocked over by Spike is the last thing to fall into the vast crater. Buffy races across rooftops and hurls herself from the cinema roof onto the school bus in which the survivors are escaping. In a brief coda, she and her core companions – the original three plus Dawn and Faith – look into the crater and memorialize what has been lost, not mentioning the dead explicitly because some feelings lie too deep for tears, and making wistful jokes about lost shops. Suddenly, Buffy is free of all the burdens of Slayerhood and Willow, Faith and Dawn in turn ask her what she plans to do next. The show ends forever not on an answer, but on the growing sunny wistful smile on her face as she considers what her answer may be. It is the smile of the Gioconda and of the Buddha and of a young woman with a life ahead of her.

Angel

The first season of *Angel* is the closest thing to a standard anthology series that Whedon and the Mutant Enemy production company have done. A number of the episodes – 'She' (A1.13) for example, or 'I Fall to Pieces' (A1.4) – contribute almost nothing to the story arc save for a sense of the building of a team that is briefly disrupted by Doyle's death in 'Hero' (A1.9) and grows to include both Wesley and Gunn, as well as hangers-on like its rich patron David Nabbit.

Still, the efficient first episode, 'City of' (A1.1), introduces new viewers to the vampire with a soul, brings in Doyle, his half-human sidekick, and has them rescue Cordelia, lumbering Angel with her as sidekick/reminder of what it is to be human. We are also introduced to Lindsey and the concept of Wolfram and Hart, law firm to the stars of evil. It also establishes the crucial question of temptation – the vampire tycoon Russell offers Angel the good things of LA, the kingdoms of the world in other words, and Angel responds by throwing him out of the window – parodying another of Satan's temptations of Christ with the sardonic 'Can you fly?'

Angel is subjected to various temptations: the Ring of Amara, in 'In the Dark' (A1.3), would allow him to walk in the day; and his brief return to humanity, in 'I Will Remember You' (A1.8), would have given him not only ice cream and a heartbeat, but also Buffy. He refuses any such soft options; his redemption has to be done the hard way without gimmicks or mere luck. By the season's end, 'To Shanshu in LA' (A1.22), he thinks that he understands the rules of the game – he resists temptation and fights the good fight and eventually he will be returned to full humanity.

Redemption is clearly an issue in the world of Angel. Doyle earlier refused to involve himself when other Brakken demons were under threat from the Scourge, then dies to save Angel, Cordelia and a shipload of half-breed demons like himself. Cordelia and Wesley manage to outgrow her solipsistic vanity and his cowardice to become fully adult. At the point where, in 'Sanctuary' (A1.19), Wesley sides with Angel and Faith against the Watcher's Council mere hours after Faith brutally tortured him, he acquires real moral grandeur. Cordelia's empathic encounter with all the suffering of Los Angeles in 'To Shanshu in LA' crystallizes her commitment to others rather than self. Faith surrenders herself to justice on potentially capital charges in order to save Angel from Kate Locksley's murderous spite.

And yet, in Season Two, Angel is tempted closer and closer to his demonic side. Part of the issue is that we find out even more about his past – we knew about the murder of his original family, the whirlwind of murder that was his time with Darla, but now we are forced to see, for example, his driving of Drusilla to mental collapse before turning her. We also discover that he returned to his vampiric family for a while after the return of his soul[16] and that at least one earlier attempt in the 1950s to do good ended in complicity with evil – 'Are You Now or Have You Ever Been?' (A2.2).

More importantly, he has failed to come entirely to terms with old relationships. Members of the evil law firm Wolfram and Hart invest considerable energy in raising Darla from Hell or non-existence; they regard their failure to destroy Cordelia and Wesley as no more than an annoyance, rightly perceiving that the answer to killing or suborning Angel lies in his long-standing commitment to Darla. Angel suffers from the delusion that redemption is simply a matter of saving enough lives to pay off the karmic debt created during his years as Angelus, staying humane while he does it. The reappearance in his life of Darla and Drusilla make it clear that things are more complicated than that – not least because of the intense romanticism of his relationship with Darla, who echoes his worst fears by saying: 'No matter how good a boy you are, God doesn't want you – but I still do.'

He tries, while Darla is human and dying, to persuade her to accept mortality and repentance; he succeeds, because of his preparedness to die to buy her a new chance, only to have her re-turned to vampire-hood by Drusilla, the mad creature they made together. In the face of this failure, he quarrels with Cordelia, Wesley and Gunn, severing his links, through Cordelia's visions, with his redemption and the Powers That Be. He claims that he is protecting his employees from danger, but later, in 'There's No Place Like Plrtz Glrb' (A2.22), he admits that he was frightened that they would see his true demonic face and reject him. When a far worse demon is revealed under alien suns, he learns to control it, and even Fred, the demented woman physicist who has no past with him at all, can see that there is more to him than the beast.

He allows Darla and Drusilla to take a terrible revenge on the lawyers who have manipulated them; he uses the utmost cruelty in an attempt to destroy Darla and Drusilla; he despairs and has sex with Darla in an attempt to lose his soul again. Once before, when he despaired, in 'Amends', the Powers intervened, preventing his suicide through sunlight with a Christmas snowstorm; now his return to his true path is rewarded by his being able to enter Kate Locksley's apartment uninvited (breaking the normal rules of his vampiric condition) to save her from suicide.

Yet he does manage to help someone redeem himself – and it is Lindsey, not Darla. In 'Dead End' (A2.18), Lindsey finally accepts that others pay the cost of his damnation: a replacement hand belonged to a former colleague condemned to Wolfram and Hart's organ bank. It is not just that his schoolboyish rivalry with (crush on?) Angel helps him find and free those mutilated prisoners who are still viable; it is that from Angel's humiliating mockery of him and Lilah in 'Blood Money', he learns how to ensure that he can never go back. He ridicules his superiors and Lilah with endless references to his 'Evil Hand' as he strokes Nathan's bald pate and gooses Lilah.

As long ago as 'Lie To Me', Cordelia delivered an impassioned defence of Marie Antoinette – 'It took a lot of effort to look that good' – and portrayed the revolution in terms of 'let's lose some heads'. A mere three years later, she finds herself – in 'There's No Place Like Plrtz Glrb' – an enlightened monarch in a sequinned bikini, freeing slaves and peremptorily banning polyester, saving the entire human population of a demon dimension by personally beheading its High Priest Silas, and abdicating in favour of the one being, the sweet, brave, dim Groosalug, whose mixed heredity means he might bring peace.

The resonance of her actions with an earlier vain, selfish Cordelia is a joke that makes us take seriously the extent of her sacrifice: she renounces love and power and glamour in favour of her duty, life-threatening visions and the uncertainties of everyday life in demon-haunted LA. Only Buffy and Angel themselves have made greater sacrifices. Her time as slave and puppet princess has sufficiently crude parallels with her life as starlet – an insolent director calls her 'Princess'; he, her mistress and Silas all tell her to be silent – that it would have been legitimate to assume that Hollywood was over for her, had not Season Three included one last twist of that particular knife.

Like *Buffy*, *Angel* is an ensemble series, and the last four episodes – the Pylaea arc – settle important matters for all of the group. Wesley, in spite of the carping of his father, discovers that he is a leader. Where once he told Angel 'I am your faithful servant', now he is the general, who is prepared if necessary to send the warrior Angel to death or damnation, the employer for whom a repentant Angel comes to work. Gunn makes his decision – his loyalties are ultimately with this group rather than with his street friends, though this decision is tested to destruction later in 'That Old Gang of Mine' (A3.3).

And the Host, the character who graduated from throwaway joke (a demon who foretells the future of those who sing karaoke in his bar) to source of magical advice to loose affiliate of the team, learns that he really does not have a home to go back to, thank Heavens! The high camp of his manner and diva-centred vocal stylings is interestingly opened out in this segment: Pylaea is a world without music; the Host always had this unnameable 'thing' in his head. Given the very precise parallel of this to a standard trope of lesbian, gay and trans coming out narratives, and the fact that in 1920s slang, 'musical' meant gay, it is all the more inventive that the Host is not necessarily coded as gay in sexual preference as opposed to style. Like family in *Buffy*, home in *Angel* is where the heart is – people come to LA to accept exile. And with a merry cry of 'There's no place like…' Angel strides into the Hyperion Hotel to find Willow waiting for him with bad news.

Season Three is *Angel*'s most paradoxical, containing some of its finest episodes while being in many ways its least effective season. Part of the reason is that its arc is broken-backed, with large parts of the first half being continuations of plot issues from Season Two and of the second half helping set up Season Four. Another problem, specifically acknowledged as such by Joss Whedon, is the decision to create a romantic relationship between Angel and Cordelia – with the exception of 'Waiting in the Wings' (A3.13), where they are playing

Angel and Cordelia possessed by long-dead lovers, Boreanaz and Carpenter have less erotic chemistry even than they have accidentally had with, say, Alexis Denisof as Wesley or Stephanie Romanov as Lilah.

Perhaps the best way to regard their aborted romance is as one of Season Three's stack of answered prayers that go horribly wrong and gift horses that should have been looked in the mouth; it is a season that is more unified thematically than it is in plot. Angel gets the son he never dared to hope for and the baby is taken from him. He compromises with dark magic to get the child back and is rewarded with a teenage boy whose first action in this world is to attempt his staking and who eventually dumps him in a coffin in the ocean. And his child is not Buffy's, or even Cordelia's – it is Darla's child which she staked herself to give birth to.

Angel has always hoped to be human again, and in 'Carpe Noctem' (A3.4) he is body-swapped with a frail and unpleasant old man, who manages to make Lilah Morgan his personal, as well as his institutional, enemy. He still thinks of himself as in love with Buffy, and resents Cordelia and Wesley's parodic mockery of the gloomy romance in 'Fredless' (A3.5), a mockery which foreshadows the equally tortured love affairs that lie in the future of both mockers.

In Fred, Gunn finds a lover and a substitute for the dead sister to save whom he was prepared to sell his soul, but it is at the expense of losing the friend who once took a bullet for him. He rejects the claim by his former friends in 'That Old Gang of Mine' that he has lost the mission by refusing to join in their random slaughter of all demons, yet he nearly betrays his new friends to them. Fred recovers from her near-insanity and rightly decides that Angel Investigations needs her forensic intelligence – she becomes, far too often for entire comfort, the damsel in jeopardy.

Wesley continues down the road of ruthlessness for the sake of the mission which made him an effective general in Pylaea, endng up with no friends, a slashed throat and a lover who is also his personal tempter. He always wanted to be respected by his abusive father; the half-demonic Billy, in 'Billy' (A3.6), awakens in him a virulent temporary misogyny which draws on the extent to which he is, after all, his father's son and which costs him any serious chance he might have had of winning Fred's love.

Wesley is proud of his intellect, but he is hoodwinked by Sahjhan's false prophesies, by Holtz's appeal to him as fellow general, by the apparently battered Justine's claims on his chivalry. In 'That Old Gang of Mine', he threatened his friend Gunn with expulsion if he endangered the mission; Wesley's arrogance and jealousy expel him from the group, and he is nearly smothered by a vengeful Angel. Lilah gives him a copy of Dante, and compares him to Judas; when she beds him, their apparently loveless passion is his nadir – like Judas, he is trapped in the coldest of places. By the end of the season, he is in truth the 'rogue demon hunter' he pretentiously claimed to be in *Angel*'s first season.

The theme of dangerously answered prayers is embodied most deeply in Cordelia. She decided to hang on to the visions in Pylaea at the expense of her romance with the Groosalug, and in 'That Vision Thing' (A3.2) they develop from pain that is slowly killing her to sympathetic wounds and burning that threaten to rob her of her beauty. She starts to learn to fight, then finds herself too soon in the position of having to kill Billy, only to have the satisfaction taken from her by her shadow, Lilah, to whom she earlier appealed in the name of 'vicious bitch' solidarity. She finds herself empathizing with the pregnant Darla – she after all has her own experiences of being impregnated against her will – only to find Darla more interested in using her as a food source. Ironies about Cordelia, Darla and motherhood continue to abound in the next season.

In the crucial 'Birthday' (A3.11), the Powers, in the shape of Billy's demon jailer Skip, tell her that her visions are killing her and that she needs to accept their gift of the life she should have had as the vision-free, impossibly successful star of the sitcom *Cordy*. Yet this version of reality, which she is only persuaded to accept by the threat of imminent death and a deceivingly edited vision of Angel apparently denying her, is overwritten on her actual reality.

The actress Cordy is haunted by a sense that there is something she needs to be doing, and goes to the Hyperion where she tears off layers of wallpaper to find an address the real Cordy scrawled earlier; she goes to save an endangered teenager and meets Wesley, Gunn and an Angel driven mad by the visions he got after Doyle's death. Even with all memory of the truth taken from her, Cordelia knows at some level that the one-armed Wesley and mad Angel have paid too high a price for her health and happiness and kisses Angel, taking the visions back. Skip warns her of death again, and Cordelia voluntarily renounces a part of her humanity to become just demon enough to hold the visions.

She gets the Groosalug back, and is briefly happy with him, only for him to announce that he can tell her destiny is Angel and then leave so as not to be in the way. She decides to tell Angel she loves him, in 'Tomorrow' (A3.22), but on the way to their assignation she is visited by Skip a second time, this time with a summons to duty elsewhere. She has passed tests, he announces with an authoritatively flattering air, and is to ascend and become a Higher Being. With the hindsight of Season Four, this looks fishy, but Cordelia is used to the path of duty being one of renunciation and makes the choice she believes is right. Vanity may be her besetting weakness, but it is venial here even given its consequences. Cordelia has evolved from being Buffy's comic counterpart – the selfish airhead – to being someone of almost equal moral grandeur, which makes her later betrayal by the Powers all the more terrible.

Season Three has one of the most interesting of Big Bads, Holtz, the off-screen vampire hunter of Season Two's flashbacks, a man whose righteousness is gradually corroded under the pressure of his lust for revenge. Angelus and Darla killed his wife and son, and turned his young daughter, so that he had to expose her to sunlight himself. Holtz tries to catch them as they rampage across Europe and he fails, even with the resources of the Roman Inquisition at his disposal. He is approached by the demon Sahjhan, an incorporeal tempter who needs a cat's-paw and brings him to the twenty-first century to seek his revenge.

Holtz is keen to distinguish what he wants from the mere vengeance of the gypsies who cursed Angelus with a soul – what he wants, he keeps saying, is justice. After all, how can Angel ever hope to atone for each and every person that Angelus tortured and killed? We already know the answer Angel learned in 'Judgement' (A2.1) – he can only do it one day and one person at a time, for eternity – but that is not an answer to which Holtz is prepared to listen. He captures Angel at the end of 'Quickening' (A3.8) and starts to torture him, but Angel escapes. At the end of 'Lullaby' (A3.9), he has a clear shot at Angel and his child by Darla but does not take it. Holtz believes that he is entitled not merely to kill Angel, but to torture him as well; now Angel has a son, he has so much more to lose. Gradually we watch Holtz cease to be a righteous man.

He affects concern to Wesley that Angel will harm his own child and indeed Connor is in danger from Angel as a result of the conspiracy between Sahjhan, Holtz's own employer, and Lilah to contaminate Angel's blood supply with the child's blood – Holtz may not know this, but his choice of allies makes him an accomplice. He uses torture and sex to turn Justine – whose sister Julia was killed by vampires – into his equally amoral lieutenant; Justine and Juliette were of course the sisters of de Sade's pornographic novels. He offers Wesley a day's grace to rescue the child, then has Justine abuse Wesley's concern for her to cut his throat treacherously and kidnap the baby.

At this point, Holtz and Sahjhan part ways – Sahjhan only wants Angel dead in order to kill Connor, whom prophesy decrees will destroy him, whereas Holtz's morals, though eroding, will not allow him to kill the child. When Sahjhan opens a door to 'the Quor-toth: the darkest of the dark worlds', Holtz seizes Connor and dives in. Sahjhan had faked the prophecy which led Wesley to believe that Angel would kill his son. Nonetheless, the fact that the prophecy was a fake did not preclude its coming true – Tim Minear has mentioned that the rewriting of Connor's entire existence in 'Home' (A4.22) is to be taken as a fulfilment of the prophecy. (Wesley did after all bother to verify its truth by asking the Loa, an oracular spirit, which briefly possesses a styrofoam hamburger advert.) Cheating on prophecy never pays – it is his pursuit of Connor that leads to Sahjhan's destruction, vengefully incarcerated in an urn for eternity by Justine, who is mourning Holtz.

She gets him back, of course – but as a tired old man, worn out by more than the eighteen years he spent in Quor-toth; ironically, Holtz skipped more than two centuries in the prime of life only to become ancient in a fortnight. Connor has become his son and instrument, but one he is perpetually at risk of losing to Angel, as the young man learns that Angel is not entirely the monster he has been brought up to believe. Holtz has his lover Justine stab him twice, fatally, in the neck in order that Connor will believe him treacherously slain by Angel. Holtz's death at her hands is an obscene parody of the sexual consummation they may never have had and a memory of the sexualized scene where he tested her resolve by nailing her hand to a table. 'Justice' has become something for which Holtz will kill himself and betray his lover and his child – rarely has a human character in the *Buffy*verse so comprehensively damned himself.

Lilah, and the rest of the employees of Wolfram and Hart, have, of course, already damned themselves and are condemned, in Season Three, to almost perpetual frustration as Angel outwits, or merely fails to notice, their every cunning plan. Lilah plays her own game much of the time, partly because she has decided that she disagrees with company policy about Angel and wants him simply dead, partly because she is smarter and more courageous than the men she works with. When Angel suggests that her turn to evil is 'a feminist thing', she says that it is 'a survival thing' – not all ironies come due in the course of Season Three. She entirely rejects any notion of redemption, regarding him as dense for even trying to appeal to her better nature:

> You think you can awaken some buried spark of decency in
> me? Is this how you 'help your helpless'? *I'm not helpless.* And
> I'm glad you showed up, 'cause I was sittin' here feeling a
> little 'what's it all about' and now I know. It's all about making
> the rest of your eternal life miserable.

Lilah becomes fascinating in the course of Season Three because,
unlike her former rival Lindsey, she has no moral ambiguity to attract
her, just intelligence, sexual charisma and verbal wit. Her name
may have originated as a mere verbal pattern – her rivals and peers
being Lindsey McDonald and Lee Masters – but she comes to live
up to its resonances – Delilah, Lilith, Morgan le Fay and the Morrigan
(the Celtic crow-goddess of war).

The season ends with Angel Investigations entirely disrupted and
dispersed. Lorne, fed up with having his club destroyed, and with
being assaulted every time the Hyperion is invaded, decamps to Las
Vegas, and a new set of problems; Cordelia ascends; Angel is dropped
into the ocean; Wesley starts having sex with Lilah. Fred and Gunn
find themselves rattling around the Hyperion saying 'Where did
everyone go?' The answer is: where they thought they wanted to
be. Fred and Gunn themselves wanted to be the perfect couple and
find themselves being it in isolation.

Season Four is an odd season, partly for practical reasons. David
Greenwalt had left; Joss Whedon and Tim Minear were concentrating on *Firefly*: a new show runner was hired outside Mutant
Enemy and left again within weeks. Towards the end of the season,
there was a serious chance that the show would not be renewed
for a fifth season and a finale had to be devised that would slingshot
a revised formula for the show and persuade the network to renew.
In addition, Charisma Carpenter, who had recently married,
became pregnant and was due to give birth towards the end of the
season's shooting schedule; the plot arc had to be rejigged to cope
with her appearance and with her stamina in the last weeks of her
term. Luckily, the two writers who ended up largely responsible

for micromanaging the season's arc, Jeffrey Bell and Steve DeKnight, work well under pressure.

This is the most arc-heavy, plot-intensive season that Mutant Enemy has ever made. It proceeds at a breakneck speed, like a skateboarder on a very steep hill, having to make endless minor changes of course if disaster is to be avoided – my metaphor, but one welcomed by Steve DeKnight in interview. It is all about energy, virtuosity and performance and includes some stunning reversals and trickery, some at least of which are probably last-minute inspirations and improvisations. It is full of *coups de théâtre* and revelations to an extent that not everyone liked; at one point even one of the characters, Gunn, refers to his life having become 'a turgid supernatural soap opera' and the knowing referentiality of the remark has a certain justice.

Structurally, it is a season in which a series of apparent Big Bads turn out to be Little Bads. The horned demonic Beast turns out to be a minion of something else; a reawakened Angelus is largely no more than a distraction; the Beast's master turns out to be Cordelia, only she is 'not in the driver's seat' and is being controlled by the child she is carrying, which is born as the adult Goddess Jasmine. Fighting her is an act of the deepest moral ambiguity – and leads to a radical change in Angel Investigations' affiliations.

It is the show's darkest, most tragic season – all of the characters end up morally compromised and most of them lose things and people important to them. Angel returns from the ocean's depths, rescued by the friend he cast out, but he loses his son, his current beloved and his comfortable sense of virtue. For five episodes, he is the monstrous Angelus again, manipulated into this very bad idea by evil Cordelia and only saved by Faith and Willow. As Angelus, he destroys his friends' emotional lives, kills a few people and definitively alienates Connor, who finally has justification for believing that Holtz was right. He also destroys the Beast and brings back the sun the Beast extinguished, but the first is an act of pique and the latter an unintended consequence.

We see Angel at his worst as well. In 'Awakening' (A4.10), the spell that takes away Angel's soul does so by giving him a perfect day and we realize just how much a perfect day for Angel consists of having his friends do, and be, exactly what he wants. Wesley is apologetic and Cordelia loving and Connor can be talked round. The Beast is killed and the sun restored after an Indiana Jones-style adventure and Cordelia falls into his bed, where he orgasms with a cry of 'Buffy' and awakens in his cage, with the sly cynical echoing laughter that proves he is now Angelus.

Faced, in 'Home', with a Connor who is almost entirely deranged after killing his 'daughter' Jasmine, Angel strikes him down and edits reality so that Connor was never his son, and grew up with a normal life and family, while none of Angel's friends remember who Connor ever was. It remains to be seen how this editing of their experience plays out over the following season; Angel's more ill-judged actions tend to have consequences and this fundamental lack of respect for his friends' autonomy is deeply disturbing. At the beginning of the season, underneath the sea, he hallucinates a family meal at which no one will pass him food; at the end, from outside, he watches Connor eat with his new family before going off to Sunnydale. Angel's flaws include never asking why these things happen to him.

We see even more versions of Angel's past than usual this season. In 'Spin the Bottle' (A4.6), he is reverted to the 17-year-old Liam, ignorant, hostile, lecherous and rather too interested in the implications of being suddenly a vampire. In 'Orpheus' (A4.15), we find how he regressed from the paranoid but socially competent Angel of the 1950s, to the seedy guilt-ridden vagrant of the 1990s; in the 1970s, he witnesses a fatal hold-up and ends up dining on the blood of the dead victim. This season's Angelus is neither Darla's ruffian-turned-aesthete toy boy nor the psychopath who was prepared to end the world to spite Buffy; here he is a lazy carnivore, lashing out as takes his fancy and trying to turn Faith into a vampire because it is fun. Setting aside the vexed question of what a soul is, precisely, in this fictional version of reality, we have the worrying possibility that Angel and Angelus are, more even than is true for most of us, both in a sense constructs, fictional selves with which the souled and unsouled person formerly known as Liam negotiates the world. In a drug dream shared with Faith, Angel and Angelus fight, and Angel wins; this is almost as worrying a 'retarded fantasy' as the perfect day which lost him his soul.

Wesley starts the season as an alienated loner, who keeps Justine locked in a cupboard while making love to Lilah and delivers the retrieved Angel to his former friends like a piece of baggage. Approached by Fred for help with her vengeance against the man who sent her to Pylaea, he helps as much to spite Gunn and Angel as for her; still loving her, he has sex with Lilah when she dresses as Fred – 'Leave the glasses on.' He is responsible for the team's worst idea – interrogating Angelus. He loses out comprehensively, having to behead Lilah's corpse in case Angelus turned her. Angelus keeps revelation of the Wesley/Lilah relationship until the moment when it will most damage Wesley's suit to Fred. It takes the evil Jasmine to repair the breach with Gunn – why should loving the same woman alienate them, she asks.

Wesley is at his best with Lilah and with Faith. He uses Faith as a weapon – becoming the ruthless Watcher he never was before – but with her entire consent; the scheme to drug Angelus with Faith's blood is her idea, to which he agrees. Faith is keen to expiate her torture of him in Season One, and there is camaraderie between them; when they escape together from her prison, she asks how he is and he answers with her own catchphrase, 'Five by five'. He is as tough on himself as on others – the scheme to drug Angelus involves his buying time by being viciously beaten – and he does a deal with Wolfram and Hart in a probably doomed attempt to save the dead Lilah's damned soul. And yet, the show undercuts the earnestness of this by having Wesley and Willow competitively discuss their dark pasts – Willow is patronizingly consoling about his minor sins. (In real life, the actors are a couple.)

In Season Four, the writers luckily remembered that Fred is a genius, unbalanced and a survivor. She taser-whips Connor in 'Deep Down' (A4.1) for deceiving her and tongue-lashes Gunn in 'Ground State' (A4.2) for getting himself temporarily killed. The title 'Supersymmetry' (A4.5) refers both to Fred's physics paper and her attempted revenge on Professor Seidel, who sent her to Pylaea; she is furious with Gunn for muscling in on her revenge and merely killing him. She cannot cope with Wesley's simultaneous feelings for her and the hyper-sexual Lilah – 'Sometimes,' he tells her, 'it's not just about holding hands.' She is the first to fight Jasmine – and competently eludes her deluded former friends to do so – and the first human to compound with Wolfram and Hart. She shares with Wesley and Willow a pride of intellect which may be her downfall.

Gunn shares with Angel an unpreparedness to cope with the complex autonomy of those he loves. He is easily tricked into jealousy by Angelus over Fred's complex feelings for Wesley, while being the first actually to be unfaithful. He contrasts interestingly with Angelus; imprisoned in the vampire's former cage by Connor, Gunn breaks out by a simple persistence Angelus was incapable of, refusing credit with a pop culture joke. ('Never give up, never surrender' is the catchphrase from the film, and imaginary show, *Galaxy Quest*.) The nature of his deal with Wolfram and Hart – he confronts a human-eyed panther in the sinister White Room – remains unclear, but he has certainly made one.

At the time of writing, it has been announced that Cordelia will not be a series regular next season, but rather a recurring character, like Giles in the last two seasons of *Buffy*. In one interview, Joss Whedon said that her story was essentially over and, if that remains true, it is interestingly one of the few major character arcs in either show to have ended in tragedy or pathos. Cordelia has, after all, gradually evolved out of her selfish immaturity in early seasons of *Buffy* towards something worryingly close to moral perfection – and her reward is to be tricked into becoming a monster and the mother of a monster, to be left in a coma and subjected to the vaguely unhealthy kindness of those Lilah hires to care for her and keep her fashionable.

As the season progresses, she becomes less and less herself. In the first episodes, she is in Heaven, bored witless, trying to get her friends to summon her home and helping them by minor adjustments of reality, in 'The House Always Wins' (A4.3). Then suddenly she returns, with amnesia, and no particular feeling that she should trust these people who claim to be her friends yet continually lie to her about who she is and what they are. She takes refuge with Connor, who is as alienated from them as she is. Lorne tries to get a sense of what is going on and is rewarded with confused and terrifying visions of Apocalypse – 'Slouching Towards Bethlehem' (A4.4). He is almost relieved when Lilah's minions steal them from his head.

Lorne casts a spell to restore Cordelia's memory; briefly, in a mixture of 'Band Candy' (3.6) and 'Tabula Rasa', he turns back all of his friend's memories to the age of 17, and then he gets things right. (The Lorne who narrates this excellent if derivative episode – Joss Whedon's only Season Four script – does so from an unspecified point in the future and is aware that this is where things went wrong.) The Cordelia who remembers everything, including vicarious experience of Angel's entire past, is oddly watchful, oddly concerned with everyone's reactions to what she says, particularly if they are not watching the flicker of her eyes. She rejects Angel – she loves him, but cannot bear Angelus's crimes – and by the end of the episode 'Apocalypse, Nowish' (A4.7) she has seduced Connor, whom she nursed as a newborn child. This outraged many viewers – and their outrage should have signalled to them that something is going on.

Over the next few episodes, the apparent Cordelia plays ever more intense games with Angel and his son without ever clearly announcing herself to us as evil. She persuades Angel to become Angelus again; she sows distrust between him and Connor. When people under Angel's protection die in locked rooms, and Angel's soul is removed from a safe, no one, including the audience, quite suspects her. In one virtuoso scene, Angelus pretending to be a re-ensouled Angel allows himself to be persuaded by an apparently good Cordelia to leave the cage in which he has spent a couple of episodes. We only know the truth for certain when Lilah hides from Angelus in a room and Cordelia stabs her through the neck. The fact that the knife is one we earlier saw the Beast present to its unseen master is just a supplementary shock.

From this point, we get to see the workings; Cordelia is her usual self, or something like it, when dealing with others, progressively harsh and dictatorial with her minion Connor and in telepathic threats to Angelus. Yet there is still something of Cordelia left – her frustration at having to be nice to her old victim Willow, when Willow arrives and works out how to replace Angel's soul without first retrieving it, is darkly funny. Finally exposed, she makes Connor sacrifice a young girl, gives birth to Jasmine and lapses into coma. She has been reduced to a puppet, or a costume, used to hurt her friends and loved ones, and then cast aside empty, an object over whom Angel, Connor and Jasmine fight. Self-sacrifice and renunciation have led her here, not her original selfishness and arrogance; if this were the end of her story arc, it would be a salutary reminder that in this universe not all stories of heroism end happily.

Her final episode as other than a coma victim is marked by the reappearance of Darla. Asked by Connor if she is his mother, Darla says, provocatively, 'I have her memories'. This seems to settle any ambiguity about Darla's eventual fate, as does her role as good angel to evil Cordelia's tempter in this scene.

Human Darla was killed by Drusilla against her will after accepting human death, and her soul winged its way to wherever the redeemed go in the *Buffy*verse. The purely vampiric Darla of Season Three makes a rational choice to die for Connor knowing that the love she feels for him is a contagion caused by his soul, an illusion, which will pass when her baby dies inside her. Her last remarks – 'This child is the one good thing we did together' and

'You died in an alley too' – are statements of something close to repentance. She stakes herself to save Connor.

We know that when a human's body is occupied by the vampiric demon, it acquires their memories – having memories is a form of identity, but not the whole truth. When Darla says 'I have her memories', she seems to be saying that she has made a similar change of state to that involved in becoming a vampire – she has become an angel, or something like one.

This should come as no surprise. She has always been one of Buffy's shadow doubles and like her, and like Cordelia, gets to move to a higher realm. Ironically, because she had no thought at all for herself, her sacrifice is as pure, and as unambiguously rewarded, as that of her descendant, Spike.

The fate of Cordelia's other shadow is less clear, though in 'Home' she too describes herself as a 'messenger'. Generally, Lilah is represented as irredeemable even by her genuine love for Wesley – she plays him and betrays him, but is like a little child with a present when he is the first to break their deal and acknowledge openly that he loves her. She wants to pull him over to the dark side of things – and is one of the show's evil truth-tellers when she tells him that his desire for moral absolutes is now alien to his nature. Wesley accepts the Wolfram and Hart deal partly so that he can break into their contracts department and free the undead, damned Lilah's soul by burning her contract. She demonstrates to him that her contract is indestructible, but thanks him for the attempt; even dead, she loves him.

And there is some ambiguity here – she spared Lorne's life, for example. She dies as a result of bringing crucial information about the Beast to the Hyperion – memory of it has been edited, like Connor at the end of the season, from this reality. There is also the mysterious unhealed wound in her side that the Beast gave her. The episode that features her death is entitled 'Calvary' (The Place of Skulls), which may refer to the demon skull retrieved for Cordelia's dark magic, or might, through its crucifixion reference and her wound, indicate that Lilah dies a martyr, perhaps even a dark Messiah. Her subsequent return, as the emissary of Wolfram and Hart, to congratulate the team on beating Jasmine and preventing her version of world peace, is a *coup de théâtre* and a wonderfully ironic reversal.

As Cordelia's 'child', Jasmine, the season's eventual Big Bad, is the media-savvy loyalty-compelling diva she originally aspired to be. She claims to be, and almost certainly is, one of the Powers for whom, supposedly, Angel and his friends have been fighting all these years – indeed, she claims, she is the only one of those Powers who really cares. Of course, there are the people she eats, and who die as part of the manipulations that ensure her 'birth' and the world of insectile monsters she wrecked for practice, but these are all sacrifices for the greater good. Connor, who never sees her as other than monstrous in appearance, is persuaded by this almost until the point when he kills her, and even Angel is tortured by the possibility that she is right, until he offers her an alliance after defeating her and she talks of destroying the world out of spite. In the end though, Cordelia, who sacrificed herself rather than others and has been used and abused, is a silent rebuke to her claims; apparently, in some early drafts, she rose from her coma and struck Jasmine down, but the later version is the better one.

And one of the show's principal assumptions gets revised – in the last episode, 'Home', an undead Lilah announces that the war is over. Wolfram and Hart have decided to give their LA office to Angel Investigations rather than fight them any more. For each of them, this is the offer they cannot refuse. It means medical care for the comatose Cordelia, a new laboratory for Fred, showbiz contacts for Lorne and something mysterious for Gunn. Wesley accepts for his own reasons; Angel does a deal for the sake of Connor and Buffy. Season Three taught us to look gift horses in the mouth, this one in particular; we know that Spike will be resurrected to serve as Angel's good conscience in the next season, which will apparently be much less arc-oriented. Yet, however sunlit the season is rendered by the vampire-safe glass of Angel's shiny new office, we can be certain that it will be as dark and morally complex as ever.

The Other Scoobies

The last point that needs making speculatively about these two series is that much of their subject matter reflects the working conditions of the people who create them. As various essays in this collection argue, the show has intensely democratic values in its portrayal of heroism and superpowers – Buffy regards herself as accountable both ethically and to her friends and Angel learns to humble himself to a subordinate role and redemption as a daily task. Leadership is a skill; the role of leader at times devolves to Giles or even, in 'The Weight of the World' (5.21) to Willow. Shows that might have been the preserve of an auteur in the old manner are instead a liberal nursery of opportunity and talent – many of the writers now direct and produce as well.

Joss Whedon's personal preoccupations and his genius are clearly dominant, but in a first among equals way. Descriptions of the writing methods of the *Buffy* and *Angel* teams sound unusually collective in the circumstances – Whedon devises the overall story arc, often some time in advance, and the others pitch for story slots within that arc, negotiating as a team the ways in which suggested stories would fit into the big picture. Various writers have cornered particular sorts of script – Marti Noxon is good on tear-jerkers, Jane Espenson at farce, Tim Minear at the darker side of Angel. Whedon always contributes, but rarely shares credits; a Whedon-credited and directed script is always something of an event. On *Angel*, indeed, he yielded leadership to David Greenwalt, Tim Minear and latterly Jeffrey Bell – his suggestions as to how the Host's cousin Numfar should perform his appalling Dance of Joy led to his casting in the role.

As director, Whedon's gift seems to be for the suggestion that actors have to find their own truth. Asked by George Herzberg how to play Adam in Season Four, he suggested that Herzberg 'find the stillness'. One of the most effective aspects of Herzberg's flawed but impressive performance is just that sense that every time Adam says anything, he pauses to invent it for the first time, and then to consider its implications.

Grand plans have a habit of being disrupted – the decision of Seth Green to leave *Buffy* made for some rapid rejigging of Season Four and the crystallization of what might have been rather nebulous plans to explore Willow's sexuality. Some elements in the arc result from chemistry; according to Joss Whedon, in an online interview:

> like the romance between Cordelia and Xander. Their arguments kept getting more and more intense until we realized that they needed to be together. We just didn't realize that we started writing them as a couple in episode two.

What is impressive about the shows' use of foreshadowing and echoing across the years is that much of it, in the nature of things, has to have been largely an opportunist improvisation and yet never fails to have emotional and metaphysical resonance. The later seasons merely confirm this.

My remarks earlier about Buffy's quintessential obstinacy apply in large measure to Whedon and the rest of his team. They have constantly stretched the limits of what is possible in popular television, both in terms of what can technically be done – the dialogue-free 'Hush' – and what can be shown – Whedon is on record as having told the WB network that the kiss between Willow and Tara in 'The Body' was simply not negotiable.

'The Body' is, as is remarked in various of the essays in this volume, one of the most extraordinary hours of television ever seen. What needs pointing out about it here is that it takes the extraordinary risk of being a homage to the memory of Whedon's own dead mother, who died of the same causes as Joyce; in interviews, he has remarked on how incidents like Willow's clothes crisis derive from actual lived experience. Whedon's mother, a 1960s radical who became a brilliant teacher, is one of the great unsung presences of his shows – when Dawn talks about 'negative space', about defining an object by where it is not rather than where it is, she is perhaps talking as much about Whedon's own loss as about his characters'. It is also remarkable that so flashy, operatic, witty and inventive a writer should be so entirely prepared to portray emotional truth as much through silence, stillness and reticence as his normal palette and to share so intensely personal envisioned series with other talents. The ultimately adult nature of these teenage shows derives from this completeness of emotional range.

Notes

1.   In, for example, John Clute and John Grant (eds), *The Encyclopaedia of Fantasy* (1997), many of whose other entries, notably that on 'pariah elites', are relevant to close readings of *Buffy* and *Angel*.

2.   Joss Whedon has been selective in which bits of vampire mythology he has chosen to use. His vampires explode when killed, taking clothes etc. with them and preventing unsightly corpses that our heroine would have to remove. They are stronger than in life, invisible to mirrors but not cameras, and vulnerable to wooden stakes, decapitation, sunlight and fire; only those victims whom the vampire forces to drink his or her blood at the moment of death from draining become vampires themselves. In the first two series, it is clearer that the vampire that results from a siring is not the person they previously were than is the case later on – to what extent does a loosely conceived of soul trump memory and identity? The tendency to spare Harmony, whom they never even liked when she was alive, and the sending of the vampire version of Willow back to her own world, raise interesting moral questions.

3.   In homage to the cartoon series *Scooby Doo*, which also features a group of (rather younger) adventurers who fight what often

appears to be supernatural evil, but is almost always rationalized away. Sarah Michelle Gellar starred in a live-action *Scooby Doo* film in 2002; a sequel is scheduled for 2004.

4. There is no inconsistency between Spike's participation in Darla's raid on the gypsy camp in 'Darla' and his later ignorance of Angel's curse; quite simply, Darla would never dream of sharing important information with Angel's unruly children, with whom she has been landed.

5. As early as 'The I in Team' (4.13), Giles suggests to Spike that the chip may be part of some greater purpose and Spike entirely ignores his remarks – which does not mean that they were not, as it happens, entirely to the point. Oddly, Giles is far more sceptical on this point in later seasons.

6. It is interesting to note that both Julie Benz (Darla) and Charisma Carpenter (Cordelia) auditioned for the role of Buffy, given that both Darla and Cordelia are in some sense shadow doubles of Buffy, and, in Angel, of each other. Cordelia is the person Buffy was before her powers; Darla is the rival Angel killed for her who perpetually casts a shadow on her relationship with him. Cordelia is Angel's self-chosen link to humanity and, after Doyle's death, his link to the Powers That Be as well; Darla is his link to his demonic past. It is not a coincidence that Cordelia in 'Darla' (A2.7) deceives an informant by referring to Darla as 'My older, like *way* older, like four hundred *years* older, blonde sister, Darla. No last name'. It is also interesting, given the comparatively minor use of Cordelia as a character in the first season, that her status as season regular can be seen as banking Charisma Carpenter for later use.

7. The film *Buffy The Vampire Slayer* was Joss Whedon's first screenplay to sell, and he had comparatively little artistic control over the film itself. Kristy Swanson's portrayal of Buffy was harder, more brittle and less sympathetic than Sarah Michelle Gellar's, though she worked hard at some of the

martial arts training scenes. The essential plot – Buffy is called, is trained by her first Watcher, Merrick, and kills the master vampire Lothos, at the cost of burning down the school gym with a lot of vampires inside it, and the death of Merrick, who kills himself rather than be turned – remains understood, though neither Lothos nor Merrick has ever been referred to explicitly in the show; an officially sanctioned comic book, 'The Origin', retains most elements of the screenplay and is, paradoxically, now more canonical about Buffy's backstory than the film itself.

8. Joss Whedon discusses this point at length in the commentary to this episode on the DVDs of Season One of *Buffy*; a useful discussion of slasher movies and their crude moralism is *Men Women and Chainsaws* by Carol Clover.

9. At the episode's end, Chanterelle/Lily takes over the waitressing job and the name 'Anne', under which she reappears, in the second series of *Angel*, running a hostel for the homeless that is not a demonic scam.

10. My thanks to Farah Mendlesohn for helping me clarify my thoughts about Season One.

11. My thanks to Tanja Kinkel for this and other points.

12. Sandy was killed and presumably sired by the vampire Willow in 'Doppelgangland'; she next turns up, entirely without comment, drinking in Willie's Bar in 'Family' almost two whole seasons later. Perhaps only a show so aware of its fanbase could possibly get away with continuity points that subtle.

13. Setting aside the question of whether he tells Buffy everything we see (does anyone believe he told her about his bad poetry?), there is the simple fact that the parallel episode of *Angel* – 'Darla' (A2.7) – throws a slightly different light on his siring by Drusilla of which he may never have been aware. Drusilla was sulking at her neglect by her 'parents'; Darla regarded Spike as 'the first drooling idiot' that came along at the right moment. Given her desire to be 'punished' and Angel's

mockery of Spike's vanilla sexual tastes, it is not entirely clear that Spike's love for her was actually consummated until the night of his killing of the Chinese Slayer. (Doug Petrie confirms this in his DVD commentary to the episode.)

14.   Is there any significance in the fact that William stays to be seduced and killed by Drusilla instead of hurrying home to look after his mother, whereas the Chinese Slayer he kills dies talking of her mother? Yes, there is – and we find it out in 'Lies My Parents Told Me'.

15.   He learned this skill from his brother Tucker, who summoned the Hellhounds in 'The Prom', a feat he echoed by siccing flying monkeys onto the school play. There is a running joke about people not remembering his name and referring to him as 'Tucker's brother'. In all the debate about Andrew's sexuality, is it not relevant that the attack on the play, one of the first things we know about him, is a reference to 'The Wizard of Oz', a Judy Garland movie?

16.   There had always been a contradiction between versions of Angel's past – he mentioned, in 'Angel' (1.7), that the last time he had seen Darla, she had been wearing a kimono, which never entirely meshed with the Romanian location of his killing of the Gypsy girl and cursing. Some similar contradictions could never be resolved – Spike's reference to Angel as 'My sire, my Yoda' ('School Hard', when in fact Spike was sired by Drusilla, being a case in point; others generate plot by being solved. The truth is that Angel simply lied to Buffy about aspects of his past.

This technique, known as 'retroactive continuity' is more common in comics than in television, but in *Buffy* and *Angel* has allowed for some neat evolution of character and of the handling of tropes.

entropy as demon

BUFFY in southern california

boyd tonkin

A day as bright and colourful as the night was black and eerie. Students pour in before first bell, talking, laughing. They could be from anywhere in America, but for the extremity of their dress and the esoteric mania of their slang. This is definitely So Cal.

Joss Whedon,
shooting script for
'Welcome to the Hellmouth' (1.1)

Through the centre, winding from left to right, was a long hill street and down it, spilling into the middle foreground, came the mob carrying baseball bats and torches. For the faces of its members, he was using the innumerable sketches he had made of the people who come to California to die; the cultists of all sorts, economic as well as religious, the wave, aeroplane, funeral and preview watchers, all those poor devils who can only be stirred by the promise of miracles and then only to violence.

Nathanael West, *The Day of the Locust*, 1939

I

Rupert Giles, ironically nostalgic for the grey skies of his English home, pretends to find the endless sunshine of Southern California terribly boring. For once, appearances deceive the watchful librarian. Through much of the last century, screenwriters, novelists and critics have relished an exemplary contrast between the relentless glare of the weather and the deep darkness and endless turbulence of the region's reputed moral climate.

Here, as nowhere else on the planet, twentieth-century culture indulged its taste for didactic dualism. In 'So Cal' shines the blinding light that hides sinister secrets. The blessed landscape is a playground that doubles as a killing field, the golden home of laid-back hedonism and deranged 'esoteric mania' alike. This phoney paradise (and paradise for phoneys) may mutate, at any moment, into a sudden inferno. Bertolt Brecht, dismayed by his joyless Hollywood exile, recalled Shelley's comparison of Hell with London, and decided that, on balance, 'it must be / Still more like Los Angeles'. *Buffy the Vampire Slayer* unfolds in a somewhere that pretends to be nowhere (which is what 'Utopia' originally means). Sunnydale stands, as Joss Whedon has remarked, somewhere close to Santa Barbara, and it shows.

The scripts' allusive and sophisticated blend of teen soap and Gothic fantasia gives a fresh, and quite distinctive, twist to a strain of Southern Californian suburban noir that has flourished at least since the 1930s. The disillusioned studio hack Nathanael West was dreaming and writing of the incineration of LA in 1937 (also, as it happens, when the action of Roman Polanski's film *Chinatown* takes place). *Buffy*'s followers will need no reminding that, in that year, the Master's blocked eruption into the sunshine of human society almost did for So Cal once and for all.

Angel, the spin-off series, draws rather more explicitly on the cultural mythology of Los Angeles, and its expression in landmarks of hard-boiled crime fiction and film. One can easily imagine Raymond Chandler's Philip Marlowe, Walter Mosley's Easy Rawlins or James Ellroy's Lieutenant Dudley Smith tussling with the supernaturally crooked, bloodsucking lawyers of Wolfram and Hart. Indeed, Ellroy even begins his acclaimed sequence of LA thrillers (in *The Big Nowhere*) with a teasingly vampiric touch, when a corpse turns out to bear mystifying teeth-marks 'too large for a human mouth biting straight down'. In a later LA novel, *White Jazz*, the showbiz floozie Gilda manages to wrap a disparate set of Californian nightmares into a single package when she works on a movie called Attack of the Atomic Vampires. As the librarian himself has said, 'this world is older than any of you know, and contrary to popular mythology, it did not begin as a paradise' – 'The Harvest' (1.2).

Once in charge of Angel Investigations, our tormented vampire-with-a-soul may have to tramp those mean sewers rather than the sun-baked streets, but his lineage as a private dick is strongly signposted. His rivals boast comparable pedigrees: the ruthless zombie cops in 'The Thin Dead Line' (A2.14) bring to mind the moody precinct warriors of Joseph Wambaugh's LAPD thrillers on a particularly bad day. Earlier in that series, Angel drops into the Hyperion Hotel for the flagrant 1950s pastiche of 'Are You Now or Have You Ever Been?' (A2.2). Here, the persecutory demons of paranoia remind us that Chandler, Ellroy, Mosley and their fellow princes of LA noir grapple not just with high-society crooks and sleazy cops but with the subterranean powers of Joseph McCarthy and the House Unamerican Activities Committee. 'They feed me their worst, and I kinda serve it right back to them,' chortles the paranoia demon, Thesulac.

Indeed, aspects of the four *Angel* seasons can sometimes recall a sort of underground theme park of Californian hard-boiled style. Readers of Thomas Pynchon will recall that, when the novelist wrote his own satirical fantasia on the restless spirits of California in 'Vineland', he actually created a 'Noir Centre' in lower Hollywood, where one could purchase furniture from the Lounge Good Buy, perfume and cosmetics at the Mall Tease Falcon and designer water at Bubble Indemnity. *Angel* has yet to slide that far into regional burlesque. Yet I would argue that the blander, brighter locales of *Buffy* itself make a more evocative, because more indirect, use of the idiosyncrasies of nature and culture in Southern California. Over time, Buffy and her Scooby gang confront and overcome most of their significant secrets.

Yet the question of where, precisely, they stand in Sunnydale often stays tantalizingly below the surface. The commercial and demographic imperative to be all things to all teens (at least in the USA) means that the series often can't, in the most literal sense, tell us where it's coming from. Joss Whedon and his fellow writers often stress the role of demons and monsters as embodiments of psychic states, or even intellectual tendencies. (He has, for instance, spoken of Angel as a version of the recovering alcoholic.) But why should these fancy beasts of the unconscious not possess an unconscious of their own as costumed markers of a distinctive, and distinctively dangerous, time and place?

II

Buffy rings the changes on Southern California's bad dreams. Its range of reference (virtually the entire corpus of Gothic narrative, plus the broad far western edge of contemporary youth culture) surpasses any models or forerunners. And, in two specific areas, it adds new resources to the rich local repertoire of myth and metaphor. These concern the shifting nature of danger and disaster on the Pacific coast: first, as a hotspot of environmental tumult and calamity; and second, as a focus for human mischief contrived by creatures at either extreme of the social scale.

A frequent commonplace of So Cal literature portrays the place as a climatic (and geophysical) wolf in sheep's clothing. The landscape looks and feels young, benign, innocent. In truth, the earth below, the skies above and the seas beyond secrete their ancient and imperishable powers of flood, fire, storm and (most notoriously) earthquake. 'Easterners commonly complain,' writes that expert watcher of So Cal's inner demons, Joan Didion, 'that the days and weeks slip by relentlessly, numbingly bland. That is quite misleading. In fact, the climate is characterised by infrequent and violent extremes.' Sudden calamities strike the coast and hinterland, some predictable (tellingly, the fire-raising Santa Ana winds blow in the weeks around Halloween) but many apparently random, and all the more fearful as a result: 'Los Angeles weather is the weather of catastrophe, of apocalypse.'

In the wake of the San Francisco earthquake and fire of 1906, one potential event spread from California to enter global myth: the idea of the Big One, a forever-imminent displacement of the San Andreas fault that will send the urban Far West to its long-awaited and (in some accounts) long-deserved perdition. Buffy's adopted town, of course, has its own original fault and its own memories and dreams of catastrophe. The thin membrane of the 'Boca del Infierno', the unstable portal between the human and demonic worlds that lies beneath the library at Sunnydale High, transforms a geological fact into the premise of fantastic drama. What anthropologists would call the liminal status of Sunnydale and its residents shifts the tectonic status quo into an endlessly resonant metaphor. Sunnydale remembers, endures or fears its own one-off catastrophes. In the show's prehistory, the Master's attempt to conquer the surface of the Earth was accompanied by a severe earthquake that flattened half the town. This was not quite the Big One, of course: The Master's plan misfired, with the senior vampire ignominiously stuck, since 'opening dimensional portals is a tricky business' – 'The Harvest'. Yet the very idea of the Harvest when all Hell really will 'come to town' preserves the concept of a very rare, but somehow inevitable, terminal event.

Joss Whedon made good on a long-standing promise, or threat, when that terminal event closed the seventh and final series of *Buffy* in 'Chosen' (7.22). After a sequence of episodes studded with millenarian imagery and dialogue, the final showdown between the Slayer's posse and the ancient evil of the 'First' saw school and town swallowed into the earth. For this demon-plagued corner of suburbia, at least, the Big One did in the end arrive, as Southern Californians always privately fear it will. Only a smoking chasm remained as the story-arc of *Buffy* reached its climactic point, and turned full circle. The entire 144-episode saga of Sunnydale emerged as little more than an interlude between tremors. This California dream ended, as many California dreams began, amid dust, storm and vacancy.

Earthquakes are not the only endemic terrors of Los Angeles and the surrounding counties which *Buffy* relocates onto the supernatural plane. Giles remarks that the Harvest 'comes once in a century'. A conscientious Watcher and Slayer can reasonably plan, if not for its exact timing or location, then at least for its overall incidence. Do Californian engineers watch *Buffy*? If so, all this will sound spookily familiar to them. For the creation of populous So Cal as an island of abundance in an unstable semi-desert ecology depends entirely on a series of calculations about the frequency of catastrophic events.

The mighty dams and irrigation networks devised by William Mulholland, that Godfather (or Master) of the inter-war Californian boom, rested on the assumption of an extreme flood once every century. This 'hundred-year event' might end the bliss of sunny suburban dales not in a 'harvest', but in an inundation. And yet this ominous meteorological hypothesis, on which much of So Cal hopefully stands, came to pass not once but twice within the single decade after 1955.

Mike Davis, the cultural historian of Southern California whose work opens the portal between places on the map and places in the mind, introduces us to the chilling notion of 'disaster deficit'. Geological probability suggests that the area has suffered fewer natural calamities than it should have done over the past century. 'Recent research on past climatic change and seismic activity,' Davis reports, 'has transformed the question "why so many recent disasters?" into the truly unnerving question, "why so few?". Put another way, twentieth-century Los Angeles has been capitalized on sheer gambler's luck.'

Buffy energetically makes up that deficit. Its regular commuter traffic of monsters and demons surge through the thin crust of the new suburbs to bring mayhem and threaten annihilation. Some of these entities clearly harbour ambitions to be, or at least to provoke, the Big One. Acathla, notably, tried to swallow the entire world with one demonic breath but was buried: 'where neither man nor demon would be wont to look. Unless, of course, they're putting up low-rent housing' – 'Becoming Part One' (2.21).

Yet, on reflection, *Buffy*'s bestiary of the underworld is memorable less for its heavyweight apocalyptic talent than for its capacity to generate interminable, medium-level annoyance. As the week-by-week, season-by-season rhythm of the television series demands, those demons just keep on breaking through. And plenty of them seem more vandalistic than strictly millenarian: the face-chewing Gavrok spiders, say; or the Hellhounds, with their grungy antipathy to formal wear. Yes, the ground beneath the Slayer's feet can still shake in traditional fashion. And when it does, awful events will certainly impend, as in 'Doomed' (4.11). All the same, the prevailing business at Sunnydale High and, later, UC Sunnydale is a form of reactive crisis management.

Mike Davis, whose work reads uncannily well as a sort of real-world translation of the supernatural disturbances in *Buffy*, has pointed out that constant, low-intensity disruption is replacing fears of a final tremor in Californian life. The Northridge earthquake outside Los Angeles in 1994, combined with a rising incidence of extreme weather events, helped replace terror of a single Big One with expectation of recurrent Middling Ones.

The supernatural Los Angeles underworld of *Angel* offers its own, distinctively metropolitan, miseries and menaces. In the fourth series, the arrival in LA of a seriously satanic 'Beast' provokes one plague or perturbation after another. 'Apocalypse, Nowish' (A4.7) rolls these threats into a single delirious package, beginning with infestations of rats and sparrows and concluding in pillars and showers of fire. 'No one's safe,' frets Angel's far from benign sidekick

Cordelia, in a very Angelena tone: 'It's coming, and no one can stop it.' The Beast's ministrations mean that, after this 'rain of fire', a smog-like darkness envelops the city, to the delight of all its demons and vampires. Only with the monster's destruction – in 'Salvage' (A4.13) – does clear air and sunshine return to LA.

For quite a long spell, in fact, the city learns to survive amid murk and flame. Sunlight is rapidly followed by that other Californian problem, the rise of a utopian religion with a leader / god, Jasmine, who brings universal peace at the cost of occasionally dining on her followers. By the season's end, of course, everything is back to normal – police sirens in the background and a hostage crisis in a mall.

Fire, flood and drought (abetted, in 2001, by the purely human disaster of power-cuts) now induce rumbling paranoia rather than once-for-all fits of panic. And one new peril has arisen as rampant urbanization stretches the 'wild edge' of Southern California to encircle and confine the local wildlife. Towns very like Sunnydale may, for the first time in the history of settlement, find themselves plagued by attacks on humans from coyotes and mountain lions. The 'freak' event has become a semi-regular occurrence, as legendary monsters stalk the affluent tracts. Unexpected daily demons now shadow the suburban dream. In *Buffy*, primal creatures such as the reluctant werewolf Oz, or the hyena folk who snack on Principal Flutie in 'The Pack' (1.6), often prompt discussions about the Beast in Man and the animal passions that beat within civilized breasts.

Yet, remarkably, wealthy communities in the Sunnydale mould have, during the 1990s, faced actual danger to life and limb from real cougars, real bears, real packs of feral coyotes. To the horror of residents and authorities, carnivorous predators on suburban streets transgress 'the essentially imaginary boundary between the human and the wild'. This being So Cal, there is now a support and therapy group for survivors of mountain lion attacks. Fancifully witty as they always are, the writers' team for *Buffy* might hesitate before they ever made that up.

In the mid 1990s, the Hispanic population of the state thrilled half in earnest, half in jest to the urban myth of the vampire of Chupacabra. This fearsome being allegedly drained dogs and goats of every drop of blood in short order. First 'described' in Puerto Rico, the goat-sucker appeared 'just like the devil, four or five feet tall with red eyes and a hideous forked tongue'. In Latino suburbs around LA, 'some people locked themselves in their houses and refused to send their children to school', while many others chuckled and cheerfully embroidered the rumour. As a plotline, it seems tailor-made for *Buffy* except that *The X-Files* managed to purloin it first.

III

Threats to suburban well-being can take human form as well, of course. Here, the demonology of *Buffy* comes closer to the murky mainstream of Californian noir. In social terms, the danger emanates both from below and from above. From below, it has periodically taken the form of gang warfare: a staple of Southern Californian reality since the 1940s, and of wider legend since the 1970s, when the Crips and Bloods of South Central Los Angeles first won national notoriety. In fact, the first post-war gangs of LA and its environs often wreaked their small-time havoc in high schools. Their fights and rackets accompanied the stresses of local class and racial conflict. One white-supremacist group of the 1950s, active around the time that California's schools desegregated, actually called itself the Spookhunters.

Inevitably, Spike and his testosterone-fuelled vampire mates often strut their stuff in gang-like guises. 'Three badass gang types hang out on a deserted corner,' runs David Greenwalt's shooting script for 'Angel' (1.7). 'You wouldn't want to meet any of them on a dark street or a sunny one.'

The school and street gangs of above-ground LA became a trigger for national panic only when their Black and Latino variants grew conspicuously larger and tougher than the rest. In general, *Buffy* refuses to encode its infernal crews with a clear racial identity – a sign of its writers' self-aware approach to the real-world reverberations of caricature in genre art. After surveying 138 depictions of the destruction of Los Angeles in film and fiction since 1908, Mike Davis concluded that 'white fear of the dark races lies at the heart of such visions (with the sardonic critique of cults and fringe culture coming in a distant second)'. Among these apocalyptic works, 'monsters' or 'alien hordes' did away with LA on 20 occasions; only earthquakes (with 28) and nuclear warfare (49) managed a higher score.

In contrast, a pretty average assassin's fraternity in *Buffy*, such as the Order of Taraka, will look like a model of multicultural inclusiveness. Its deadly ranks welcome all sorts of human and demonic malefactors, even, in 'What's My Line? Part Two' (2.10), the aesthetically challenged Mr Pfister, who is made up entirely of maggots. Yet the most exhilarating *Buffy* scripts sometimes confront genre clichés and typologies face on, rather than tiptoeing around them.

And the ethnic marking of a demonic troublemaker becomes exuberantly in your face (even over the top) in the figure of the African-American vampire hoodlum, Mr Trick, in 'Faith, Hope and Trick' (3.3). This undead homeboy, come straight outta Hell and Compton to organize the 'Slayerfest', rather labours the obvious when he points out that Buffy's textbook 'white flight' neighbourhood is 'not a haven for the brothers? Strictly the Caucasian persuasion in the Dale? But you gotta stand up and salute their death rate'. Indeed you have: funnily enough, the most homicidal community in Southern California turns out to be not Compton, Watts or any other infamous inner-city wilderness, but the classic (if decayed) 'bungalow suburb' of Pomona. In this ruined idyll, 'since 1970 nearly 1 per cent of the population has been murdered'.

Yet the greatest menace to society always comes from creatures a lot further up the scale of human (and demonic) privilege. Mr Trick eventually goes to work for Richard Wilkins III, Mayor of Sunnydale for 100 years, and the superbly depraved heir to a vast literary and cinematic canon of corrupt officials in the state of

California. The Mayor, indeed, has a goal for his municipal villainy that rather puts the traditional West Coast pursuit of bribes, land and girls in the shade – ascension to the status of a pure demon.

Warner Brothers, the network which, until May 2001, showed *Buffy*, illustrated the mischievous way in which the show's creators connect dark fantasy to daylight reality when they pulled transmission of the Mayor's big moment in 'Graduation Day Part Two' (3.22). Ostensibly, the postponement came about because the episode's scenes of wholesale destruction on a high-school campus chimed uneasily with fears of classroom carnage perpetrated by rifle-toting, Goth-clad teens. Fans, however, quickly spotted a WB publicity stunt. They asked, reasonably enough, how many elected officials had recently metamorphosed into 60-foot demon serpents during high-school ceremonials. The incident reminds us that, though *Buffy* can indeed be read in the light of an underlying social truth, it is also a clever and knowing enough enterprise to be able to mock (in this case, pre-emptively) its own more pedestrian analysts.

The Mayor (who is also, incidentally, an avatar of Richard III) does not act alone in his century-long devotion to the powers of Hell. Running allusions to a malign conspiracy of local notables, including Bob the police chief and, inevitably, Principal Snyder, draw on every confidential tale of skulduggery in high places to have emerged from LA and its hinterland since Philip Marlowe first trod its streets. And one customary tactic of all such plotters is to blame every dark deed on the disorganized crime of the nearest underclass. 'I'll need to say something for the media,' pleads Sheriff Bob after a vampire raid on the Parent-Teacher Evening. 'Usual Story? Gang-related, PCP?' – 'School Hard' (2.3).

After the Mayor's transfiguration, and the blitzing of Sunnydale High, the motif of elite conspiracy moves to the sinister Initiative. This demon-hunting, federally funded programme turns out to be promoting its own, much more infernal agenda. Its crack team of tooled-up law-enforcers gradually emerges as champion lawbreakers in hi-tech disguise. Professor Maggie Walsh's Frankenstein-flavoured creation of the monster 'Adam', and his projected hybrid army of 'demonoids', are scheduled to fight a final battle between the powers of sunshine and of night: 'the war that no one can win' – 'Who Are You?' (4.16).

Well funded, lavishly equipped, secretive and ruthless, the Initiative has affinities of style and method with the technology-driven 'wars' on gangs and drugs that helped undermine the social peace of Southern California in the 1980s and early 1990s. Bankrolled by populist politicians, and often led by an out-of-control Los Angeles Police Department, these initiatives sailed under minatory acronyms such as HAMMER and GRATS. They licensed an explosive mixture of condign violence, street harassment, provocation and entrapment (sending undercover 'drug dealers' into schools, for example). Predictably, they also hastened LA's most recent dress rehearsal for a purely human Armageddon: the pandemic rioting and looting that followed the LAPD assault on Rodney King in May 1992.

Since the 1950s, the Department has pioneered the research and application of high-tech policing methods in pursuit of 'pathbreaking substitutions of technological capital for patrol manpower'. Senior officers fashioned their force not as sweaty neighbourhood beat-pounders, but as remote and well-armed avengers: as 'Marines', in fact (a term also used to describe the Initiative's soldiers). As for the street-level targets of their hardware and hubris, the 'war on drugs' came to mean that 'every non-Anglo teenager in Southern California is now a prisoner of gang paranoia and associated demonology'. Demonology, indeed.

IV

Buffy, as I have argued, hangs out with the undead, struggles against her demons and endures a multiply haunted adolescence in a somewhere that purports to be nowhere. In addition to an encyclopaedic repertoire of allusion to fantasy and horror genres,

Buffy draws more covertly on local sources, notably the physical and social threats to peace and prosperity that lurk on the shadow-side of the Southern Californian dream. *Buffy* taps into the rich vein of anxiety that imagines this balmy civilization as not merely cosmetic, but positively fraudulent. Built on lies or evasions about its safety and permanence, this lotus-eating bliss must periodically fray to reveal the darker continuities beneath. 'No other place,' admonishes Marc Reisner, historian of California's perennial water wars, 'has put as many people where they probably have no business being.' Its superficial bounty, in other words, stems from a fundamental act of trespass.

In *Buffy*, the recurrent challenges to the pursuit of happiness posed by monsters, demons and vampires mimic this So Cal predicament. A surface mood of blithe optimism is tempered by constant, worried vigilance. To adapt the old Austro-Hungarian quip, the current situation in mythical Sunnydale, as much as in its real, opulent but water-deficient neighbour, Santa Barbara, can often be desperate but not serious.

Interestingly, Buffy herself makes this prevailing temper explicit when she grasps that the Vahrall demons represent a clear and present danger to the future of the planet: 'I said "end of the world", and you're all like, pooh pooh. Southern California pooh pooh' – 'Doomed'. Here, Giles has to remind the blasé, seen-it-all-before Scooby gang that Armageddon will probably entail more than a little local nuisance: 'Hell itself flows into our lives like a sea of fire.' It's a striking image, as that 'sea of fire' has sometimes taken more than a metaphorical shape around those parts. At Halloween 1993, a sudden forest conflagration swept by the Santa Ana winds made short work of the oceanfront millionaire mansions of Malibu. One witness to this high tide of flame anticipated the peculiar climate and language of the *Buffy*verse very exactly. 'This is Hell, dude,' he told the *Los Angeles Times*. 'I'm expecting to see Satan come out any time now.'

In some respects, *Buffy* breaks away from the Gothic tradition with which it so deliriously plays. It masks, or allegorizes, few of its abiding themes. To take the most glaring example: vampires can hardly function as merely an erotic, Freudian 'return of the repressed' in a context that foregrounds sexual desire in such an endearingly matter-of-fact way.

Unlike many of its models, the series has very little to hide. As Giles says on one occasion, 'I believe the subtext here is rapidly becoming text' – 'Ted' (2.11). Rather, the fantastic machinery of *Buffy* works so well because the hard truths that may be swiftly said about sex, power, parents, identity and community still have to be imagined with a force and depth that more realistic popular art will seldom match. The show does all that, and more. But one can still suggest that it contains one semi-occluded terrain of hints, nuances and even disguises.

This area belongs, precisely, to Southern California: to the specific somewhere that must be translated into a generic nowhere for the series to stake its claim as a national, now international, cult success. In time, even the strong local signal of Valley Girl slang, with its 'esoteric mania', begins to sound like the routine argot of trend-hopping teens in the USA and beyond. Yet traces of a peculiar place, with a peculiar physical and social geography, do rupture the surface. Like the demons themselves, they may burst unbidden through the flimsy portal of the Boca del Infierno.

'This is definitely So Cal,' as Joss Whedon wrote: forever the land of uprooted incomers, which in the case of *Buffy* include Celtic vampires who might once have fed in Anne Rice's New Orleans and the ancient, malignant 'Old Ones' blown in from H.P. Lovecraft's New England. 'In spite of all the healthful sunshine and ocean breezes,' wrote Louis Adamic (the social critic, and a real Slavic immigrant to Southern California), 'it is a bad place full of old, dying people, who were born of old, tired pioneer parents, victims of America full of curious, wild and poisonous growths, decadent religious cults and fake science, a jungle.'

Even the wilfully eclectic modes of supernatural style in *Buffy* can be seen as a So Cal trademark, just as the region's vernacular architecture may famously shunt Spanish Mission next to Scots Baronial next to Bauhaus Streamlined, lot by lot and cheek by jowl. Kevin Starr, state librarian of California and its de facto official historian, stresses the state's hunger for a recreated past rather than its flight from the old world. 'Let others speak of California, Los Angeles especially, as the erasure of memory,' he recently wrote. Just as characteristic is 'the persistence of memory on this far American shore, the way California hungered for history and orthodoxy along with a sense of new beginnings'.

You can, of course, hunger for ancient heterodoxy as well: the Goth cult among schoolkids caught on in So Cal earlier than anywhere else. In summer 1997, police arrested many teenage Goths for drug offences at night in the Disneyworld park at Anaheim. 'It's a great way to get out of the house,' a young friend of the fanged told the *LA Times*.

This yearning for dark, Old World mysteries amid the brightness and blandness of the New perhaps helps to explain the development of Willow Rosenberg's character across the seven series. This anxious, obedient computer ace forsakes first her heterosexuality and then, after the killing of her lover Tara by the whiny geeks of the Troika, every trapping of social conformity. The terrifyingly powerful witch that Willow eventually becomes lends a world-shaking glamour to the vengeful Goth fantasies nurtured in a thousand adolescent bedrooms. As she descends into the state of a gaunt, grey magic-junkie, she sheds all vestiges of sun-kissed West Coast health and hope. 'Bad' Willow raises the dead in a cultural as well as a corporeal sense.

Her Poe-like resurrection of Buffy at the start of the sixth series triggers a consistently gloomy, Euro-Gothic atmosphere. West Coast skies seem to darken while the disoriented Buffy herself, now more Faustus than cheerleader, imagines Sunnydale itself as Hell. Significantly, before her (somewhat soppy) redemption by Xander's love in 'Grave' (6.22), Willow has also turned into a sort of weather-witch, brewing violent storms, hurling fiery bolts and rocking the

very ground beneath her anxious pals' feet. Also typically
Californian, after a period of nervous anxiety about her powers, is
Willow's self-reinvention as the even more powerful White Witch
of 'Chosen' – there are second acts in American lives.

Buffy flies, I would maintain, under the double flag of Southern
California: on the one hand, a far-reaching cultural eclecticism and,
on the other, a stubborn bedrock of sheer natural wildness and
terror. 'Gingerbread' (3.11), written by series co-producer Jane
Espenson, deftly grafts the German Gothic figures of Hansel and
Gretel onto an up-to-the-minute scare about child abuse and ritual
magic. Driven to paranoid hysteria by the demon who has adopted
these eerie children as his guise, Joyce Summers and other Sunnydale
moms found 'Mothers Opposed to the Occult'. Their ill-fated
campaign emulates the moral panics that have swept large tracts of
affluent suburbia over the past decade especially, perhaps, the long-
running McMartin Preschool case in Southern California, when day-
care centres stood accused of mass 'satanic' rituals. At the McMartin
trial, 'children testified about molester-teachers who flew around
on broomsticks, and other manifestations of the evil one'.

Yet underneath the 'Gingerbread' witch-hunt, with its mingled
flavour of borrowed folklore and headline news, Jane Espenson
envisaged another force, an inchoate, primeval demon of chaos.
Below social morality and collective paranoia, nature itself seethes
in a distinctly So Cal way with a blind urge towards breakdown and
mayhem. 'The world is full of disorder,' Espenson has said
(interviewed in Golden, Bissette and Sniegoski, *Buffy the Vampire
Slayer: The Monster Book*):

> Human beings are constantly trying to bring it into some
> semblance of order, and the world fights back. Disorder
> became demonized, as if it were an actual entity against which
> we struggle. Entropy as demon. I think that's why so many of
> our demons have that function. They just want to get in and
> mess things up.

'The world fights back.' It's a pretty serviceable motto for anyone who watches *Buffy*, or who lives in Southern California.

Bibliography

Brecht, Bertolt, 'On thinking about Hell', in *Poems 1913–1956*, ed. John Willett and Ralph Manheim (London, 1994)

Buffy the Vampire Slayer Script Book: Season One, Volume One (New York, 2000)

Davenport-Hines, Richard, *Gothic: Four Hundred Years of Excess, Horror, Evil and Ruin* (London, 1998)

Davis, Mike, *City of Quartz: Excavating the Future in Los Angeles* (New York, 1992)

Davis, Mike, *Ecology of Fear: Los Angeles and the Imagination of Disaster* (London, 1999)

Didion, Joan, 'Los Angeles Notebook', in *Slouching Towards Bethlehem* (London, 1993)

Ellroy, James, *The Big Nowhere* (London, 1990)

Golden, Christopher, Stephen R. Bissette and Thomas E. Sniegoski, *Buffy the Vampire Slayer: The Monster Book* (New York, 2000)

Pynchon, Thomas, *Vineland* (London, 1990)

Reisner, Marc, *Cadillac Desert: The American West and Its Disappearing Water* (London, 2001)

Starr, Kevin, 'The Musso and Frank Grill in Hollywood', in William E. Leuchtenberg (ed.), *American Place: Encounters With History* (New York, 2001)

West, Nathanael, *The Collected Works of Nathanael West* (London, 1969)

writing the vampire slayer

interviews with
jane espenson and steven s. deknight

roz kaveney

1. Jane Espenson

JE   I grew up in Ames, a small town in Iowa very far from the TV industry, and I always knew I wanted to write for TV. I was a big fan of *Barney Miller* and *Starsky and Hutch*, and *The Love Boat*. I knew which shows were guilty pleasures and which were the well-written ones.

RK   Define the difference between guilty pleasures and well-written television shows.

JE   The nice thing about *Barney Miller* or *M*A*S*H* or *The Odd Couple* is that the characters are well defined. You knew how the characters would react: you could imagine a scenario in your head and have an insight as to how it would play out. A show that is a guilty pleasure has wonderful moments that make you laugh and fall around but does not have such well-defined characters.

RK   So you see television as character-defined?

JE   You would think so, but *Law and Order* is one of my favourite shows and is completely story-driven. You don't fall asleep at night imagining scenarios for it, or saying, 'Boy, here's the episode of *Law and Order* I have been waiting for'.

RK   What about *24*?

JE   Well, exactly. I was surprised that *CSI* became the top show because it is completely without an arc. This is the era of the arc – character-driven turmoil that keeps you coming back next week to see that this person is OK and to find what happens to them next. People come back to *CSI* for the little puzzles. There is nothing better or worse about this – the shows I watched as a kid were shows like *M*A*S*H*, which is why, when I was 12 or 13, I wrote a spec *M*A*S*H* episode. It was terrible in most respects, but I think even then that I got the voices. Getting voices is something I get easily without effort – there are other parts of the job I find harder. I have been thinking about it a lot because I am writing my first episode of *Firefly* – which is going to be one of the first ones written – by looking at the three hours so far written for the characters voices. Book has only 30 or 40 lines so far and I have to look at the words on the page that have already been written for him in the most mechanical of ways – how much does he hesitate, how much does he use colloquialisms? – and just get the mechanics of it right. What you do effortlessly when a show has been on the air for a long time and you hear the voices, is the same thing you do effortfully when you are trying to do it off written exemplars with not a lot of input.

RK   So what bits of the job do you find hard?

JE   Plotting. I find breaking a story hard. On *Buffy* even though we break the story as a staff, it is so Joss's show. Joss or Marti will come up with the beats of the story with inputs from us. If they are not in the room, we will try and break the story, but if we do it rarely stays the same as we left it. Joss or Marti, particularly Joss, will come in and with laser-like insight completely re-envision the story and it will be that 'Doh!' moment of 'Oh, of course! why didn't we see that?' When I have had to do it recently has been when I have been doing comic books and some have gone well and others less so. It is not my primary skill – what I am good at is the funny and the voices.

RK   Talking of comics, I loved your Jane Austen segment in 'Tales of the Slayer.'

JE   When Joss came in and offered us any literary period or style, Doug was all over 1970s Blaxploitation and I said Jane Austen. When I got down to writing it, I realized that Jane Austen would never ever have written about vampires and that after all it is not a very comic-book world she lived in. It is all talk and almost nothing happens. It is all internal and it doesn't lend itself naturally to comic books and I had to go, 'What have I got myself into?' and figure out how to make it work. I had almost written the whole thing before I finally had that twist ending. Which, thank goodness, because there was not much there without it, I was banging my head against – of course it's a party and of course there's dancing and of course we know there is a vampire and how do I make this anything other than the dashing young man who is a vampire. And then I came up with my little identity twist and thank goodness because I would have been pretty flummoxed without it.

RK   So, funny...

JE   Gotta be funny...

RK   Except when not...

JE   Knowing when not to be funny is one of the last lessons of funny that I've learned. I come out of sitcoms – *Ellen*'s last season for example – and the more jokes per page the better. Three jokes per page good, four fabulous. On *Buffy* you want whimsy more than hard jokes and you only want them where it's right. You want to break the tension with them and spice up exposition with humour, but you don't want it thrown in for the sake of funny when that's not appropriate to what everyone is feeling. Which is a lesson I had to learn.

When I wrote 'Gingerbread' (3.11), I put in inappropriate funny about the dead children and had to take it out, and by the time I wrote 'After Life' (6.3) I had learned that lesson and didn't put funny and tried to write scary and just put the funny in where it fitted and that worked really well even though I still find it scary when I look at a page and don't see funny on it. When you finish a script your first instinct is to hold it in your hand and are just about ready to turn it in, almost everybody will flip it open a couple of times and read a page and try to see it through Joss's eyes.

If he looked at this page is there funny? is there anything that would make him chuckle? and it's scary if you open and there's not. I get very nervous, I had a chance to turn in my *Firefly* early and at the last minute I held it back and said that I need more time. I opened at sample pages and saw clumps of three or four lines that were just people exchanging greetings or information without funny, and I couldn't bear it, it was dull. I needed to take it back because it wasn't done.

Plot funny I do have to work on – it doesn't come naturally – nothing to do with plot comes particularly naturally to me; gag funny does – it seems pretty natural – but it's in the voices. There is something that you're doing almost formulaically, but that you are not conscious of. When you sit in a sitcom room and you pay attention to how people are structuring the jokes that they are pitching, you start to notice that there are certain patterns to them. You look for a funny word or an association with the word in the previous line and you look for 'How do I turn it around? Is there some play off the opposite of this situation? Is there some metaphor that the person could call on in the situation?' You do end up with a little checklist of places to go to look for funny in gag-writing and when you are sitting in a room you find yourself using such a list, but when you are at home and the funny is coming naturally. It's probably the same list and you are doing it unconsciously and that comes pretty easily for me.

As long as people like my humour... There is a thing that happens when styles of humour get outmoded. We were talking the other day about the old Jack Benny show and there is a structure there that Doug described as punch-line, setup, setup, where there'd be a joke like: 'My boyfriends at home dancing the can't-can't – Don't you mean the can-can? – Not the way he does it.' The joke comes first and then you set it up and that was a very standard structure that you hear in work of that period: *Mad Magazine* used it too.

Humour is not just universal, it has fashions that come and go. So far I am grooving with the funny, and when I am 80 I have a feeling that it won't be working no more. But then who cares, I'll only have to entertain the other 80-year-olds in the home and they'll still like it.

RK   Let's go through the actual mechanics of developing a script. Tell me about pitching.

JE   Pitching is something you do at *Buffy* when you come in for your job interview – you pitch story ideas. Once in a great while there may be a freelance who comes in and pitches ideas and those are full-fledged story ideas already beaten out which means that you have act breaks and the whole story, beginning, middle and end.

But when we're pitching stories, we tend to be much more informal, we'll say something like maybe this story is about Willow setting fires with her mind and she doesn't realize it, because that's a metaphorical symbol of inner turmoil, and we'll pitch it like that, but we won't have it all broken down because there's a point of diminishing returns because if you flesh out a story fully, you're doing what Joss and the rest will do as a group and taking it down the wrong road. And very often pitches come not from any of us but from Marti or Joss. Joss will come up with an amazing thing to happen to Spike that will progress Spike's story in a way none of us were thinking. Usually the pitch goes past before you notice it. And then you start breaking the idea.

You have to know where the story is headed, and then you come up with the act breaks – within that story what's the big turning point in the middle, the second act break? What are good first and third act breaks? What's our teaser? And then the little beats along the way.

There has to be a scene where they share information, because that has to be before Xander goes to the place, so there's probably a meeting scene at the top of Act Three or perhaps it's in the middle of Act Two. There will be a big debate among all of us about where the events should go. There's probably a girl who is attacked but she gets away – at the top of Act One? Should it be someone we know? Should it be Xander and not a girl at all? Discussions like that and it all gets written down on the whiteboard with comments from Marti and Joss so we all know it's the final structure. All the scenes and who is in them and what happens in that scene. When that's done, the whiteboard is full, and it's all broken down into acts and scenes, it is given to whoever is down to write that episode to go and write the outline.

RK   How does assignment of scripts work?

JE   We generally know when a story is being broken who is going to write it. We generally go in a descending order through the ranks of the writers, so Marti will write and then Fury and then me and then Doug will, down by titles from higher to lowest. It rotates through that cycle throughout the season. It may get messed up because someone is not available because they are writing an *Angel* or a *Firefly* at the same time, so they get jogged out of the rotation. Or they have to share an episode because they have got some personal thing. The order can get a little messed up. Sometimes Joss will say that a script is too big and ambitious for a new writer, or offer me a particularly funny one, but generally we go in order.

RK   The outline?

JE   The outline normally only takes a day – some do it in the office, but I always take it home – and it is a matter of taking what is on the whiteboard and turning it into sentences and it can be anything from nine to 14 pages. It will have a little more structure about the order things come in within a scene and about transition from topic to topic and a few sample jokes – here's something funny Willow might say in this scene – and it will give you more sense of attitude and tone than you would get from the whiteboard. You turn that in and you get notes from Joss on your outline.

RK   Notes?

JE   Notes from Joss are usually minor because he tends not to change things away from what was decided in the meeting. But he will usually catch something you've done where you misinterpreted something he said, or have got a character in the wrong mood, and then you get another day to change the outline, and more often he tells you so you understand what you need to do – you often don't have to do a second draft of the outline – and you go away and write the draft.

And now you're writing the draft and you get anything from four days to two weeks, and sometimes it will be as little as three days, but you really can't do it in less than that. If we are in that kind of time crunch we will usually split things so that one person writes one half of the script and the other writes the rest. You write a draft and you are fleshing it out from ten pages to 52, and everything goes in. People standing outside might think that we do drafts with placeholders in – a joke to be decided on goes here – but we don't. It's all down there when we turn it in; some beginning writers think a first draft should be like a first draft – it shouldn't – it should be your idealized version of what you'd like to see on the scene. That first draft should say 'Here's your reason to renew my contract', even if you know it is going to be rewritten over and over again. 'Here's what I bring to the show, here's how I see the show.'

And then you have to wait for Joss to read it, which can be agony because sometimes he takes as much as a week to get back to you with notes. It can be nerve-racking – and then he gives you notes on the first draft and they are very specific – the vaguest note you will ever get is 'This joke doesn't feel right, come up with a better one'. Sometimes they are as specific as 'Use "in place of" rather than "instead of"', and they get more and more specific as you go through the note process. On the third draft you can tell towards the end whether he will go in and do a pass at the script himself, because, if he is not going to, he will be down getting you to fix punctuation and word choice because he is not going to have a chance to do it himself, and then he will take what you hand him and give it straight to the production people. And usually he makes his own last pass, you get the shooting draft and find the bits he has changed and what is stunning is how uniformly amazing his stuff is. At this point you have agonized for three weeks over a scene and he just went in and you see what he was trying to get you to do.

RK   How consciously have you all made shadow doubles – not just duplicates, as in 'The Replacement' (5.3) – but characters echoing each other across time and so on, a part of the shows?

JE   Some of that is conscious – these characters have histories and we know what will push their buttons and we know that the audience knows their history and we love that stuff.

RK   But what about the whole light/dark, Madonna/whore, William/Liam thing?

JE   Much of that just happened without its being thought through. There was a lot going on and inattention and we try to keep Spike and Angel as far apart as possible and we would not consciously have given them the same name. I didn't even know that Liam is short for William.

RK   It's the Irish form.

JE   Some of it is conscious and some of it is not conscious, but is clearly there anyway, and sometimes it's just sloppy and a dynamic that is going on in *Angel* will be in someone's mind when we are writing *Buffy*. We throw out a lot of stories for being too close in story or feel to what we are doing in another show. We have two crazy characters – one in *Firefly* and one in *Buffy* – and we are working really hard at distinguishing kinds of craziness. So much of this comes out of Joss's brain that sometimes if you spot parallels it is that something is on his mind and finds expression in two shows at once. But some of it is conscious – echoes across time – take Spike getting his soul back – there will be differences but he and Angel are in the same world with the same rules.

RK   The act of creating difference also creates similarities. What about inadvertent foreshadowing? Say, Willow's hubris over Faith's murderousness – all that 'You have to have it in you' stuff she says in 'Doppelgangland' (3.16)?

JE   The only way to make it happen is after the fact – it is like the Willow gay thing. In 'Doppelgangland', she notices that her vampire self is 'kind of gay'. When we started plotting the Tara arc in Season Four, Joss said, 'Were we planning this back then?'

And even he didn't know for sure. When it first came up, the Spike thing about torturing people to death with railway spikes was not funny and that episode has a joke in it now, after 'Fool For Love' (5.7), that it didn't use to have.

It is a matter of texture. Sometimes you try to be prophetic and it can be a little precious and fourth wall. We can echo but on the basis that audience remembers and not that they have forgotten. Characters experience the same thing differently because they have changed across time.

RK   Plus that you can make characters refer to the fact that they have been through this before – in 'Waiting in the Wings' (A3.13), there is an echo of 'I Only Have Eyes For You' (2.19), when Angel acknowledges that he has been possessed by young lovers before.

JE   I love it when shows acknowledge that they have created a world and try to keep it consistent. The *Young Indiana Jones Chronicles* have a scene to explain where Indy got his scar – which is Harrison Ford's scar and not the character's – we did the same with Spike to explain James's scar. I love to write a joke about the appearance of the actor – that was what happened with Buffy's haircut – Sarah wanted to get a haircut and so we could put in this whole wonderful moment of her hacking her hair off. We were able to use the fact that she wanted a haircut to do this quite shocking thing. Here is a difference between TV and novels – we have real people acting it out, and everyone sees the same Buffy and we can comment on how she looks and she is short and thin. It makes it a world you can step into.

RK   In 'Intervention' (5.18), you had the Buffybot saying 'Angel… has hair that sticks up and he's bloody stupid'.

JE   I think that was Joss – no, it was me and he liked it – since it was a fun comment and also a bit of Spike's programming. It had the Englishness of saying 'bloody stupid' and also Spike's obsession with Angel's hair. Doug, back in 'In the Dark' (A1.3), put in all that stuff about nancy-boy hair gel.

RK   *Buffy* and *Angel* are among the first big shows of the DVD era – which means that it is possible to read them like novels.

JE I've been thinking a lot about parallels between novels and what we do. What we write is not a hundred-part movie, but more like an episode novel. What used to distinguish television was its ephemerality and simultaneity. Everyone experienced it at the same time and then it went away and you didn't see it any more and there was something beautiful about that. And now every piece of work exists at the same time in everyone's heads, and it doesn't go away, and it is not simultaneous because of VHS and TIVO. You don't get the same thing of people calling between act breaks to go 'How Cool!', and the existence of a spoiler culture on the net means that people's expectations are far more varied. It is all much more like a novel. The only reason television is more aggressively censored is that you can't walk in a room and see what your child is imagining out of a book.

RK How do you explain the intense quotability of what you all write?

JE Quite simply, it's Joss, and the rest of us trying to write like Joss. If you see a *Variety* interview with a bunch of show runners and one of them is Joss, Joss will always be prominent because he gives great quotes in real life. You will ask him about something and he will come up with some statement that sums up the times we live in – his quotes are very precise and he always says exactly what he means. We try to sound like him. In *Firefly*, I am throwing out perfectly good jokes because they are not yet the Joss thing, the right words for the character and situation. You don't save jokes for reuse – if they are not right for that moment, they are not right for anything else. There is that 'Yes!' moment, when you have written the right line. And sometimes you get a note from Joss about that moment and then you have to accept you are still learning and turn the hubris back down to seven.

RK Let's run through your actual scripts.

JE 'Band Candy' (3.6) was the first one – I pitched it at my job interview – I had this notion that we think our parents would be better if not so responsible, but actually it is scary and dangerous. In my pitch there was no Giles/Joyce sex, just fooling around. It was my first lesson in – in this show we can really go there. On most shows, it would be too extreme for mentor and mom to have sex – we played it for a joke and we could go to a place like that. And then Buffy finds out in 'Earshot' (3.18). There is the criticism that all the adults sounded the same age – I pulled on the language of my own youth – Snyder's personality is the guy who gets left behind.

RK   Besides Giles's teens are Ethan's teens and Ethan is the magician, so it sort of makes poetic sense.

JE   I got to throw in British slang – Joss rewrote the music scene – I loved having Joyce saying breaking the window was brave. I was so happy when Joss thought of echoing the music scene in 'Forever' (5.17) with 'Tales of Brave Ulysses'. I am not good on music – but when something is added to your script you come to feel responsible for it, and proud when it gets echoed later.

RK   'Gingerbread'?

JE   'Gingerbread' was my hardest episode – lots of rewrites and even plot changes like Amy getting turned into a rat. It was a troubling episode and I never really got the groove of it – Willow's mom was smothering in my version – I made a lot of mistakes but it was only my second show. It was a shock after doing well with 'Band Candy'. I thought of it as a surface funny romp and it is not.

RK   It has Cordelia getting to be heroic.

JE   When I got the job, I was most worried about writing Cordelia. I didn't get her, I don't think that I approved of her, and I felt that showing such a frivolous, fashion-obsessed girl was bad for all of us, and I didn't get that she had depths. When I started writing her, I realized that she is not everything that is wrong about how men see women, she is a girl who has created a persona for herself that has less depth than she has. I was happy to get to do 'Rm W/a Vu' (A1.5) and do her justice again. I gave her the SAT line – 'I can't have layers?' I was still trying to find her then. I love giving characters the line that is not what you'd expect and show how it completely fits.

RK   'Earshot'.

JE   'Earshot' was my breakthrough, the first one where I really made Joss happy. He really loved that script and it made me feel confident in the job. I felt that I had cracked it and was employable. It had stuff for Jonathan and a really strong metaphor and Buffy in pain. Also it turned out to be an episode that had a comment on real world events and what we said was relevant – everyone is in pain and if teenagers knew that it would be better.

RK   Also, it had Freddie the newspaper editor…

JE   I wish we could have brought him back.

RK   … and Willow the great detective.

JE   Look at it now and you see for the first time Willow handing out assignments and her idea that detective work involves work sheets. I identify with intense school-oriented Willow.

RK   I love the intense emotions in 'The Harsh Light of Day' (4.3).

JE   There was a line in the coda that we cut for length – Buffy is being feeble and Willow calls her on it and then Buffy says: 'I was so proud that I was in a relationship that was not about Angel; and every moment I was in it, I was thinking, look at me, it isn't about Angel, look at how it isn't about Angel now. How come I didn't see that it was all about Angel? I wouldn't have been thinking about him if it wasn't about Angel.' I wanted to show her vulnerable. Harmony and Spike were Joss's idea. This was a script I lay in bed thinking about and realizing that every scene was going to be a joy to write – the most fan-ficcy script I have ever got to do except for 'Superstar' (4.17). Getting to write Spike and Harmony and then the Buffy-Spike fight was a joy to write.

Joss gave me a particular assignment, which was: 'Make me fall in love with Parker, because we are not going to buy Buffy doing this if he is not off the chart charming.' I had to do what I don't normally do – my gift is for doing the voices – create a character that charming that we would fall in love with him.

And now, about 'Pangs' (4.8) – this was one where the core of it was something Joss had wanted to do for a long time, which is have a dead Indian at Thanksgiving – a very poetic illustration, I think, that we do kind of live in this country by virtue of some very ugly conquest. And the next thing you know we had a very non-threatening bear and some funny syphilis. I loved writing this one, because it was jam-packed with humour. This one also, however, was one of the most extensive rewrites I've ever seen Joss do. After I turned in the draft, he noticed a structural problem, which is rare on this show… we usually don't touch structure after a script has gone to draft. Anyway, there was a problem in that Act Three didn't really advance the story. So he started rewriting at that point… much of Acts Three and Four are pure Joss, not me.

RK   You co-wrote 'Doomed' (4.11)…

JE   It was a pile of scenes that I barely remember writing over a weekend. I loved writing 'A New Man' (4.12) – it has Spike and Giles together and all the stuff in the car – Ethan and Giles and that strange edge between them – 'a couple of old sorcerers' and that misleading moment with 'You're really very attractive'. That was originally a much longer scene, with Ethan complaining about people trying to sell him synthetic eye of newt.

And yes, I have always felt that there was something between those two when they were younger. It is one of the places where slash and canon merge – much like Jonathan and Xander in 'Superstar'. I am not trying to hide anything. Run with it, kids.

RK   Was it known in advance that Danny Strong was available to play Jonathan in 'Superstar'?

JE   It came to Joss in a dream or something. We were down in the *Angel* conference room and he gave us the whole teaser with the vamp nest and the mansion and the swivel chair and Jonathan. Joss had this notion and I asked to be allowed to write it. Also because I love alternate universes – you can do anything – it made me happy. I like changing dynamics, and getting to see what's Buffy like when she's no. 2. We packed it with jokes – the women's soccer team and Danny in basketball uniform – that so tickled me.

RK   What about the reworking of the opening credits?

JE   Joss said write little moments to insert. It was Doug's idea to do new credits – I wanted Jonathan kissing a just-rescued girl.

RK   It is interesting that somehow having Jonathan cheating to make the rules of the world suit him makes the appearance of Dawn, who has no responsibility for what has happened, more emotionally acceptable to the others.

JE   Yes it does help with Dawn; it also meant that Anya got to set out some of the 'rules' of alternate universes.

RK   'The Replacement' is a perfect version of a standard episode.

JE   When I pitched for the job, I suggested this episode and ones like it just because of the existence of Nick Brendon's twin – it's an amazing resource. I knew it would be funny. 'The Replacement' was the third or fourth title for that episode – I felt that it didn't work as a way of misleading the audience. It had a great scary looking demon with a molten cracked face. I liked the joke about his name – I saw it on the page and decided to go with the joke about Buffy bluffing when she thinks it is English slang. I love the joke about Buffy exhibiting hubris.

In 'Triangle' (5.11), everything the Big Troll said had Capital Letters in the script. It was never an episode that got up and ran. It was tooth-pully – I never felt how did that get written, because I had written every word… Anya driving Giles's car was one of my favourite jokes though – I often end up doing driving scenes – driving scenes always have 'why can't you drive faster stuff?', because of the need for urgency.

'I Was Made to Love You' (5.15) gave us the first meeting with Warren, and ended up being funny and poignant. April breaks your heart at the end – I like that scene – I tried to show that scene in a seminar at Santa Barbara, but their equipment gave the wrong balance between the words and the music. I love the girl we got because she was so very robotty…

RK   I can't imagine anyone playing her better.

JE   I know, I can't either…

RK   We can't have that conversation, can we?

JE   No, we can't. She was great and it ended up being really good. It started off as lets do the little abandoned robot and ended up being so much more – Buffy and boys and not needing one.

'Intervention', the Buffybot episode, was the rare case where by cool luck that I got assigned to do a second robot episode and poor Spike! Marti came up with making Buffybot, not Spike, going 'Repeat the programme' – Marti has the best instinct for romantic beats. Certain things are just mythic and true. Sarah was brilliant and really consistent with the actress who played April, with that unbreakable smile. In retrospect, all this helps set up Warren's bad attitude to women.

'After Life' was my first non-comedy episode since 'Gingerbread', which was very scary for me: I was very relieved how it turned out. 'Flooded' (6.4) was written as alternating drafts between me and Doug and he took it over rather. 'Life Serial' (6.5) was me and Fury – I got to write the mummy hand and kitten poker sequences. Marti came up with playing for living things and Joss said they were kittens. That episode was fun to go down and watch and meet the kittens. Writing the mummy hand was hard, it involved a long time in the editing room. I was very worried about how countable the loops needed to be, how the audience would follow them. In this episode we do the geeks for comedy – which is easy because we are all geeks. The boys on the show do the *Star Wars* references. They are a different generation, but geeks are eternal.

RK   Who was the James Bond source?

JE   It was me, but I got it off fan websites. For 'Doublemeat Palace' (6.12), Joss made me look at a Randy Quaid movie, *Parents*, in which a clean-cut family of mom and dad and kid has the parents indoctrinating the kid into cannibalism. There are odd moments where the movie is staring into space and the episode has this same odd pacing...

RK   It has a thousand-yard stare...

JE   Between me and the director, we put that feel into the episode. We wanted to capture the feeling of fast food. This was the Buffy hits bottom episode. Fast food is good honest money but a job for someone younger and it is greasy which she hates – wrong for her to be standing over a fryer and we made it as bad as we could. The giant penis came out of the old woman's head and attacked her and it was not supposed to look like that – it was supposed to be a lamprey – but when it turned out to be a penis we got mileage out of it later with our trademark of unintentional foreshadowing and Tara and Willow laughing about it. Now it is harder to claim we didn't mean it to look that way. There exist two versions of the sex in alley scene – the first version is even grittier.

RK   When we talked before, your Willow Returns was going to be about inadvertent fire-starting. Talk me through the process of changing your mind/someone coming up with this better idea? Just how difficult was it, in 'Same Time, Same Place' (7.3) to write the same scene twice from two points of view? Can you wing it, or do you have to plot and block every moment very carefully?

JE   I have no recollection of a version of this with inadvertent fire-starting. Isn't that interesting? I must've blocked it out. The mutual no-see-'em idea was definitely Joss… I remember he said it early on, and we all kept trying to come up with other things, and then it came back around to Joss's idea again… it always does. It was clearly the perfect metaphor for their situations.

Writing the double scenes for this was tricky and took some planning, but even more of a challenge was after it was shot, cutting length from the double-Spike scene in the basement, since anything you cut from one half of the scene had to come out of the other half too. Very tough for the editor.

RK   I gather that 'Conversations With Dead People' (7.7) was one where, instead of each person getting an act, each of you got a storyline. Which one was yours and why?

JE   I wrote the Dawn-alone storyline. Goddard wrote Jonathan/Andrew, Marti wrote Willow, and Joss wrote Buffy. I'm not sure why I was assigned Dawn… I would've expected Drew and I to be assigned the other way round.

RK   This was that hitherto unheard of thing, an episode without Xander – any particular reason?

JE   Xander fell out of this episode simply because we couldn't find a way to fit him in that was significant for his character, and in light of that, it felt more respectful to the character to leave him out.

RK   Talk to me about juggling different storylines in 'First Date' (7.14).

JE   This was fun because I loved the reveal of Wood's identity, and because it had an interesting domestic feel to it in the midst of building chaos. As far as juggling storylines... that's part of the story-breaking process and is done by the whole team... by the time it was *me* that was all settled, and I just had to make each scene the best I could.

RK   'Storyteller' (7.16) is, let me say, one of my favourite episodes of all time – technically it strikes a perfect balance between fantasy and plot and between the needs of the character and the needs of the overall story arc. Why did you pick this particular way of centring an episode on this character?

JE   The idea of centring an episode on Andrew was Joss's, of course, and I was happy to run with it. This sort of emerged full-blown from Joss's head... I was very concerned about the mix of film and video and fantasy and flashback... I thought the varieties of storytelling would be confusing... I was amazed to see how well it came together. It also allowed me to address some things that I wanted to do personally, like discuss the high percentage of murderers on Buffy's team.

RK   Which bits of 'End of Days' (7.21) are you and which are Doug? How did it feel knowing this was your last chance to write any of these characters? Anything here you are particularly proud of?

JE   The bits I started out writing were all the Andrew/Anya bits. Then I ended up taking the bulk of the first rewrite, and Doug took the final pass and supervised the shooting/post production... it's the kind of hand-off team writing that I usually have little faith in, but it worked out fine in this case. I'm especially proud of the Anya/

Andrew hospital interaction, in which we finished up Andrew's three-part 'Show me the ____' joke run.

RK Your two *Angel* scripts?

JE 'Rm W/a Vu' is a big old comedy – my friend Michelle helped me get 'You always hurt the one you love' as the background for the mother bricking up her son in the wall. It was another hits bottom episode. Every scene had something funny in it. Dennis was named by me so I could make that silly Phantom Dennis joke.

'Guise Will Be Guise' (A2.6) was co-written with Minear – he did the Tish Magev stuff and I did Wesley – this was one episode that came off a pitch of mine. I had the idea and went downstairs to *Angel* and told David Greenwalt about it. I wasn't expecting to do a second episode. I like the way it gives Wesley a chance to work on his father issues. Virginia was originally named Georgia and we had to give her another geographical name to keep the dirty joke about 'Were you in Georgia?' – 'I don't see that's relevant'. We were going to call her Dakota, but then we realized that no one says that, it's North Dakota or South Dakota…

RK Lets not go there…

JE It just gets dirtier all the time. It was important that we get Wesley a girl and have another girl around. Joss pitched the thing about sunlight, about how, if you are impersonating a vampire, you are bound by the same rules as if you were one.

2. Steven S. DeKnight

SDK I did a screenwriting Masters degree at UCLA but my first actual job was on MTV's *Undressed* with Roland Joffe. It was a sex-comedy show and not by any stretch of the imagination a great show. Part of the issue was the sheer volume we had to put out. The actual production season was 13 weeks long and in that we would do 30 half-hour episodes of the show. Unlike a normal TV show, where you get a six-week hiatus for the writers, we would get a couple of weeks off and then go right back into it, with no assurance that the show would be renewed during the latter part of each session. By the end of my year-and-a-half stint there we did 140 half-hour shows, which is a gigantic volume.

We had three sound stages working every day. When the show was on air, it was on four nights a week. My time there really did help with learning to write fast; you worked 12 hours a day and you had really to crank out material.

In the middle of all of this, I decided I needed a new agent so that I could get a better job, and so I wrote a *Buffy* spec script called 'Xander the Slayer', where Xander accidentally absorbs Buffy's powers and we find out why men can't be Slayers. I'd tell you more but there is a chance that it might end up as an episode of the animated show.

RK   So, you got a job on *Buffy*? What were your first impressions coming into a show that had been running for some years by that point?

SDK   My first impression was that I was surrounded by brilliant people – it was a shock and a relief to find yourself working on a show where the higher-ups are actually better than you are, something to strive for. Often in TV the head person is someone you look at and say how did this person get here? Because everything that is going through that head person is getting ruined. I came here and everything was completely different because Joss is actually the guy who is running the show and he is brilliant, his notes are brilliant – it is the only time I have got notes from higher up that actually make a script better – usually the notes you get from higher up are six of one and half a dozen of the other or just make things worse. Hierarchy-wise it is definitely Joss who was running the show – this was in season five before he pulled back a bit to work on *Firefly*, and other projects.

He was here every day, he was the guy in editing, he was the guy on the sets, he had a really close eye on the show. That being said, he gave us all a real opportunity to be creative on the show. Generally how it would work is that he would have the broad points of the season mapped out – he would know its beginning, its middle and its end. And then, episode by episode, we would talk and he would explain the general areas we need to concentrate on in each particular episode – this happens to Buffy or Buffy is going through this or this has to be addressed with Xander. He would say kick it around and go off and run the show. And so we would be in the room for a couple of days kicking around ideas and when we finally had something we thought was pitchable, we would flag him down and call him and Marti in. Then he would say 'Yes, that's great' or, more often, 'That's interesting and this little section of it is interesting and you should work on that', and so we would kick it around some more and this would cycle through a couple of times until we were generally in the area and then we would start to map out beats on the board and then we would call him in and finalize the outline. Before this happens, you know which writer is going to write the episode and so they are pretty much helming it.

RK   I gather this is pretty much a rotational thing.

SDK   It is – on posting boards, people say this person always gets the funny episodes, this person always gets the serious episodes, but actually this is not true. It is purely rotational and who's up next, which is great because that is not how other shows work and Joss believes in giving everyone a fair shake.

RK   I would like you to clarify job descriptions – for example, what is a story editor? What do they actually do?

SDK   The job titles can be a bit misleading. On the writers' side, they indicate what level you are – it's an advancement level. Staff writer means you are on the staff and writing scripts – the big difference is that a staff writer is not getting paid extra for scripts, they are just on salary. It's kind of a hell position because you do just as much work and get paid a lot less. Then the next step up is story editor, which does not mean you edit the stories – I used to assume that, but absolutely not – they edit nothing. The work is exactly the same as that of a staff writer except that you get paid for each script. Then executive story editor, producer, supervising producer, co-executive producer and executive producer at the top.

Once you get up to co-executive, you have some show-running responsibility. People at a lower level will usually defer to a higher, but it doesn't mean you are running anything. Usually the show runner is the exec producer and in that case I could be a producer on *Angel* and not be producing anything except scripts.

On the other hand, usually in TV, the higher up you get the more physical producing you get to do – it is only then that you get involved in casting and special effects and so on. On *Buffy* and *Angel*, even at a lower level, you get invited in to work on the bigger creative picture. The writers are often sent down to the sets to watch vital scenes – they are sent into the editing suite to help fix problems – we are often asked into casting – you don't get that in other shows where the writers are kept much more insular.

RK   Let's talk about some of the assumptions involved in the ways the shows are written. Is the constant twinning of characters conscious or accidental?

SDK   A lot of the stuff you will see is conscious and a lot is happy coincidences that work. People will post after an episode that something you did was cool because it referred back to Season One, Episode Three, and I think, 'Yeah, that works neatly, but it is not like I did it consciously' – but on the other hand, I have watched all the episodes. One of the things that keeps us from planning that deeply is the time constraint; by mid season you have three or four days to write an episode – but quite a lot of planning is involved, so a lot of stuff gets layered in earlier. Whether consciously or unconsciously, it's all there.

We do make big major decisions like that – following through lines for entire seasons – but other moments are just chance and luck. But there is a lot of sitting in a room for nine hours a day tearing your hair out and making all the pieces fit together. No matter how detailed the overall plan is at the beginning of a season, the devil is in the detail and it always takes so much effort to have things not only be good but make sense. Once you are in deep, things stop making sense because you are just trying to jam in pieces. I always try not to explain everything exactly – give the audience everything they need to work it out but not spell it out in detail – which is always a little boring.

Sometimes we lean to cutting too much out. In 'Spiral' (5.20), when the Knights of Byzantium were chasing the Winnebago, it was clear in our mind how they located the car, because the Knights have the clerics, who could sense Dawn in the Winnebago, but we cut too much out and the audience were saying how did they find the Winnebago? Constraints of time and things get past you, because it's often such a whirlwind. Not that bad at the beginning of a season because for the first five or six episodes of a season we have plenty of time to think everything out. Mid season is where the crunch starts happening. By the end you are right up against it. The schedule once you start filming means you are finishing an episode every eight or nine days and it is faster to film an episode than to write it which means that the gap is continually closing. That is one of the reasons why we really need the month and a half with no new episodes. It is just impossible to write and polish, I wish we didn't have to have that gap but it is really necessary.

If you watch the shows in the UK on satellite with each episode a week after another, what you might miss is that those gaps of four to six weeks are usually preceded by a cliffhanger. If you look at a season and find an episode with a big cliffhanger like Angel sleeping with Darla – we do something like that and then we break.

RK   Could you explain about 'Sweeps' episodes?

SDK   Sweeps are the period in American television where they tabulate the demographics of who is watching and use it to sell advertising time. Usually the juiciest episodes are designed to be during sweeps so every show does this, because if you do well in sweeps it keeps your show on TV. This means we have to come up with really juicy episodes three times a year. Sweeps episodes always lead to extended sessions trying to come up with the big story – they have tremendous allure for you as a writer, and there is a huge mythology about them which you try to live up to.

RK   There is a fair amount of conscious or accidental foreshadowing on the shows.

SDK   Some things are planned far enough in advance that there is conscious foreshadowing that operates even from one season to another. The appearance of Dawn was one of these; the thing at the start of Season Five with Willow and the fire on the beach is a neat little marker that her powers are getting out of control. On the other hand, a lot of unintentional things fit together beautifully; the structure Joss has set up has a deep texture that lends itself to this.

RK   Is there anything else you would like to say about coming to the shows when they had been running for some time?

SDK   It was all so very comfortable. At *Buffy*, it was a given that the show was going to stay on the air, and so all our concern was purely a creative need for bigger and better stuff. There was less pressure than I was used to and more concern for the creative side. There was a little bit of worry about the negotiations with the WB, but ultimately we decided to use that as a very positive thing and to try new things and some of it worked and some didn't. The biggest thing is just the feeling of family – we get along really well most of the time. We have a deep love for each other that you don't find on other shows. When the writers aren't breaking story on *Buffy* or working on scripts, we are hanging out in a room together and going down to the comic store together and it's a little culture.

RK   Let's talk about the individual episodes you wrote.

SDK   'Blood Ties' (5.13) was my trial run, the nail-biter. When I first had my interview with Joss, I was interviewing to write for the animated show and he liked my spec so much that he asked if I would like a freelance episode with the live action show and I said 'Hell, yes'. A few months went by while they were looking to bring me in for a standalone, an episode not concentrated on the story arc.

Eventually they called me in and by this point they had pretty much finished with standalones and I was writing for the arc and for the one character I didn't know at all, which was Dawn, the new character. It was going to be the episode where she finds out that she isn't real, or rather that she is real now but used to be a bubble of energy and it was a very passionate agonizing episode for Dawn, which scared the hell out of me because I was all prepared to write a nice, light, fun monster episode.

It was the deep tormented teenage girl adoption metaphor episode which, not being a teenage girl or adopted, gave me some pause, but once we laid out the episode I realized that there are common emotions here which everyone can relate to. I wrote that up and got half of it hideously wrong and then had to do a rewrite. I had decided for some odd reason to do something that wasn't in the outline and go back to the diaries in her first episode, the diaries she burns halfway through 'Blood Ties' that she had been writing ever since she could write. And I thought it would be cool to start with that diary voiceover and have her talk about her relationship with everybody... What I didn't realize was that everyone had hated her voiceover with the diaries in the second episode so much that they had made a decree never to do the diary voiceover ever again. And so an act and a half had to be majorly rewritten. I learned a valuable lesson, which is if it's not in the outline, don't put it in.

After much white-knuckling and typing, I finished it up and it was Episode 13 and I got to do most of the rewrites myself. Then we did this thing we call gangbanging a script where someone takes the teaser and someone takes each act and then you break apart and write really fast and the poor script coordinator has to make sense of it. Then Joss gives notes and we break apart again and it's down to the wire. One of the great things about this show is that it is very rare that you will be here late – it's very civilized hours and not the one or two in the morning you sometimes hear about on sitcoms. Once I was here until 11 and that was for rewrites on something that had to be filmed next day. The rewrite came together – I was so impressed with the crew up there because there were scenes they fixed that I would not have known how to do. I always say one of the reasons I am here is that OK the script went well, but Michelle

Trachtenberg's performance and Michael Gershman's direction helped seal my fate here and get me in.

I was invited in for the rest of the season right before we started filming that episode. I was asked in for the back nine – usually if you get a bump in pay or title you get them for the back nine. The day it happened I was asked in for the production meeting and Marti asks me to wait around. And then I am summoned down to Joss on the set and I think there is a problem, and Joss said, 'We like you and your work. Would you like to join the show full time?' And I thought well it's like winning the lottery – it's my favourite show on TV.

'Spiral' went through the usual process. Joss says: 'Here's what we know – the Knights are after the Key and want to destroy it. Glory now knows Dawn is the key – figure out what happens.' We came up with the idea of the classic 'family on the run' situation – Spike, Buffy and Dawn in wigs and disguises in a motel to lay low – we are always thinking about budget issues. Joss blows in and listens and then says how about everyone's in a Winnebago being chased by the knights on horseback and I look at him and say, 'Oh yeah, I'm all for it.' It was one of the most expensive episodes we ever filmed – it was our *Mad Max* meets *Stagecoach* episode. Gareth Davies, the physical producer, wanted to kill me over that script because, whereas most episodes have 30–35 scenes, this had 70. It was huge, gigantic, movie-size stuff, and it was a great storyline because it put Buffy in a battle she couldn't win and made her realize that. We take a character and tear them down and then build them back up.

Some fans had problems with the next episode, where Buffy is comatose. I thought it was a really cool idea that Willow goes into her mind to snap her out of it. One of the reasons we did that was that Sarah was doing *Scooby Doo* at the time and we only had her for two days and we had to figure out how to do a Buffy-centric story with no Buffy. That's how we came up with the idea of the repeated scenes inside her head, which we filmed once from several angles with Willow watching.

RK   I hadn't known that, I just assumed it was a tour de force.

SDK Yes, it was a great story that came out of necessity and Doug Petrie did an amazing job on it.

RK Even though they are moving, for large stretches 'Spiral' is a bottle episode.

SDK They are in the Winnebago, or the gas station, and it is a contained story. All the characters – I don't have a favourite to write for because there are all the others to write for and it never gets boring.

RK How was it writing for the newly mad Tara?

SDK I am not completely convinced that I got that right – Joss had more thoughts later in the season. I was writing her nuts not so much lucid one moment and not the next. Amber made gold of it.

'All the Way' (6.6) was the Season Six Halloween episode – somehow I became the Dawn specialist. I am always thrilled to write for Michelle – this season she was more reactive and complainy than some people like but that was a matter of what we were doing for a season with the character. There was a nice strong metaphor about the guy who can't control himself and goes bad. That episode had quite a few challenges, not least the previous two Halloween episodes, which were great and thus hard acts to follow. I don't think this was quite up to par, partly because it was not as intrinsically a Halloween episode. This was about Dawn sneaking out, and Halloween was a McGuffin for that. The episode has a nice exception to the rule we had created about vampires not being around at Halloween – it had vampires breaking rules and a seventies vamp refusing to follow the rules. It's a nice bit of misdirection…

RK Both at the level of episodes and that of seasons, 'bait and switch' seems to be the standard Joss manoeuvre.

SDK Originally the vamp boyfriend had a leather jacket and it was going to bring a little cool to Dawn – but the jacket we got didn't work on the actor, so we went with a letter jacket instead. Dawn got to kill her first vamp-boy. Michelle loved doing that.

The next episode was my favourite, 'Dead Things' (6.13). I was so worried about this episode because it was one of those crunch times and a solid draft was needed in two and a half weeks and it was the Thanksgiving holiday season and everyone was busy and disappearing and the night before everyone left I got Joss and Marti and Doug and I realize that I have three and a half days and tried to share it and I got stuck with it. I was writing non-stop and doing an outline by e-mail with notes from Joss and Marti over the phone. I just had to crank it out and came in on Monday bleary-eyed and white as a ghost. It was the best thing I'd done and I took chances I would not have done without the pressure.

It includes great ideas from other people – Joss had the idea of Warren's killing a girl and its being Katrina, and I had a problem because Buffy looks a little dim for not recognizing the corpse, but then she did only meet her for a while. Marti had the idea of the scene with Buffy and Spike on opposite sides of a door and Lisa Lassek, the editor, picked the song which was put in originally as a temp track and we fell in love with it and it was monstrously expensive and so worth it.

Warren is the evil human guy in the *Buffy*verse. You don't always need a monster – he commits two of the most unspeakable acts – killing Katrina and Tara. Buffy confessing to Tara was Joss's idea. This was one of those rare episodes where everything came together, the actors were all spot on and the editing of the time-switching was something made in the editing suite, especially considering the scenes were shot in a forest at night. It took several passes to get it clear – Lisa Lassek was just so amazing – she has moved to *Firefly*.

'Seeing Red' (6.19) – we all loved having this strong lesbian relationship on the show, but everything is up for grabs with Joss. The episode was so juicy – Warren becoming explicitly the misogynist super-villain he always wanted to be – his big problem was always that he hates and fears women. That's why he makes robots and they are such twerps, and why he makes love-slaves and why he wants to kill Buffy. I got to layer in the heart-wrenching story of Buffy and Xander not being as close and of Spike being so desperate that he crosses a serious line. That idea came from Marti – the entire scene was gruelling and upsetting to shoot and it took a lot of time in the editing room. It was Marti's idea not to have any music. Some people complained that it was too realistic – we wanted it not to have any fantasy element, to be nasty and violent. Some people assume it is the end of Buffy and Spike's story – at the very least it ends that phase of it. And then there was the infamous stray bullet that kills Tara...

RK   Earlier in the episode you wrote Dawn being excited that Willow and Tara were back together so well that it is hard to see how people can accuse you of being homophobic.

SDK   The censors had been always so difficult about gay and lesbian characters in bed together – in this episode we got to do that loving physical relationship between them which makes the final act more tragic. The line about the shirt was something Joss came up with at the end of Season Five – it had been planned for many months. The reaction from sections of the audience was extreme. Whoever had been with Willow needed to die to trigger her grief and that grief's consequences. I can understand why people are upset because of the departure of the one loving lesbian relationship on television, but that ought to be a criticism of all the shows that have always excluded the topic. What I do regret is the radio interview I did the next day. I was nervous and made use of inappropriate humour, but people were saying pretty bloody things and I was upset.

RK   How much of a shock was moving across to *Angel*?

SDK   Working upstairs on *Buffy* meant I got to know the people on *Angel*, and would come down to talk to them and rave about the show. Often I thought *Angel* as a show looked better because it was always filmed widescreen and had darker cinematography. I got talking about doing an episode but was so busy I never got the chance. Then I got the offer to move and was keen to accept. Whenever you move to a new show, it is like changing high school; you may think you know what you are in for and they throw you in at the deep end.

RK   How difficult was it moving into a complex situation where show-runners were coming and going and where a story arc had to be devised in spite of that?

SDK I got asked to do the season opener, 'Deep Down' (A4.1), which was a great opportunity, because I had twice as long to work on it – I was feeling out the show. There was an executive shuffle – David Greenwalt had left and David Simkins came and then left on the first day of shooting on 'Deep Down'. Not everyone who moves into a Whedon show gets the working style and the combination of humour and emotion.

RK To what extent did you know where Season Four was going from the beginning and to what extent did the arc get substantially revised as you went?

SDK There were minor corrections to details – we had decided to have Charisma as the Big Bad. Liz and Sarah had the idea of a Fallen Power... Joss liked that idea. He said it was in Cordelia – that was our plan all the way through and then we learned she was pregnant and that Charisma was going to be gone for the last four episodes because of giving birth. This gave the opportunity to address the Connor question. We envisaged much of this as a way of retconning Season Three.

RK 'Deep Down' is a triumph of organizing all the material that had to be got through in the first episode – how much of that is excellent work by everyone at the breakdown phase, and how much specifically you?

SDK The story was broken by Joss and Greenwalt and I got their breakdown, which was somewhat vague in places – I started working on it and did various alterations when no one else was here and I was left to my own devices. I sent Joss the outline and then did the script – I got the longest script notes ever, because a *New York Times* writer was present – it also turned into an induction session for new writers. The script got rethought a lot. Gunn and Fred were coping as foster parents but there was no search for the female vampire. On the rewrite, I realized that too little happened to Gunn and Fred, so I put in the search for a witness to the disappearances and Connor covering himself. Then it fell into place – the witness had to be a vampire so Connor had an excuse for killing them.

RK   Did you collectively always know, when you did the meal at the start, that a similar shot would recur at season end?

SDK   No – the meal at the start resonated and Joss went with it later...

RK   Wesley and Lilah – how hot did you all know they were going to be and going to go on being and how did you write so effectively to the actors' chemistry?

SDK   They scorch the screen and there are scenes, especially in episode seven, that got so steamy that they will never be shown. I love Lilah's playfulness and that she is bothered by Wesley's Fred obsession and that she cares about the dollar in his wallet...

RK   You very much remembered, as did others this season, that Fred is a tough cookie who survived Pylaea and can eat a kid like Connor for breakfast – was this a joint decision?

SDK   We did some tinkering with the character – we wanted her to have had responsibility over summer, and become battle-hardened. The taser-whipping of Connor shows how on the edge she is.

RK   When did you decide to start doing the Wesley as a John Woo character you do in 'Apocalypse, Nowish' (A4.7) and in 'Inside Out' (A4.17)?

SDK   We wanted to design the biggest fight we could afford. We wrote out the beats – there was a time crunch so everything had to come in waves – each person had to have a particular mode of attack. Was Wes's thing magic? – Joss said a grenade, and then he said guns, and guns John Woo style. No one would have said that because guns are normally a no-no on Joss's shows, but Wesley is on the grey side here. The slo-mo shot was my idea.

RK   Here you and the others start the slow process of dropping hints that something is very wrong with Cordy. How much do you think was hinted in the script and how much by acting and direction?

SDK   It was largely a matter of what was said and what was scripted in. The odd watchfulness was layered into the scripts and by the time the possession became explicit, most people had started to get it. The interesting path not taken is Cordelia's dream – we were going to have the real Cordelia seeping through in Jasmine's sleep – but we never had the opportunity to follow up on that. At one point Jasmine was going to stop Angel killing her by saying Cordy was still inside her.

RK   The Connor/Cordy sex scene is brilliantly ambiguous – it upset a lot of people. Were you amused by getting flak again?

SDK   It was so frustrating – I wanted to scream 'Wait and see'.

RK   You collaborated on several mid season episodes with a bunch of your colleagues. Roughly, what was the division of labour on those episodes and what are you proudest about of the bits that are yours?

SDK   'Awakening' (A4.10) was a Joss pitch.

RK   Interesting that Angel's perfect day involves sock puppet versions of the people he loves most.

SDK   Yes. I'm proud of 'Calvary' (A4.12), which was written over a weekend – we did a third each but it fit together with very little revision, fortunately since we had to start shooting. Mere Smith wrote the mutual playing scene.

RK   What was the collective brief on writing Faith this season, with the possibility of a spin-off show; how much was it decided that she had grown up in jail?

SDK   The possibility of a spin-off really did not affect anything we wrote. The 'Release' (A4.14) cliffhanger came from Mere, that Angelus should bite her and plan to turn her.

RK   How was it writing 'Inside Out', a script that you were going to direct?

SDK   It was terrifying – originally I had been pitching a standalone ghost story for my directorial debut, but we needed a last episode for Charisma. She was eight-and-a-half-months pregnant and so this became the birth episode. Charisma was great to work with, but I only had her for six hours a day instead of 14. There are scenes where the others are acting at her and it's a body double. I had trouble writing it and then I had to just get the script done. There is this one very specific image I put in for myself to direct of Connor dragging the girl to her death.

RK   Did you try to play to your possible strengths or otherwise?

SDK   I had just done one day of second unit experience. I have no directorial style yet – I was just winging it.

RK   Are we to take it that some of what Skip says is untrue – this is a massive retcon which makes most sense if only parts of it are the truth?

SDK   I wanted to leave that ambiguous – hence Gunn's big speech, which I filmed very simply to let J work his magic – by then I was two hours behind, no matter what did. J knew the speech and did it perfectly straight off.

RK   Anything else you want to add about Season Four?

SDK   Like Faith says somewhere, it was quite a ride. Gunn's line about 'a turgid supernatural soap opera' was a shout-out to David Greenwalt, who had said it when visiting the office – and Mere wrote it down.

this was our world and they made it theirs

reading space and place in BUFFY THE VAMPIRE SLAYER and ANGEL

karen sayer

Act I

Prologue

What is space? How can we 'read' space and place? What does it mean to read space and place in the context of watching TV series like *Buffy the Vampire Slayer* or *Angel*? The best way to begin is perhaps to think of a moment in *Buffy*, a moment when Xander is running – something he frequently does – running from place to place, space to space, searching for meaning.

Scene 1

Buffy and her friends are dreaming. It's the end of the fourth series and the Scoobies have just beaten Adam, the season's resident enemy and reworked Frankenstein's monster, and now they're sleeping it off. As they dream, so we enter an unreal world, a world of portents made up of their lives, hopes and fears. We've just been reminded (via 'Previously on Buffy') of each friend's role – Willow: spirit; Xander: heart; Giles: mind; Buffy: hand – now we're entering a world in which we learn about their desires, writ large in bedroom, desert, jungle, high school, theatre and suburbia.

As Xander dreams, we see him move from scene to scene, each scene set within the sets of *Buffy*: from upstairs in Buffy's house to a lab, across a corridor to his (dark) basement, then suddenly to a daylight playground. We swing through the desert (via Buffy's point of view) and an ice-cream truck driving along a Sunnydale street, his basement again, Sunnydale High, a jungle à la *Apocalypse Now*, the courtyard outside Giles's apartment, and Giles's place itself. As the tension mounts, as he's repeatedly threatened and warned of danger, so he moves faster and faster: from Giles's condo to Buffy and Willow's college dorm, through a closet into a dark hallway and out into his basement where the First Slayer takes his heart.

Each dream in 'Restless' (4.22), like Xander's, is linked by a journey, chaotic though that journey may at first seem. While he's on this journey, Xander moves around and beyond the Sunnydale we are familiar with. But, at the same time, he moves between sets that are ever more closely connected. The faster he moves between these spaces, the more we realize that there might be an alternative map at work here, not the broadcast Sunnydale map, but the studio map. As he dreams, so the show fleetingly reveals suggestive, hidden spaces and we're drawn backstage into places we don't normally see. Through Xander's dream, the show's setting perversely collapses to give us a peak at the real world.

Scene 2

It's the Boxer Rebellion; we're hearing Spike's story of his first Slayer kill in *Buffy* Season Five. At the end of Spike's fight he, Dru, Angelus and Darla meet up and leave at Angelus's request; Angelus is bored. Spike is full of himself, Drusilla proud, Darla compliant. There is no reason for the audience to doubt the scene, unless they doubt that Spike is a reliable witness.

Now it's *Angel* Season Two and the Boxer Rebellion is being reprised. The setting and action are exactly the same, but, this time, seen from Darla's point of view, the scene seems to end differently. We should bear in mind here that each episode belongs in a relationship to every other episode, a relationship that in *Buffy* and *Angel* operates between series not just within them. As Laurel Brake has argued, 'the element of time' is key 'in serial publication'. The characters move through the same space, in the same way, with the same words, but this time we know what Spike does not: that Angelus has already been cursed and regained his soul. He has already begged Darla to take him back, but backed away from a kill (of a missionary, his wife and baby). And now, as they leave, Angel seems sickened by the violence that surrounds them, Darla suspicious, the others oblivious because of Spike's triumph.

In the cases of Angel/Angelus's, Spike's, Drusilla's and Darla's back-stories, both series share the same space, if sometimes seen from different points of view. In other words, both shows are perfectly comfortable with the idea of hybridity, the idea that places are multiple, contingent and plural, and that 'place' is not simply a location or a territory, but is a phenomenon that 'is inseparable from the consciousness of people who occupy it'. No place has ever had a single rooted identity; every community has always been characterized by diversity and by the links between it and the rest of the world. In one sense or another, most apparently distinct, bounded spaces and places are 'meeting places' and this is used effectively on both shows.

Scene 3

It's Season Seven. Andrew is filming *Buffy the Slayer of Vampyres* on his camcorder and we're in the kitchen as he grabs interviews. As Andrew pans round, we see the Potential Slayers and Scoobies at breakfast, open boxes of unknown cereal scattered about the place, and Buffy (from Andrew's point of view) slo-mo tipping a completely fictional box of cornflakes into her bowl as the wind blows her hair. There's something weird here: the 'completely fictional' cereals.

We've already seen that both *Buffy* and *Angel* co-opt places outside their normal bounds so that their use of space actually extends to the real world and world history, including: (Spike's nineteenth-century) London; (Angelus's eighteenth-century) Ireland; China (the Boxer Rebellion); and New York (a subway in 1977). But the real world equally penetrates both shows. Perhaps this becomes clearest when we consider that advertising 'messages' selling real products and services constantly intersect the actual, broadcast space of each series. Each 'act' is so constructed as to allow this to take place. But, even in the UK where *Buffy* airs on the (non-commercial) BBC, or on video and DVD where the advertising is erased, you will find commonplace commodities embedded in the show's space.

In any one episode of any US TV series, characters may eat, drink or wear clothes that are branded, read known magazines, or shop in named stores. In *The Truman Show* (1998), one of several slightly angst-ridden movies – including *The Matrix* (1999) and *Dark City* (1998) – broadcast around the same which questioned the nature of reality, the principle characters name and show off 'fake' products (beer, cocoa powder, a kitchen knife). When the director of the TV show is interviewed, it's made clear that all the revenue comes from product placement, which in this instance is taken to an extreme: all the products used in the show, including homes, can be bought from a catalogue. By performing a role that is commonplace in US sitcoms and soaps, the principles of *The Truman Show* highlight the commercialism of TV shows via parody. The film also points to itself as advertising space, given that it still uses actual product placement alongside the fakes (e.g. the use of Ford cars). The same thing happens when Andrew films all those fake cereal boxes. But, we can still see Apple computers and laptops throughout all seven seasons of *Buffy*. Indeed, product placement is something that Apple celebrates on the web, via insider articles and a list of films and series, including *Buffy*, in which its products appear.

When considering the value of such a placement, companies like Apple read shows like *Buffy* and *Angel* with a commercial eye to the audience's demographic. Though *Buffy* and *Angel* are ostensibly aimed at different target groups – namely, *Buffy*'s audience is expected to be younger than *Angel*'s, as suggested by the original ages of the protagonists, the language and the content – both shows, like *Beverly Hills 90210* and *Charmed*, which also used Apple product-placement, are/were aimed at the 'youth' market. (Apple is so impressed by *Angel* that it has recently become involved in sponsoring as well as advertising on the show in the USA.) In this sense, the shows address their audiences as consumers.

This insertion of commercial objects into the fictional and broadcast space of a show has a number of effects. Aside from helping sell Apple, the products we see belong to an actual time and a genuine place (late twentieth-/early twenty-first-century California, USA) and so link the fictional setting (Sunnydale/*Angel*'s LA) to that time and place. In this way *Buffy* and *Angel* create the illusion, as any realist text would, that they encompass, represent and belong to the real world. So, both the series and their audiences belong to wider cultural and commercial contexts, of which they make use, which act as sites of inter-textuality and which allow both *Buffy* and *Angel* to seem 'real' because they're grounded in what their audiences know. In the meantime, spotting locations and matching them to 'real' places has become a lucrative move for Hollywood guides.

Scene 4

This time we're walking, walking down a corridor. The characters seem careworn, sad, somehow involved in an everyday moment of grief, a moment that is unlike any that we've experienced so far. Whereas in 'Restless' we moved rapidly between spaces, in 'The Body' (5.16) the spaces we see seem enlarged, the corridors impossibly long, movement too slow. In 'Restless' we watched in dreamtime, in 'The Body' we're watching in real time. Normally, though we opt not to realize this, we never see a character travel down a complete corridor; the sets/the spaces are usually sliced to pieces/cut up, even when someone is running. This time, however, we see the characters walk, the ordinariness of their walking simply feels odd compared to the way in which the show is usually produced. Their walking, the show taking time, has the effect of expanding the spaces that the characters inhabit, and of making their actions, their feelings, quite mundane. This separates Joyce's death from all the other deaths on the show, and it intensifies the experience so that her death becomes 'real'.

For TV shows like *Buffy* and *Angel*, space is certainly material, about sets and setting. But, it is also about the way that the shows are filmed, about how those sets are/that setting is used, and about time. And because in *Buffy* and *Angel* space is constructed, it is also something that is imagined. In reading shows like *Buffy* and *Angel*, it is each show's use of this imaginative space that is key: the subjective qualities of the world constructed in the show and the audience's access to that world.

As David Herbert has argued (in 'Place and Society'), with respect to literature, fictional texts may allude to actual places, to real topography, 'but... imaginative literature goes well beyond area, landscape and environment and touches upon topics such as quality of life, social class divisions, women in society and sources of inequality; all of these are relevant to... meanings of place'. The ensemble of lighting, setting and scale, theme and mode of address directs the audience's access to each broadcast. To become aware of and read each show's imaginative space, the subjective qualities of the places constructed, we need to be sensitive to their use of language, the impact of convention, their methods of narration and motifs.

Act II

Prologue

Buffy and *Angel* differ in their use of imaginative space. First of all, *Buffy* is set in Sunnydale, a completely fictional location to be found somewhere on the coast of Southern California, while *Angel* is set, appropriately enough, in Los Angeles, a 'real' place. Secondly, where

Sunnydale is apparently characterized by open bright suburban pleasantness, the LA of *Angel* is darker, more urban, erotically claustrophobic and explicitly seedy. Let's break this down, how do the shows create and then give access to their imaginative space?

Scene 1

It's Season Seven, 'The Killer Inside Me' (7.13), Spike and Buffy are talking in the basement. Spike's chip – the hardware that the Initiative implanted in his brain to stop him killing – is playing up, causing him pain, and the two of them need to figure out what to do to fix it. He asks Buffy 'Who ya gonna call?' and continues, 'God, that phrase is never gonna be useable again, is it?', sparking off memories of and passing comment on the original *Ghostbusters* film (1984) and the anime cartoon series *The Real Ghostbusters*.

In 'fat' popular texts like *Buffy* and *Angel* there's nearly always a comfortable recognition of the extra-textual relationships built into the mode of address; just like product placement, these references ground the shows in the audience's world. Thanks, normally, to Andrew's SF-nerdishness, Season Seven of *Buffy* is riddled with references to films, TV shows and graphic novels. But *Buffy* always relies on its audience being well versed in contemporary culture and this reliance is entirely explicit, as Rhonda Wilcox has noted; Buffy actually apologizes to Giles in 'I, Robot – You, Jane' (1.8) for a 'pop culture reference' when she says 'My spider sense is tingling'.

In the last episode, Andrew gamemasters a session of Dungeons and Dragons that replicates the Scoobies' everyday lives – right down to Giles being knocked out. Via a real role-playing game, Andrew maps out a fictional world of monsters within a fictional world of monsters – which to those in the know nods to the *Buffy* RPG and gives us a warm glow. In *Angel* it's Cordelia and Gunn – both being worldlier than the other characters – that give us most of these cues.

On top of this, this extra-textuality extends in *Buffy* and *Angel* to each show's look and feel, each show's space. For instance, in its iconography, *Angel* predominantly draws on references to the hard-boiled conventions of film noir. It's this that makes it different to *Buffy*. Though, as a real city, LA lends *Angel* additional authenticity and weight, *Angel*'s rain-soaked streets and low lighting do not represent the 'real' LA, 'real' crimes or 'real' detection; they reflect a stylistic attempt to present thematic ambiguities around good/ evil, corruption, social disintegration and disillusion in an imagined LA. Meanwhile, *Buffy*'s visual feel and mode of address are drawn from a mix of action, horror and soap better suited to the themes of teen angst that dominated the earlier series. Hence the Initiative's deep underground bunker in Season Four, overwhelmingly Bond-like and built for destruction, could stand equally for the operation of covert government structures and/or adult power.

Scene 2

We've had the adverts, we've had 'Previously on', now we're into the teaser. We enter Sunnydale or LA – perhaps China, London or New York – in darkness or conflict. If our entry is in daylight we find ourselves in the middle of a relaxed spell – friends talking, brief romantic interlude, office gossip – but suddenly we're thrown into a night scene for suspense. Now we're into the credits; even without a cut to violence, any happy moment in the teaser is being obliterated; *Buffy* is being introduced through cut-up recycled scenes overlain by sudden action. *Angel*'s principals are framed: Angel in white, Cordelia in green, Doyle then Wesley in yellow/gold, Gunn in red; we look for new colours round the new leads. From the beginning light contrasts with dark, the territories of good vs. evil are mapped out.

In terms of consumption, the teasers keep the audience tuned in. But, beyond this, the 'Previously' teaser and credits give us information and access to the show, they give us a feel for what's about to come next; they act as a door. So, the credit colours in *Angel* remind us of the key attributes of each character – Angel's essential innocence, Cordelia's *naïveté*, Doyle/Wesley's cowardice and comic timing, Gunn's death wish. After this, we know where we're going. Once in, we move through the episode, through its architecture.

In 'Are You Now or Have You Ever Been?' (A2.2), for instance, a photograph of a hotel is used to draw the audience into a 'flashback'. As Wesley studies it, so the picture becomes animated and resolves into a new scene. Meanwhile, as Angel moves through the hotel his centrality as protagonist is used to link 'past' with 'present', each inter-cut with the other. This points up Angel's longevity and the biological fixity of his body, in contrast to his psychological or emotional development – possibly the inverse of what most teenagers experience as growth. At the same time, we're introduced to a new space, the Hyperion, the new base of operations for Season Two.

Though well-versed in the conventions of genre TV, on the whole *Angel* is nearly always more cinematic than *Buffy*, and more willing to draw on those recent experiments that allude to the fact of cinematography for its effects. It was only in Season Five that *Buffy* began to opt for this more experimental approach – for example, the use of dislocating cuts to represent Glory's inter-dimensional instability. *Angel* on the other hand has always made explicit play, through its rapidity, of the necessary editing that normally stands for time passing. Doyle's and later Cordelia's vision headaches – until she is 'demonized' by the 'Powers That Be' – are similarly characterized by almost painful stroboscopic cuts. As well as adopting some of the compressed conventions of timescale used in film noir, this draws attention to the show's artificiality, it breaks the realist mode by drawing attention to itself, while simultaneously gesturing towards Angel's own heightened awareness, or Doyle's and Cordelia's fragmented point of view.

Scene 3

Look at Buffy running, as she does through credit after credit, coat flying, along the corridor of the old Sunnydale High. What do you see behind her? An uncanny lip-like fretwork. A screen of mouths.

Aside from the editing, the design details contribute to the connotations or available meanings connected with each and every scene. The organization of space on screen, exterior shots of key buildings and subsequent sight of their interiors, tells the audience something about the characters that live/work in them, their wider relevance to the community they belong to, and the relationships the protagonists have. Shots are carefully delineated in the scripts to reflect the audience's or a character's point of view, to reveal and hide information. New settings, like the Hyperion, are added to each neighbourhood as the plot demands. This enlargement of the fictive map is noticed by Riley in *Buffy* during the first episode of Season Five, when he wonders why he has never come across a large castle in Sunnydale before. (It's introduced simply to house Dracula.) In each case, Sunnydale's zoo, museum and college are only mentioned as and when it becomes necessary to take the protagonists out of school and/or bring in fresh foes – hyenas at the zoo, mummy girl at the museum, Adam under the college. Once introduced, however, these new locations add to the overall scale and feel of Sunnydale as cultured and well to do. In both series, the viewing audience is therefore moved between and around these sites as required; and, as the imaginative map gains detail and becomes clear, so a sense of place is gradually built up. Between audience and screen, the specific apparatus used by each show therefore helps direct the audience's experience of Sunnydale and LA. What the audience is given, in a sense, is a spatial script.

As each series has evolved, so their audiences have come to know the spaces that the characters inhabit, the social conventions of the places they're set in and local relationships based on age, class, race, sex and species. We learn very quickly in *Buffy* that the old Sunnydale High school library, for example, is the oldest building on campus. Though it's built over the Hellmouth, it's also representative of what might be called Sunnydale's 'polite' society, its values and its norms. Libraries, like museums, are never simply neutral buildings/rooms in which books/artefacts are housed, but are, in and of themselves, invested with cultural authority. The old Sunnydale High library's age alone guarantees its cultural capital. This is equally suggested through its colonialist design, which echoes Carnegie's social imperative, and holdings that comprise most obviously ancient leather-bound tomes. As in a 'real' museum it has what L. McTavish in 'Shopping in the Museum' calls 'spatial organization... and the installation of selected pieces within specific sites contribute to the meanings of the artworks and shape the experiences of diverse museum visitors'. This association of the old Sunnydale High library with authority is also suggested by the noticeable absence of most of the high school's students. When two students do turn up to look for some textbooks, Xander's initial reaction is hostile; he has forgotten that this is a public space that his peers might want to use.

Meanwhile that authority is reinforced by Giles, the school librarian who, though he himself is a repository of occult knowledge, was previously a curator at the British Museum. Each setting thus carries its own connotations and is productive of its own meanings, derived from the 'real' world as well as the show; each setting can therefore be treated as a highly complex text in its own right. Beyond questions of extra- and inter-textuality, this in itself opens both shows up to multiple readings as their audiences work to negotiate their way through.

Act III

Prologue

So far my argument has concentrated on what the reading of space/ place in *Buffy* and *Angel* might entail, and to some extent the deployment of imaginative spaces on screen. What I want to do now is focus in on one space and to consider its impact on the available meanings in each show. The space I have chosen is 'home'. Neither the homes nor the meanings they produce in *Buffy* and *Angel* are necessarily conventional, yet the treatment of home lies at the heart of an overriding thematic concern with, as Susan Own suggests, 'friendship as family', the maintenance and loss of community. At the same time, *Buffy*'s dialogue and use of 'social monsters' clearly relates to a generation divide, so that teenagers and adults fail to communicate because adults fail to understand the realities of teen life. As Wilcox puts it, 'the horror of becoming a vampire often correlates with the dread of becoming an adult'. Bringing these two points together, what I want to suggest is that as the shows have progressed, it is not simply adulthood that is questioned, but the (masculine) individualism of becoming grown up in contrast to the (feminine) companionship of youth.

Scene 1

Spike has been out on the town, he's just wrecked the High School, had a run in with Buffy's mom – 'Get the hell away from my daughter' – and has messed up the Anointed One's plans. He talks to Dru and says he'll 'make nice'. He crouches on bended knee, asks for forgiveness, but suddenly changes his mind. He grabs the Anointed One, throws him in a cage and raises him into the sunlight, where he dies. What Spike wants is 'a little less ritual and a bit more fun'. It's Revolution.

In *Buffy*, adults and adult figures fail to connect. Though the 'Old Ones' in Season One work as a community of sorts, it is a community grounded explicitly in patriarchal dominance, abuse and submission, one that seems to write large the realities of family life from a teen point of view. The next generation of vampires, Spike and Drusilla, though apparently devoted to each other and more equal, subsequently struggle and fail to form and re-form their own 'family'. Indeed, as the show progresses the audience learns that that family has already been shattered, firstly by Angelus having been cursed and secondly by Darla's death at the beginning of Season One. In the end, even Drusilla and Spike split up and, by Season Five, though Darla has been reborn, Drusilla cannot bring them all back together again.

This inadequacy might be expected of monsters, but the human adults fair just as badly, if not worse. Joyce's attempts to find a new man not only result in her having a relationship with a Stepford husband, but also a complaint, after she has invited Dracula into her home, that she finds it hard to meet men. Just as she starts dating again, she dies. Giles forms one steady relationship with Miss Calendar, but just as love is beginning to blossom she is killed. Though Joyce and Giles have a fling, this is in a regressed state as teens and they cannot maintain the attachment once they've 'grown up'. What is perhaps worse is that none of the adults in the show seem to have any ordinary, everyday friends.

This is in direct contrast to the relationships built up by the young protagonists, the Scoobies. Their friendship is founded on a set of common experiences, in part against a common set of enemies, but also a common set of expectations, shared culture and references. Moreover, as each gang member ages and develops, so they work to take their friends with them. This is tested almost to destruction in Season Four and wins out in that season's finale. In Season Five, Spike – now living alone – makes it clear that Buffy's will to live resides in her family and friends, and that if they're taken away she could be killed. In the same series, Tara is rejected by her biological family and replaces them with the family of Buffy, Willow, Xander, Anya – and, peripherally, Spike – while Riley's absence at this point foreshadows his departure from the show. This moment is also important because until this point Tara has felt that she is an outsider, not one of the gang; sitting on the margins, she is all too aware of the centre's location and wants desperately to belong. The fact that in the end she does belong shows that though the group is tested and proven to be strong, it is not immutable, passive or fixed.

This is highlighted in the middle of Season Five when, though he has been absent since the middle of Season Four, Xander wistfully remembers Oz's companionship as another man who'd get his jokes. (When he gets a male friend again, it is Andrew, repentant survivor of a rival, evil group, who survives in the finale as a result of the self-sacrifice of Xander's former fiancée, Anya.) Incidentally pointing up the strong female bias of the Scoobies in this series, this also reminds us that this Scooby gang, unlike its cartoon namesake, is yielding, shifting and adaptable. Hence, though Dawn – introduced in Season Five as Buffy's sister, when the audience knows full well that she doesn't have one – is discovered to not even be human, the Scoobies can still take her in as an innocent to be protected for her own sake. In the final episode of Season Seven, Faith, Anya, Andrew and Spike are just as important as Willow, Xander and Giles in making Buffy's plan come together.

In *Buffy*, friendship is key and in the first three seasons it is the school library that frames the friends' actions and thereby emphasizes their strength. In this conversion of public into private we see the malleability of architecture, its ability to adapt and shift from one use to another. People remake places to their own liking; buildings are not as fixed as we might think. In the case of the library, its structure (which should mark it out as separate from the world because what it houses is timeless and universal) is used against the grain. This is why Xander has forgotten that other students might want to come in. The library is treated by the Scoobies as a sanctuary. It provides them with a protective, even cloistered, space that they can defend.

Though it sits over the Hellmouth and is subject to repeated incursions, it is the most secure place that the Scoobies can go. During the day its fanlights allow the sun to stream in, while at night its yellow lamps, mahogany desks, circular door-panes, layered hexagonal patterns, offer a womb-like, homely kind of comfort and warmth. It is because of this that despite all previous assaults – principally directed at the library as symbol of authority and in one case largely off screen – the Mayor's entry to taunt them in 'Graduation Day Part One' (3.21) is still shocking. This moment foreshadows the library's ultimate penetration, his and its final destruction. Even then, in Season Four, Riley turns to it as a safe haven, while in the Season Five episode 'Out of My Mind' (5.4) Willow suggests that he has run there again because it feels nostalgically 'homey'.

Scene 2

After the old High School has been blown up, the friends search for a new 'home'. In parallel to the emphasis on friendship as family, the characters continue to make and remake their own space. Their friendship and its sanctuaries stand in contrast to the status of their 'real' families and 'real' homes, which are consistently threatened or destroyed, and normally fail in the face of repeated attack. In 'Bewitched, Bothered and Bewildered' (2.16), when Xander runs to Buffy and her mother's home with Cordelia for protection, all the girls/women who have fallen in love with him break in and attack – even Buffy's mom, Joyce, joins in. In 'Ted' (2.11), Joyce's new Stepford man beats Buffy up in her own room – a reference to domestic violence. In 'Bad Eggs' (2.12), in which we see the mother/child relationship represented as inherently parasitic, again Buffy is attacked in her room – this time by a spider-like hatchling. When Angel goes bad, he abuses his invitation to both Buffy's and Willow's homes in order to drive Buffy mad. His preferred mode of operation is to kill his victims' family and friends before finally turning on them individualized and alone, in effect, making them grow up. In Season Four, once Buffy has goes to college, her home is abruptly taken from her as her mom converts her old room for storage. Though materially her home withstands these incursions, it never works as a safe haven, a place to which she can run and hide. In Season Five, it isn't secure enough to hide Dawn and needs to be protected with spells provided by Tara and Willow.

In the earlier seasons we therefore see the instabilities of growing up and of being the child of a single parent written into domestic space. In Season Five this is emphasized by Joyce's death. But Buffy's dorm, her new home at college in Season Four, is equally unstable. In fact, the stress placed on the Scoobies' friendship is emphasized in this season by the failure to find them a real base/home. They colonize Giles's flat, but also cycle through Buffy's room, her old home and Xander's basement. Xander has such a poor relationship with his own family that he sleeps in the garden during holidays and, though we see no actual violence, we hear and therefore imagine why he wants to get out. It is only once the Scoobies' crisis is resolved at the end of the season that they can settle again.

At this point, Giles becomes steadily more dissatisfied with both the loss of identity he has suffered in losing his old job (when the library is blown up) and the loss of his own individual space in the Scoobies' use of his condo. In buying the magic shop he initially finds (if unwittingly) a new sense of purpose. Then, pointing up the group's investment in the project as well as his newfound skill as a carpenter, Xander helps in its refurbishment. Subsequently, in reflection of the Scoobies' recovered strength, it is finally adopted as their new centre of operations.

Private space therefore consistently gives way to public space in *Buffy*; public space is remade by the group, and though never truly secure, it is always more secure than any individual's 'real' home. Hence, in Season Six, Buffy wonders how her mom managed to pay for all the repairs that must have needed doing, their home having been smashed up so many times, and Tara is shot dead in Willow's bedroom. In Season Seven, though the gang spend most of their time at Buffy's house, the place is besieged several times and there are numerous allusions to the work that Xander has had to do to fix the place up.

Just as the biological family, reliant as it is on detached, particularized adults, is unstable and insufficient, so the biological family home is represented as a site of conflict and pain, rather than nostalgia or comfort. In counterpoint to this argument, vampires regularly trespass in the public space of the Bronze, using the nightclub as a handy feeding ground on the wrong side of town. As such it's a convenient allegorical site for a variety of conventional 'just say no' messages. But, as they are able to ignore these attacks, the teenage protagonists continue to meet here to work up their own social maps beyond adult sight. They still feel at 'home'. Again, in opposition to what's been presented so far, and as noted, the old school library is ironically located directly over the Hellmouth from which/through which monsters emerge throughout Seasons One to Three, suggesting that you can never be sure that you know what is lying beneath a respectable surface.

Indeed, to take a more psychoanalytic stance, if the library is 'home' then it is also womb, in which case the Hellmouth is its vagina/cervix. Given that in the first season the Master is initially trapped in there – 'like a cork in a bottle' – this adds to his initially foetal-like, unborn (as much as undead) status. Alternatively, his Nosferatu-like appearance – Nosferatu being notably linear, rigid and erect – provides a more penetrative reading. In Season Three, this makes the Mayor's explosive entrance as snake-like demon, albeit via the school rather than the Hellmouth, more creative than destructive; the end of that season closes perhaps not on graduation so much as conception or birth. In which case, the end of Season Seven is truly climactic.

Or, perhaps the library is representative of the conscious/ego, while the Hellmouth is the unconscious/id, the Master the embodiment of that which is repressed and uncannily returns. This would be reinforced by the way in which the spaces under the new school shift, the way in which Buffy opts to go down into the Hellmouth to confront her (and all Slayers') demons, in order to generate closure. But, this is just to highlight the ambiguities of space. Some of Andrew's diagrammatic representations of the dangers of the Hellmouth – by Season Seven located under the Principal's office in the new school – are suggestive of more anal readings.

The library is patently not 'home', yet it becomes home because it is used as such: home as function not simply as place. To paraphrase Xander in 'Pangs' (4.8) – probably quoting Stephen King paraphrasing Robert Frost – 'Home is where they need to take you in when you need to go there.' This function in part works because of and in part is reinforced by the increasingly female bias of the Scoobies, which by Season Five is central to the construction of the group. Over the course of the show, it is primarily the men (Angel, Oz, Riley, Giles and to some extent Spike) who have left, suggesting a higher degree of activity on their part. Though Angel and Riley move away and join new communities (Angel Investigations and Special Ops), there is a sense in which they have reluctantly grown up and left home.

Oz fails in his relationship with Willow and leaves town, and, until he regains his soul, Spike is doomed to act out an equally lonely, individual life. Giles leaves because he feels he is no longer needed, though he does mention that he has made at least one new friend in England, which is almost unheard of at his age. The one woman to have left, Cordelia, is represented as consistently ambitious with an almost excessive masculine drive, only later learning to value friendship once she joins Angel in LA. Xander, the only man to remain, is in direct contrast passive, the heart of the group, identified at the end of Season Four as 'Anima' – though translated at the time as 'heart', this also stands for the feminine principle. Meanwhile, Andrew, the new addition to the group in Season Seven, is, it's implied, gay, at least in desire, if not action – Xander's 'That's my girl' with a hand on his shoulder at the end of Season Seven, while ostensibly referring to Anya, adds an extra layer to this.

The community of friends, then, the Scooby gang itself, like home and family, is coded feminine, in opposition to the fractured, driven, individualized and consequently masculine world of vampires and adults. However, this community, far from being natural and static, is always at risk and in flux. Community/friendship as family has to be worked and fought for, as Season Four and then Season Five, which rests on the statement 'they get to you through your family', both show.

Scene 3

A similar balance can be found in *Angel*. However, as in the last two seasons of *Buffy*, because the relationships are already adult, more is at risk for the friendships made and the communities formed. Here the protagonists have more baggage, and friendship/communal 'home' becomes a place for the discovery of one's self. As something of an outsider, for instance, we don't get to see Wesley's place until he has acquired a girl (whom he soon loses). But he nonetheless belongs to Angel Investigations, a group which continues to persist once he, Gunn and Cordelia are fired and until Angel returns to the fold. Wesley is initially brought in from the cold as a lone 'rogue demon hunter', an identity that he constructs for himself having failed as Watcher, but which he never lives out alone. Wesley can only grow, find strength and self-belief in friendship as family, and it is only paradoxically by walking in Angel's shoes for a day that he finally discovers his self-esteem.

In Season One, Angel uses the basement of his LA office as his home. Once this is destroyed, he uses the hotel as both home and office in Season Two. At the end of Season Four, the team move to the old offices of Wolfram and Hart – from art nouveau with a noirish twist to glass and steel modernity. It is in these public spaces that much of the ensemble work takes place and here that 'Angel Investigations' takes form. Failed private homes in *Angel* include Cordelia's first place, Doyle's apartment and Gunn's underground hideout. These locations represent the characters, map out their emotional conditions and relationships with the rest of the team. A key story in Season One is therefore Cordelia's fight to make her new and suspiciously cheap flat her own by expelling the original occupants' ghosts – or rather ridding the flat of the mother and moving in with the son. The acquisition is a rite of passage and through it she too finds herself.

In the same episode, Doyle rejects such a journey and it's made clear that only those who feel that they deserve to be punished live in squalor. Potentially this is a conservative message, particularly as Doyle's sense of self subsequently crystallizes as literal self-sacrifice; on this occasion it might have been better to 'grow up' much sooner.

In both series, this idea of 'home' is constructed against the spaces that the shows' Others inhabit. The secure spaces of each programme help determine alienation as they lie opposite the deep chilling world of the night. It is in part because of this that both home and family become especially problematic in *Angel* and help emphasize the tensions around Angel himself as vampire with a soul. Angel perpetually inhabits dark spaces. Though his basement and hotel room are both annexed to the group's 'home', though some of his homes are well furnished, these spaces, in and of themselves, are quite barren. Yes, he is a vampire and needs to avoid sunlight, yet the rooms he occupies seem chosen more for darkly aesthetic effect than necessity – after all, he works close to the light all day long. His 'homes' if they can be called such, are a reflection of his own darkness, demonic aspect and self-loathing.

As already noted, Doyle observes in 'Rm W/a Vu' (A1.5) that sometimes people deliberately live in ways and places which don't get their expectations up. In Season Two, Gunn's hideout works the same way. In living in the same places as vampires, Gunn risks death, which he does want, and becoming one of them, which he may not know that he wants. Both men seek redemption, both live on the margins. As this becomes clear, so Angel descends into this darkness, becoming steadily more and more alienated from the group, so that he finally fires Gunn, Wesley and Cordelia. This is prompted by the return of Darla – his lover and 'sire'.

As she haunts him, so Angel descends into and starts to explore his deepest dreams and worst desires, alone, drawn on by memories of his old vampire 'family' – Drusilla, Spike, Angelus, Darla. In fighting this battle, he increasingly works alone and, in the end, in 'Epiphany' (A2.16), discovers that what he really needs to fight evil is company. He therefore seeks to return to his friends and must work to regain their trust. Again, in friendship there is strength, but it must be valued and fought for. Meanwhile, Darla dies by her own hand in a rain-soaked alley in order to give birth to her and Angel's son. And later, Wesley goes on a similar journey, via an affair with Lilah.

In *Angel*, of course, the city the characters inhabit is 'real' – some of it known or knowable to audiences, other elements redrawn. The fixity of location – as signalled by the continued existence of the hotel, as well as LA – is important in reinforcing the values of the show, and this fixity in itself is reinforced by the stability of Angel's body. As noted earlier, though on a road to redemption, physiologically he remains unchanged. At the same time, though people and society shift around him, what he learns to hold dear apparently remains constant and, thereby, universal.

The values he represents are typified in his transformation into a knight in Season Two. Here the Powers That Be – themselves apparently timeless, as well as all-knowing – rewrite downtown LA into the site of a ritualized medieval joust. Like Doyle and Gunn, he is prepared to sacrifice himself for the greater good. That Angel's values might be awry, or misplaced, is suggested by that fact that he is there at all. He has killed when he should have helped and he has had to take on a battle that is not his own. He wins, the episode plays with the idea of the convergence of ancient and modern evil, but the battle itself is absurd. His values, meanwhile, are paralleled by the fixed values of the city itself, vested in certain kinds of property (such as the hotel), exploitation and conceit. The city's corporate architecture stands implacable and proud against his assaults. On descending to Hell, what he learns is that as an individual he can do nothing, he learns that he has been tilting at windmills.

In *Angel*, this search for home and family can be read fundamentally as the search for a lost feminine, womb-like space of rebirth. Contextually, in the search for home there is the desire for a lost territory, an idealization of the family relationship that binds us to the home and of the home itself as 'Woman/Mother/Lover'. 'Home' has become a place that we tend to look back to as having come from, and is therefore generally constructed through the lens of nostalgia and the search for vanished perfection. Though it does not literally have to be a domestic space, it has come primarily to be associated with maternal imagery, and it is that imagery that normally makes it 'comfortable'. (In the nineteenth century, that comfort came to be established through women's naturalized (hidden) domestic work – inextricably linked to a woman's respectability and competence – and by men's cultured (conspicuous) acquisition of homely commodities.)

Angel and *Buffy* use these images. Yet the most protective spaces in both shows seem to be found in what are traditionally much more masculine domains: the school library, a shop, an office and a hotel. In both, the preference for companionship over individualism, even in adulthood, remakes these spaces into sanctuaries and therefore overturns the usual opposition of public and private, so that public and private are subverted and transgressed or transformed.

Act IV

Willow is covered in blood, chanting; we cut to a half-decayed body in a coffin; the body is renewed and suddenly we see it's Buffy. Buffy, like Spike, like the vampires she has slain, has just 'woken up in a box', reborn.

The maternal imagery that remains in the continued association of 'home' with 'family', whether that home be 'public' or 'private', sits alongside the womb-like grave, the dark, dank underground spaces that, in *Buffy* and *Angel*, keep spawning monsters. As Thoreau, and a whole pattern of traditional imagery before him, suggests, the architecture of the grave and the architecture of the home can be uncomfortably close.

Here, we meet the wider issue of the establishment of boundaries with respect to the vampires. As Owen observes, vampires are also able to 'lurk' disguised in quite ordinary places, as long as it's dark.

Not only is the Master trapped in the Hellmouth, vampires in general cannot cross into a home without invitation – though that invitation might be spoken or written, hence the general invitation written onto the fabric of the school building to those seeking knowledge. Moreover, the fictive spaces of *Buffy* include dreamscapes. The last episode in *Buffy* Season Four is not the finale we might expect, i.e. the destruction of the Initiative's base, but a journey into dreamtime. In an earlier series, a little boy dreams and traps everyone in his nightmares as he seeks to flee the 'monster' he fears: his coach. The boy's dreams rewrite all the spaces of the series, inside and out. For Buffy herself, dream is often as concrete as reality given that her predictions often come true. In *Angel*, Cordy and Doyle shatter the show with their visions, and we are taken to alternative universes, different dimensions, Heaven and Hell. These aspects of each show's organization of space, the fact that Buffy and Angel themselves occupy space differently to their friends – thanks to Slayer and vampire agility, speed and strength – open both shows up to a psychoanalytic reading, which I have not attempted here. Rather, I have surveyed the shows' organization of space on screen and the meanings produced in and around one particular site: home.

Both shows are playful in their use of space. In *Buffy*'s 'Once More With Feeling' (6.7), Broadway manners overrun the norms of the show; in Seasons Seven of *Buffy* and Four of *Angel*, fights are deliberately and literally staged: one under floodlights as Buffy does away with an Ubervamp in textbook style, the other in a renovated theatre as Faith and Wesley capture Angelus.

But looked at as a simultaneously realist text, it's perhaps odd that Buffy and co rarely inhabit spaces typical of their age group, e.g. the mall or the movie theatre. Both attract large numbers of people, suitable victims of vampiric incursions, one might assume. Instead, teen socializing focuses on the Bronze and, until it's destroyed, high-school students hang out in the quad. Occasionally we have a visit to the high street, which still seems to boast independent cafes (the Expresso Pump) and stores, and which can support lavish boutiques and a gallery. There is a mall, a very fine one in fact, but we rarely see it. There is one example of Buffy slaying there, one episode where she shops there with her mom and one with her sister Dawn – as Dawn returns shoplifted items. This, coupled with the Spanish-style architecture of its older buildings and its 43 churches (perhaps 44), adds to the almost nostalgic sense of Sunnydale as a 'nice' place.

Until it's destroyed at he end of Season Seven, Sunnydale has well-appointed Mediterranean-style condos, such as Giles's place, a mansion, a castle and tidy neighbourhoods like Revello Drive. Its manufacturing district mostly gone, except for the docks, the Sunnydale we see is primarily a privileged white neighbourhood à la Beverly Hills – a fact which Principal Wood's introduction as the first black protagonist, only serves to highlight. Sunnydale's population works and plays in the sun, on the beach, in playgrounds, on the sports field. It has an ice rink as well as a museum, a zoo and an Ivy League college. This might be adaptive on the part of its residents, but it also works to heighten the tension between Sunnydale as perfected community and Sunnydale as access to hell. Like *The Stepford Wives*, Sunnydale's imaginative space plays with the long-standing tradition of revealing the rotten or even vicious underbelly of (white, Christian, wealthy) suburban USA.

Space is a social construct that is dynamic and unstable, and spatial categories such as 'suburban' and 'urban' have significance in everyday life, constructed in and through culturally and spatially specific social practices. In Sunnydale, we therefore have what in Jane Austen's time might have been called a division between 'polite' and 'impolite' society. *Angel*, set as it is in LA, has no more authenticity and the same division exists. In both cases, humans ('polite society') constantly do battle with demons ('impolite society') for the same turf, because once upon a time, this was their world. And that, in an American show, always begs the uneasy question – do they then have the right to take it back?

For Molly and Emily

what you are, what's to come

feminisms, citizenship and the divine in BUFFY

zoe-jane playdon

Eve am I, great Adam's wife,
I killed Jesus long ago...

Irish lament

Theoretically there would be no such thing as woman. She would
not exist.

Luce Irigaray, *Speculum of the Other Woman*

Invitation

'As a woman, I have no country. As a woman I want no country. As
a woman my country is the whole world.' This famous declaration
is Virginia Woolf's, championing women's rights both to education
and entry into the professions, in a seminal feminist manifesto,
important aspects of which are reflected in *Buffy the Vampire Slayer*.
Buffy's particular combination of knowledge and power places her
outside the mainstream of superheroes and leads to particular ideas
of learning, of spirituality, and of citizenship, which challenge the
dominant discourses of western patriarchy.

Over the years, the feminist project has been concerned to slay
its own vampires, in the form of ideas that, hundreds of years old,

have prowled and fed on society's marginalized communities, especially women. My invitation, therefore, is to come on patrol with a select group of Slayers, to join Buffy, the Scoobies and feminist thinkers and to help in doing the dusting.

Cemeteries and Sunlight

Let me map out the territory you will be working in. On the one hand is a monumental cemetery full of undead white males, the grand narrative of western thought from Freud back to Plato, which, as Irigaray points out, consistently excludes women by denying them subjectivity, that is, an existence of their own, in language, thought and imagination. They provide the patriarchy, that is, state-sanctioned patterns of thought and action, which consistently cast out from social identity marginalized groups and individuals who do not meet their economic or political definitions.

Such works are not only the product of men – the tradition may be typified by works such as Janice Raymond's *The Transsexual Empire* and Germaine Greer's *The Whole Woman*. Both of those female writers provide deterministic, dystopian accounts of woman as having an homogenous identity which is inescapably constructed by white, capitalist, male heterosexism.

Judged by standards such as Raymond's and Greer's, Buffy is another degrading sexploitation of the patriarchy, a woman who is objectified as a function – 'the Slayer' – and controlled to serve ends which are not her own. She is a constructed woman, a kind of 'cyborg', 'a creature of social reality as well as science fiction': constructed within the terms of the series, as the means for a male élite, the Council, to get their dangerous work done; constructed by the entertainment industry as soft SM porn, disguised as an adventure story to legitimize scenes of violence against women; and constructed within media capitalism to provide image-branding and related merchandizing opportunities, whether as tie-in 'Buff-Stuff' or generic halter-neck tops for 11-year-old girls.

Exposing these ideas to sunlight, though, is the job of a more recent literature. Feminist writing reclaims the agency of marginalized individuals, it recognizes subjectivity as valuable, and it resists the fixity of state-sanctioned patterns of thought and behaviour. Trans theory – the use of the lived experience of intersexed and transgendered people to critique contemporary notions of gender and sexuality – provides a further means of exploring liminality, that is, the 'in-between' areas that constitute the physical and intellectual boundaries of society. These ideas, and feminist thought in general, are accessible to everyone, not just women: male writers such as Deleuze and Foucault contribute to feminist thought, which is concerned with the circumstances of all people, just as Giles and Xander are part of the Scoobies, who protect all Sunnydale.

The stakes are these ideas against those of the patriarchy. Read any further, and you will be involved in an argument that *Buffy* offers not degrading readings of woman in society, but emancipatory ones, and that the series is suggestive of a series of feminisms: feminist theory, feminist mythology and lesbian feminist politics.

In Giles's Library: Philosophy

Education and training

My starting point is that Slayers are both born and made. As Giles tries to tell Buffy in the first episode of the series, 'Welcome to the Hellmouth' (1.1):

Giles	Into each generation, a Slayer is born. One girl, in all the world, a Chosen One. One born with the…
Buffy	… the strength and skill to hunt the vampires, to stop the spread of evil, blah, blah. I've heard it, okay?

Not only is Buffy born as the Chosen One, however, but also part of Giles's role as her Watcher is to teach her how to slay vampires, as a scene in 'Angel' (1.7) makes clear:

> *Buffy*   *(looking at some crossbow bolts)* Huh, check out these babies; goodbye, stakes, hello, flying fatality. What can I shoot?
>
> *Giles*   Nothing. The crossbow comes later. You must become proficient with the basic tools of combat. And let's begin with the quarterstaff. Which, incidentally, requires countless hours of rigorous training. I speak from experience.
>
> *Buffy*   Giles, twentieth century. I'm not gonna be fighting Friar Tuck.
>
> *Giles*   You never know with whom – or what – you may be fighting. And these traditions have been handed down through the ages. Now, show me good, steady progress with the quarterstaff and in due time we'll discuss the crossbow.
>
> *(Buffy demolishes him with the quarterstaff)*
>
> *Giles*   *(on the floor, breathing hard)* Good. Let's move on to the crossbow.

The undercutting of Giles's role in controlling Buffy's learning, provides part of the humour of the series and indicates that the means by which Buffy learns to *become* a Slayer, as well as being *born* the Slayer, is a particular one, negotiated between them. The introduction of another Slayer, Kendra, in 'What's My Line? Part Two' (2.10) makes this point. Kendra has been trained in what is to be understood as the traditional way:

> *Kendra*   My parents – they sent me to my Watcher when I was very young.
>
> *Buffy*   How young?
>
> *Kendra*   I don't remember them actually… I've seen

> pictures. But that's how seriously the calling is taken
> by my people. My mother and father gave me to my
> Watcher because they believed they were doing the
> right thing for me – and for the world.

By contrast, Buffy's single-parent mother is unaware that she is the Slayer, while Giles has made specific decisions not to intervene in Buffy's learning in the usual way. So, in 'What's My Line? Part 2', he has not objected to her having friends who know that she is the Slayer:

Giles	Kendra. There are a few people – civilians if you like – who know Buffy's identity. Willow is one of them. And they also spend time together. Socially.
Kendra	And you allow this, sir?
Giles	Well...
Kendra	But the Slayer must work in secret. For security...
Giles	Of course. With Buffy, however, its... some flexibility is required.

And he has not even bothered to introduce her to the Slayer handbook:

Kendra	I study because it is required. The Slayer handbook insists on it.
Willow	There's a Slayer handbook?
Buffy	Handbook? What handbook? How come I don't have a handbook?
Giles	After meeting you, Buffy, I was quite sure the handbook would be of no use in your case.

The need for Giles to support Buffy's learning in a particular way is a continual theme, so that when, in the fifth season, Giles decides to leave for England, since he believes he is no longer needed by Buffy, she makes it clear that she still needs his support in 'Buffy vs Dracula' (5.1):

Buffy	You haven't been my Watcher for a while. I haven't been training and I haven't really needed to come to you for help.
Giles	I agree.
Buffy	And then this whole thing with Dracula. It made me face up to some stuff. Ever since we did that spell where we called on the First Slayer, I've been going out a lot. Every night.
Giles	Patrolling.
Buffy	Hunting. That's what Dracula called it, and he was right. He understood my power better than I do. He saw darkness in it. I need to know more, about where I come from, about the other Slayers. Maybe, maybe if I learn to control this thing, I could be stronger and I could be better. But I'm scared. I know it's going to be hard and I can't do it without you. I need your help. I need you to be my Watcher again.

This negotiated learning relationship between Buffy and Giles may be described as education rather than training. As Peters points out, training is concerned with 'some specifiable type of performance that has to be mastered'. Its focus is on transmission of skills, from an authority to a passive recipient, where the authority knows why the work has to be performed and the recipient simply does it.

Education, though, takes place through 'conversation' rather than 'courses', in which 'lecturing to others is bad form; so is using the remarks of others as springboards for self-display. The point is to create a common world to which all bring their distinctive contributions'. The goal of education is 'transformation', since 'education implies that a man's outlook is transformed by what he knows', rather than 'transmission' of a set of behaviours. It is clear from what has been said so far, that the relationship between Buffy and Giles is one of education: she doesn't need training in the quarterstaff, but she does need his distinctive contribution of esoteric knowledge and she needs the relationality of friendships to achieve personal growth and transformation.

For Buffy, her role as Slayer is fundamental to her being, as Kendra recognizes ('What's My Line? Part Two'):

> *Kendra*   You talk about slaying like it's a job. It's not. It's who you are.
>
> *Buffy*   Did you get that from your handbook?
>
> *Kendra*   From you.

Knowing and being

The philosophical concept lying behind the distinctions between education and training is a division between 'knowing' and 'being', which has been fundamental to western civilization since Plato. Feminist thinking has taken these two philosophical categories into new areas. Now, a distinction may be made between 'praxis', knowledge developed from lived experience, including that of marginalized groups, and the 'Academy', knowledge hallowed by the patriarchy, which foregrounds objectivity and the unquestionable 'truths' of scientism. Similarly, being is typically seen by patriarchal thought as ranking ideas in strict layers of importance in a Copernican, regulated universe. Feminism, though, places community and the organization of ideas in webs of relationship in the foreground. Virginia Woolf developed this idea in her utopian notion of a group of women, which:

> would have no honorary treasurer, for it would need no funds. It would have no office, no committee, no secretary; it would call no meetings; it would hold no conferences. If name it must have, it could be called the Outsiders' Society.

To contextualize this, most superheroes are *either* born *or* made. Into the first category fall figures such as Superman, whose powers result from the accident that has placed him on Earth, and those, such as Spiderman, whose powers come about as a result of a physical accident like a radioactive spider bite. Their superiority arises from their simple physical being. Into the second category fall figures such as Batman, who teaches himself physical skills and scientific knowledge, and Xena Warrior Princess, who has learned special skills in combat, healing and esoteric knowledge. Their strength comes through knowledge.

For Slayers, though, there is no division between being and knowing: they are born Slayers and simultaneously they learn to slay, they have inherent physical gifts of strength, stamina and recovery from injury and they have to learn to fight effectively so as not to be killed. Their actions reflect both their being in the world and their approach to learning about the world: Kendra is trained; Kendra is mesmerized and killed. Buffy is educated: Buffy survives. By reconciling knowing and being, therefore, Buffy falls outside the mainstream of superheroes. This position is underlined in the series by a constant stream of references to popular culture, with the implication that those icons are less real than the (fictional) characters who are referring to them: Power Girl – 'Killed by Death' (2.18); Clark Kent – 'Never Kill a Boy on a First Date' (1.5); Human Torch – 'The Witch' (1.3); Xena Warrior Princess – 'Halloween' (2.6); and, of course, 'the Scoobies' – 'What's My Line? Part One' (2.9).

Plato's world

This distinction between knowing and being, reconciled by Buffy, is fundamental to reading the series' religious symbolism and political significance. It finds its origins in Greek thought. In Plato's worldview, that which is best in human life is just a shadow of 'Ideal Forms', which exist out of this world and are only accessible to those with spiritual intuition. Ordinary people, who simply are, are never going to know transcendence; only philosophers, men who know, can pierce the veil and are therefore the only ones qualified to rule. 'Those who are now called kings and potentates must learn to seek wisdom like true and genuine philosophers, and so political power and intellectual wisdom will be joined in one... it is the proper nature of these to keep hold of true wisdom and to lead in the city,' Plato says in *The Republic*, whereas the others must 'leave philosophy alone and follow their leader'.

Knowledge and power

For Plato, knowledge is power, 'most mighty of all powers' and he reserves power by restricting knowledge. Herein lies the political distinction between 'training' and 'education': training is an act of subjugation, education an act of empowerment. When Buffy refuses to acknowledge the power of the Council in 'Graduation Day Part One' (3.21) – 'The council is not welcome here. I have no time for orders' – she is challenging a political philosophy which is more than two thousand years old, and championing a feminism which has existed for less than a century.

This challenge is particularly important because the idea of demo-cracy, in western civilization, consistently refers itself to ancient Greek states, particularly Athens, and to principles propounded by its philosophers, especially Plato, who hated democracy. The challenge provided by Buffy is significant, therefore, both because she combines knowing and being and because she is a woman.

In Athenian society, the model for modern western democracy, women had no status as citizens: the 'brothers in the city', whether Philosopher-Kings or farmers or shoemakers, were all brothers. Spiritual power and political authority were purely patriarchal, with women, at best, having a handmaiden role in religion as a servant of a god – such as the Pythoness who spoke for Apollo at Delphi – in a pantheon which was understood as a patriarchal structure with Zeus as its head.

Other superheroes consult and take guidance from the male head of society who knows best how to use their special powers of being – Superman talks to the President and Batman to Commissioner Gordon, for instance. Buffy herself knows best how to use her being, and also knows what assistance she needs to learn more, to live and be more effective. This is demonstrated conclusively in 'Checkpoint' (5.12), where Buffy tells the Council that their claims to have power over her are false, and where she reverses the balance of power by giving them orders, which they must take, including the re-employment of Giles. Unlike other pop-culture heroes, therefore, the character of Buffy the Vampire Slayer is highly suggestive of alternative spiritual values and political relationships.

On Patrol, First Shift: Religious Symbolism

Beastly women

In the western myth of Paradise, there were two trees, one the tree of life (and being) and the other the tree of knowledge of good and evil. The Fall, the expulsion from Paradise, arose from eating one fruit and not the other, an action used by the orthodox Christian Church to create the doctrine of Original Sin, and to erect a power system to provide salvation, through the divine agency of Christ. Such salvation was available to all those with souls, which, to the medieval Church, did not necessarily include women: Eve had been created out of Adam's spare rib, in the creation story they preferred, and while she shared his body, did not necessarily share his soul. Rather, like the vampires slain by Buffy, women had more in common with animals: *habet mulier animum?* – has woman a soul? – was the perplexing debate of the European Middle Ages.

The numinous female

Buffy, however, reaches through this traditional Christian interpretation, to alternative viewpoints. Buffy herself dies and is resurrected, and thus becomes a kind of woman-Christ, an idea of the divine feminine which follows the mystical Christian tradition exemplified by Juliana of Norwich. She exemplifies the redemptive potential which is an important theme of the series and which, arguably, operates for all of its central characters, on different levels.

It is a particular idea of redemption, however, and one which, as Buffy's status as 'woman-Christ' hints, belongs to earlier theologies than that of contemporary state-endorsed Christianities. As Elaine Pagels points out, the doctrine of the bodily resurrection of Christ is a political one, which 'legitimizes the authority of certain men who claim to exercise exclusive leadership over the churches as the successors of the apostle Peter'.

Plato's Philosopher-King, with special spiritual intuition, is translated into a Bishop of Rome, divinely ordained by God and legitimized by the apostolic succession instituted by a resurrected Christ. This position reflects a struggle for power in the early Christian church, led by Irenaeus on behalf of the 'orthodox' – literally, 'straight thinking' – Christians, which was won by that group when they gained the military support from the converted Emperor Constantine in the fourth century.

It eradicated a different theological and intellectual tradition, that of the Gnostics, who believed that divinity was not transcendent but was immanent, that God was not in Heaven but was present in everyone on Earth. So, as Pagels explains, in the Gnostic tradition, 'self-knowledge is knowledge of God; the self and the divine are identical'; when the disciple attains enlightenment, Jesus no longer serves as his spiritual master: the two have become equal – even identical'. Gnosis, literally 'knowledge', is a particular kind of knowledge: not the 'straight thinking' of mathematics or logic, but self-knowledge and intuitive understanding of others, a discipline of reflection and compassion.

It is this sensibility which informs the spiritual dimension of *Buffy* and of *Angel*. Redemption – not a salvation from a transcendent god, but a here-and-now personal wholeness – is always possible and available, here on Earth. This is exemplified by Buffy herself, who, as the Slayer, must face and deal with vampires and demons – powerful symbols for the darkness encountered on any private inward journey. She dies – more than once; she rises from death; she harrows Hell. In an iconographic reference to another tradition entirely, she does so with a hammer and a sickle-like axe – 'Anne' (3.1).

This sensibility is true, too, for those that she saves physically, for they are her friends and neighbours, rather than people from whom she is emotionally distant. These people, though, are not reliant on Buffy for anything other than their physical safety: their spiritual journey is their own work, and a personal redemptive experience equal to that of Buffy's is accessible to them, as the principal characters demonstrate, through their own particular sensibilities. So, Angel explicitly, continually seeks atonement and redemption; Giles leaves the orthodoxy of the Council; Oz seeks control of his werewolf side through yogic meditation; Willow develops spiritually through Wicca; Buffy's mother learns financial and emotional independence; Cordelia develops selflessness and responsibility; Xander finds self-respect through craftsmanship; Tara realizes her complete humanity; Spike's evil becomes ambiguous and then turns to a love for Buffy that is at once bawdily profane and entirely selfless; and Faith embarks on a journey of self-discovery and ethical reconstruction.

To underline the point that Buffy's death and resurrection are not reserved for her alone, Angel, too, dies and is resurrected, becoming a further 'Christ-analogue'. This identity is emphasized by the scene in 'City of' (A1.1), evocative of Christ's temptation, when, in the high place represented by the top floor of corporate offices, he refuses worldly authority with his question to Russell Winters – 'Can you fly?'

The Gnostic writings that remain, known as the Nag Hammadi Library, point to earlier traditions, in which Eve gave life to Adam, at the bidding of a female godhead. The tractate *On the Origin of the World* tells that:

> After the day of rest, Sophia sent Zoë, her daughter, being called Eve, as an instructor in order that she might make Adam, who had no soul, arise... she said, 'Adam, become

alive! Arise up upon the Earth!' Immediately her word
became accomplished fact.

Female subjectivity is writ large here, in a Christian account of the
creation myth which transsexualizes the orthodox tradition, and
challenges patriarchal political authority, just as other texts replace
the apostle Peter's delegated authority with a primary relationship
between Christ and Mary Magdalene.

Buffy provides an interplay between the redemptive and the
creationary aspects of the sacred female. The recreation of Angel,
naked like Adam, is brought about by Buffy-Zoë's silent invocation
of him, symbolized by the placing of her Claddagh ring at the place
where she killed him – 'Faith, Hope and Trick' (3.3). Angel-Adam,
returned from hell, is also Angel-Christ, on an equal footing to Buffy-
Christ, whose death and return to life is emphasized in the same
episode by her mother being told of it. As in the Gnostic sensibility,
therefore, the relationship between Buffy and Angel is not only
primary, but also equal, so that Angel's redemption is of his own
willing as well as of Buffy's action – as Giles points out: 'There are
two kinds of monster. The first can be redeemed, or more
importantly, wants to be redeemed.' – 'Beauty and the Beasts' (3.4).

The moon

Baring and Cashford point out that the Gnostic tradition draws on
earlier theologies centred on the divine female, the earliest written
account of which, in western civilization, is the collection of myths,
verse and hymns from Sumeria in 2000 BC, concerning Inanna. The
relationship between Faith, Buffy and Angel seems to find resonances
with the longest of those hymns, *The Descent of Inanna*. In the Sumerian
account, the goddess Inanna turns her attention to her 'dark side', to
her sister-goddess, Ereshkigal: 'My Lady abandoned heaven and earth
to descend to the underworld.' Her entry into the underworld is a
process of progressive stripping of authority and power, and Ereshkigal
fiercely kills Inanna and hangs her corpse on a hook, to rot.

At the pleading of her faithful woman-servant, Ninshubur, the gods allow Inanna to be rescued by tiny, cross-gendered creatures, the *kurgarra* and *galator*, who bring Inanna back to the world above. But Ereshkigal must have a sacrifice of some sort, and Inanna is pursued by the *galla*, demons of the underworld. In her place, therefore, Inanna first gives Ereshkigal her husband, Dumuzi, and then, on the lamentations of his sister, Geshtinanna, agrees that for half the year, Dumuzi will dwell in the underworld, while for the other half of the year, Geshtinanna will take his place.

The secular explanation for the myth is that it reflects the universal concern with the cycle of the moon – which goes into darkness each month for three days, as Inanna lies dead in the underworld – and the cycle of the seasons, with the Earth lying fallow during autumn and winter. Its analogues with orthodox Christian belief are obvious – the three days spent in Hell by Christ, the theme of resurrection – and indeed, the same preoccupations with new life, death and resurrection form a central motif in western theologies from Inanna onwards, with some of the same language: Inanna, like the Virgin Mary, was Queen of Heaven and Star of the Morning, and Dumuzi, like Christ, was the shepherd.

The *Buffy* series, too, echoes the same themes. Buffy must visit her 'dark sister', not once but time and again. Ereshkigal is represented most obviously by Faith, the Slayer-gone-bad, who figuratively kills Buffy by taking her body from her in 'Who Are You?' (4.16). But that darkness is also represented by the First Slayer – in 'Restless' (4.22) – who haunts Buffy's dreams; by her negative reaction to Willow coming out as a lesbian, so that her 'sister' becomes sexually threatening – 'New Moon Rising' (4.19); by Glory, whose giant snake Sobek stands in place of the *galla*, pursuing Buffy's sister, Dawn – 'Shadow' (5.8); and most explicitly by the 'death-wish' which, Spike tells Buffy, led to the death of previous Slayers – 'Fool For Love' (5.7).

A similar journey towards understanding the hidden aspects of the self, as part of a necessary movement towards spiritual growth and wholeness, affects other key characters in the series. Willow first becomes aware of her lesbian identity when her 'dark side' enters the world as Vampire Willow in 'Doppelgangland' (3.16), while in his past Giles was known as 'Ripper' and was a member of the dark cult of Eyghon – 'The Dark Age' (2.8). Angel perpetually holds in balance his dual identity as vampire and human, literally lives in Hell for an unspecified period of time and, on his return, finds it necessary to leave Sunnydale for Los Angeles, where he is joined by Buffy's sister-Slayer, Faith, for whom he provides a release from her darkness, as Dumuzi does for Geshtinanna.

To move to a more generally familiar mythology, Buffy is like that Greek aspect of the moon-goddess which was personified as Artemis. Like Artemis, Buffy is a hunter, with the Scoobies – named after the cartoon Great Dane – acting as the dogs that traditionally accompany Artemis. Like Artemis, too, she is chaste – her primary relationship, with Angel, is obliged by his curse to exclude sexual intercourse, after their first time with its disastrous consequences. As Artemis's slaying of animals represents the natural apotheosis of life, so Buffy's slaying of vampires restores them to the natural order of life and death.

Artemis has other aspects, as goddess of childbirth and as Hecate, death-hag of the crossroads, because she is a moon-goddess, representing, like Inanna, the transformation of the moon from new, to full, to waning, darkness and rebirth. It is this transformative potential, this cycling through dark and light – enacted literally by Buffy's daytime school and college, and her night-time slaying – that is the theologically and philosophically important aspect of Buffy. Spiritually, it is what keeps her alive, where other Slayers die, since she is 'tied in' to the world of loving relationality, as Spike tells her: 'The only reason you've lasted as long as you have is you've got ties to the world… your mum, your brat kid sister, the Scoobies. They all tie you here but you're just putting off the inevitable' ('Fool For Love').

Archetypes

It is not that there are exact correspondences between the spiritual universe of *Buffy the Vampire Slayer* and either Gnostic Christianity or goddess theologies. Rather, it is that the sensibilities of *Buffy* resonate far more convincingly with those earlier spiritual traditions than they do with orthodox Christianity. Indeed, it might be argued that the artefacts of orthodox Christianity – the Cross, Holy Water – belong more forcefully to the world of the vampires and demons, since they have an obvious effect on them, which is not extended to the Scoobies. Buffy and her team use these icons but they do not worship them, or attend a place where they are worshipped, any more than they worship the other esoteric artefacts which appear in the series, such as the Glove of Myhnegon, or the Orb of Thesulah.

Rather, recognition of the virtuous nature of Christian artefacts and use of them, means that they take on an archetypal nature, and are given universal significance. The orthodox Christian cross and crucifix become translucent to the universal Tree of Life, the erica-tree of Osiris, the pine-tree of Attis, Odin's world-ash, the Shaman's journey, the Maypole of country ritual. Similarly, Holy Water becomes translucent to the tears of Christ, the Flood from which the world was reborn, the blood of the Grail, the Water of Life, which has represented the generative power of the natural world from the European Upper Palaeolithic period onwards.

Equally, the spiritual vision of *Buffy* is an immanent one, one which exists on Earth, not a transcendent one in an unattainable Heaven. The demons and monsters exist in the present, on Earth, and although other dimensions are acknowledged, their existence is parallel with, not separate from, the lived, daily one of Sunnydale. Sunnydale is, literally, the site of the Hellmouth, the point at which Earth and other dimensions meet, and the regular fighting of monsters takes place on its streets. Spiritual pain and spiritual loss are perpetually present, just as spiritual grace is perpetually accessible, in the here and now. Transformation is achieved at an individual level, by the use of personal agency, and by the extension of that agency to others, through compassion.

A universal dimension of this is the resonance which the series sets up with earlier theologies than that of orthodox Christianity. Gnosticism was only one of the religious beliefs that the orthodox Church outlawed: its monotheism and its vigorous creation of a politically dominant, patriarchal structure meant that all other beliefs were equally outlawed and ruthlessly suppressed. So, for example, another set of beliefs, at one time a dominant theology of the western world, were the Eleusinian Mysteries, sacred to Demeter and Persephone, enacting, like the *Descent of Inanna*, the lawfulness of the natural world and its cycles, and supporting adherents in the human necessity of making friends with death. The little we know about them comes, in the main, from the attacks made on them by early Christian writers, before their final destruction. These mysteries were, therefore, part of the enduring consciousness of western civilization, reappearing in many different forms, but always with the same principle of the numinous female at their centre, as Apuleius points out in the wonderful Eleusinian invocation he provides in *The Golden Ass*.

The point is that Buffy represents a feminist spirituality which locates the sacred in the personal, and which accepts personal responsibility, within a subjective, relational framework, for individual actions. By contrast, at the point at which Angel leaves Buffy and moves to Los Angeles, he leaves his point of access to the immanent. His reason for leaving signals this: he does it because he is persuaded that it is for Buffy's own good, that is, he removes from her the reasonable right to speak for herself, to identify her own desires, and instead invokes some transcendent ideal of right behaviour – a paternalistic, 'daddy knows best' ideal of women as obedient to men – by which to guide his actions.

Angel demonstrates the limitations of the orthodox Christian ideas by which Angel the character then measures his conduct. He actively seeks atonement for what he now understands to have been his sins, hovering on despair and constantly thwarted in his attempts to 'earn' some mechanistic redemption, by one good act or another. Instead of the dark, inward journey Buffy takes to meet her inner guide in the form of the First Slayer, her most fundamental self, when she believes herself unable to love, in 'Intervention' (5.18), Angel is deluded into objectifying his inner dilemma as 'sin' and projecting it onto externalized others, whom he tries to save in the same way that he tried to 'save' Buffy – by his agency, not theirs. If the series runs true to the myth, then it will be only when Angel returns to the simple, human scale of values, that he will be redeemed. [Editorial note – this part of the text is exactly as Zoe-Jane wrote it in January 2001 – long before the broadcast of 'Epiphany' (A2.16), in which precisely this occurs – with the addition of his humbling himself to work for his former assistants.]

On Patrol, Second Shift: Political Significance

Citizenship

Politics may be understood, on the one hand, as the politics of public life, the state and political parties, with Sunnydale as a microcosm of western democracy. On the other hand, though, politics may be understood as relationship, located less narrowly in the public sphere and, in feminist interpretations, focusing on gendered systems, the distribution of resources and the location of power. These two ideas are conjoined in the notion of citizenship, which represents the relationship between public and private life. The issues of frontiers and boundaries are important in all three ideas, both in physical terms of crossing borders and in moral terms.

At the heart of the relationship between politics and citizenship, too, lies the question of 'whether the citizen is conceptualized as merely a subject of an absolute authority or as an active political agent'. The thrust of Platonic democracy, I have argued, is towards citizens as subjects of an absolute authority, while the thrust of the Scoobies – especially Buffy and Willow – I shall argue, is towards citizen as active political agent. This agency, I wish to show, is demonstrated by their transgression of boundaries, their rejection of authoritarian systems of control, their exclusion from socially accepted norms and their creation of alternative ways of living.

Participation

Buffy herself is implicitly transgressive, because of her unique, embodied reconciliation of epistemology and ontology, and thus she provides an immediate political challenge to the order of life in Sunnydale. This political challenge is extended by the community formed by herself and her friends, which, like Gnostic communities, is based on a participative model rather than a hierarchical one. Leadership shifts, from Buffy to Giles to Willow to Angel to Oz to Xander to Riley, depending on who is functionally appropriate at any one time.

They form a group which, like that envisioned by Virginia Woolf, has no funds, no office, no committee and no secretary. Rather, each person is valued for different qualities, as the collaborative spell used to destroy Adam – the monster created by the army and thus the personification of a male, hierarchical, authoritarian viewpoint – demonstrates, to which Willow contributes 'Spiritus' (spirit), Xander contributes 'Animus' (heart), Giles contributes 'Sophus' (mind) and Buffy contributes 'Manus' (hand) – 'Primeval' (4.21). This integrated, equal participation provides a deliberate contrast to the political order represented by Adam. Buffy says 'You could never hope to grasp the source of our power', as she pulls out Adam's mechanical power supply.

The Scoobies' contingent, contextualized, functional form of participative management is in strong contrast to the enforced, patriarchal, hierarchical structures which typify the series' evil leaders – the Master, Principal Snyder, the Mayor – and which are embodied in the terms of vampirism: vampires 'sire' other vampires, in a linguistic association of rape, insemination and kingship. The Master kills retainers who under-perform, as the Three did

('Angel'). Principal Snyder rejoices in using his public position to violate the personal rights of individuals: 'This is a glorious day for principals everywhere. No pathetic whining about students' rights. Just a long row of lockers and a man with a key' – 'Gingerbread' (3.11) – and the Mayor continues to seek power and control from beyond the grave, leaving a videotape of instructions for Faith – 'This Year's Girl' (4.15).

Surveillance

As Foucault points out, it is by watching the worker, or the mad, or the imprisoned that authority maintains its power over them; you can only police what you can see. It is a surveillance arrangement such as this that Buffy explicitly refuses at the start of her relationship with Giles ('Welcome to the Hellmouth'):

Buffy	First of all, I'm a Vampire Slayer. And secondly, I'm retired. Hey, I know! Why don't you kill 'em?
Giles	I-I'm a Watcher, I-I haven't the skill…
Buffy	Oh, come on, stake through the heart, a little sunlight… It's like falling off a log.
Giles	A, a Slayer slays, a Watcher…
Buffy	Watches?
Giles	Yes. No! *(sets down the books)* He, he trains her, he, he, he prepares her…
Buffy	Prepares me for what? For getting kicked out of school? For losing all of my friends? For having to spend all of my time fighting for my life and never getting to tell anyone because I might endanger them? Go ahead! Prepare me.

(They just look at each other for a moment. Buffy exhales, turns and leaves the library in disgust.)

Even when Buffy does quit, and retires to Los Angeles, her return, in 'Anne', is sparked off by a demon which enslaves humans into absolutely degraded labour – 'You work, and you live. That is all.' – in a dark, brutalizing ironworks, lit by vats of molten metal and flying sparks, an image of industrialized hell used from Charles Dickens onwards. That it is Buffy's agency which creates a different relationship from the usual surveillance one, rather than a quality implicit in Slayers, is made clear by the way in which Kendra accepts the surveillance and control of her Watcher, just as Faith does with the Mayor.

Kendra's self-abasement to authority and Faith's preparedness to sell herself to evil just to find acceptance from the fatherly Mayor differ entirely from Buffy's constantly tested and negotiated relationship with Giles. Autonomy is available, but action is required to gain it, otherwise, Slayers and other citizens are merely pawns of an absolute authority. While Buffy provides an implicit political challenge, therefore, Willow provides the series' most explicit challenges. Her 'nomadism', her crossing of social and moral boundaries, is frequently underlined. She transgresses usual school social expectations by having an unusually able intellect, by being unfashionably dressed ('Welcome to the Hellmouth') and by dating a werewolf. She transgresses her family's religious boundaries, in 'Passion' (2.17):

Willow	*(nailing crosses around her French doors)* I'm going to have a hard time explaining this to my dad.
Buffy	You really think this'll bother him?
Willow	Ira Rosenberg's only daughter nailing crucifixes to her bedroom wall? I have to go to Xander's house just to watch 'A Charlie Brown Christmas' every year.

She subsequently goes through a deeply personal, inward journey, to find a further transgressive identity as a lesbian Wiccan. In this context, it is clear that Willow's Wiccan identification is a political one, rather than a religious one. As *Buffy the Vampire Slayer: The Monster Book* points out, Wicca is 'an established and legitimate religion' into which it would be an anomaly 'to keep throwing demons', since 'they do not believe in demons or the Christian mythology of devils'. Further, representations of Wicca in the influential works of Gerald Gardner and of Vivianne Crowley are fundamentally heterosexist, rather than lesbian, developing from the notion of a union of male and female principles, rather than one of female and female. Finally, Willow makes it clear that she is concerned with the alternative powerbase that the craft offers, and it is that shared interest which attracts her to Tara, from 'Hush' (4.10) onwards:

Willow	Talk! All talk: blah blah Gaia blah blah moon, menstrual lifeforce power... I thought after a few sessions we'd get into something real but...
Buffy	No actual witches in your witch group.
Willow	Buncha wannablessedbe's. It's just a fad. Nowadays every girl with a henna tattoo and a spice rack thinks she's a sister to the dark ones.

And later:

Tara	I thought maybe we could do a spell – make people talk again. I'd seen you in the group, the Wicca group you were... you were different than them. I mean they didn't seem to know...
Willow	What they were talking about.
Tara	I think if they saw a witch they would run the other way.

She smiles and laughs.

Willow	How long have you been practising?
Tara	Always, I mean, since I um, was little... my, my mom used to, she had a lot of power, like you.

The political orientation of that power is demonstrated in 'Family' (5.6), when Tara's father tries to persuade her that she will become possessed by a demon when she reaches 21 and that she should therefore give up her independent life in Sunnydale and return to keep house for the men of the family. It becomes clear that this demonization is a lie, aimed at the subjugation of women who have power, one through which Tara's mother was suborned, a literal piece of the patriarchy which Tara breaks.

That all of the Scoobies belong to Virginia Woolf's 'Outsiders' Society', by association with Willow, is demonstrated in 'Gingerbread'. There, Willow is linked to Buffy, through 'the monsters, and the witches, and the Slayers', to Xander via the generic 'freaks and losers', to Giles, who has his books confiscated and burned, and to the 'dozens of others [who] are persecuted by a righteous mob. It's happened all throughout history'.

Interestingly, though, the patriarchal authority which the mob are exercising in their witch-persecution is delusional, the product of a (literal) demonization, which initiates the moral panic. In a political context, the episode seems to be suggesting that the subjugation of women is equally delusional, that the apparently 'objective' evidence collected by Principal Snyder by invading the privacy of students' lockers has no truth in fact. Rather, a radical, feminist view of history, history as affinity, is foregrounded, in a process that 'refuses the various positions of detachment which define the historian' and 'values highly emotional, involved, personal pleasure and engagement'. Willow and Buffy are saved from burning by their friends, especially by Cordelia (whose swift action with a hose contrasts with Xander and Oz's clumsiness), and both share and refuse their demonization, and create both a counter-discourse to it and a counter-action.

Similarly, in 'Checkpoint', the 'Previously on *Buffy*' recapitulation provides a montage of Giles objecting to Buffy's 'test' in 'Helpless' (3.12); of Buffy rejecting the Council in 'Graduation Day Part One'; and Buffy, Giles and Joyce discussing Dawn in 'Triangle' (5.11).

These views of education, hierarchy and community are reiterated and extended in the episode itself, where Buffy advances a 'different perspective' of history and is publicly humiliated by her male teacher for doing so; the Council attempts to impose a surveillance model of management on the Scoobies by inspecting them; and Buffy understands and rejects this as a power-play, and asserts an 'alternative government' of relationality, allowing willing Council members to join the group to fight Glory.

Back in the Library: Conclusion

In a world where woman is so abjected that she is virtually non-existent in political and psychological terms, *Buffy* may be read as an attempt to call her into being and knowledge. The struggle that takes place, the killing of vampires, then, is a political struggle, in which the spiritual, as well as the personal, is political. As simple allegory, the girl-Slayer fights against the problematics of growing up in a patriarchy, with her interior conflicts expressed as literal demons and vampires, which she must slay. As more complex symbol, she reflects a western culture in which successive waves of feminism have analysed these problematics, where woman is now valorized, as having both knowledge and existence, which is self-authenticating. The Slayer thus embodies the combination of knowing and being, and the challenge to western male capitalism which this represents: Buffy's secret night-time slaying, done alongside her public attendance at school, stands for women's unacknowledged labour of reproduction, which provides a central feminist criticism of Marxist analysis.

Buffy herself is an embodiment of what Grosz calls the 'wayward philosophies', which refuse a mind/body split and insist on alternative readings of what it is to be human. It is not sufficient to construct an idea of 'woman' from that which exists already, since what exists already is objectified woman, as the robot April demonstrates: she is literally man-made, made by Warren to love and obey him, so that 'I'm only supposed to love him. If I can't do that, what am I for?' and 'if you call her and she doesn't answer, it hurts her' – 'I Was Made to Love You' (5.15). Rather, autonomy within relationality is required: as Buffy realizes in the same episode: 'I don't need a guy right now. I need me. I need to get comfortable being alone with Buffy.'

Like Virginia Woolf's women's committee, Buffy and the Scoobies are all Outsiders. Individually, they all transgress established boundaries: Xander, a failure in the prescribed learning of state education, turns out to be a skilled craftsperson in adult life; Willow is a lesbian and a witch; Angel a 'good vampire'; and so on. Collectively, they form the Scoobies, the Outsiders' Society, and move between the interpenetrating worlds of humans and demons, Heaven and Hell, the sanctioned and unsanctioned social, political, spiritual worlds. In relation to each other, they are almost always in a position of forbidden love, between women, between demon and human, between Slayer and vampire.

The solution of *Buffy* is inclusivity. What is required is for individuals to wish to enter, to want to become part of that community. Dawn, the Key, is as much a created being as is robot-April, but she identifies at a fundamental, personal level with the Scoobies: she is Buffy's political sister as well as her literal sister, standing up to be counted in defence of Tara in 'Family'. This alternative government, then, is one in which, in Irigaray's formulation, citizenship comes as a right of existing within the community, outside hierarchies of money or birth. Thus, Anya is a vengeance demon, but she may also lawfully join the alternative community of the Scoobies; and Tara, rejected by her own father and brother for being a disobedient female, is re-identified as part of Buffy's 'family'.

In terms of feminist theory, this position reflects the de-stabilization of categories brought about by trans theory. For intersexed people, gender identity can *only* be found through identification, at a personal, essential level. The transitions made between male and female, in response to that personal essentialism, has extended fundamentalist 'fortress feminism' notions of what constitutes woman in terms of sex, and what constitutes lesbian in terms of sexuality.

In spiritual terms, the transgression of boundaries is exemplified by what Campbell calls the hero's journey:

> A hero ventures forth from the world of common day into a region of supernatural wonder: fabulous forces are there encountered and a decisive victory is won: the hero comes back from this mysterious adventure with the power to bestow boons on his fellow man.

In this journey to the land below the sea, the world inside the mountain, the dark forest, the 'decisive victory' is one of will, not necessarily of action. Often, the hero fails to perform the task: she drinks what she should not, he cannot answer the question, or, like Buffy, there is an endless production-line of vampires, more than she could possibly ever kill. But the mono-myth tells us that to try is enough, that intention rather than achievement is the measure of human relationality.

At the heart of this worldview lies the idea not of a fallen humanity separated from the godhead by inherited sin, but the idea of what radical educationist A.S. Neill called 'original good', the view that 'a child is innately wise and realistic'. Where it is accepted that the automatic impulse of people is towards their own happiness, through the love and friendship of others, then they may be judged by their intentions, the bond of the heart, by an intentionality which holds the actor's ethical position.

Finally, then, it is this essentially ethical standpoint, this continuous working-out of what individuals need to do and be in order to find personal apotheosis, which marks out *Buffy* from other beat-'em-ups. Usually, the face-off is between the black hats and the white ones, with a decisive victory for the white hats. As early as the last scene of 'Lie To Me' (2.7), *Buffy* explicitly rejected any such easy conclusion. *Buffy* subverts set conventions, creating a new articulation of what it is to be autonomous woman. This is done in a context of inclusion, not separation from the world of men, on terms which refuse the dominant cultural ideologies of woman as secondary, sinful and subordinate.

Postscript: The First Slayer

When the First Slayer walked the Earth, in the Palaeolithic period, a new sensibility appeared all across the world. Incised stone, engraved bone, carved figures and decorated cave walls testify to a new relationality, explored through art, which, in France's Dordogne, produced a remarkable sculpture and set of cave paintings.

The paintings show the myth of the hunter, the drama of survival: in one notable scene, a speared bison dies, while a rhinoceros shits the manure of new life, and the shaman-hunter dreams their mutual interdependence.

Outside, a sculpture shows a woman, pointing to her pregnant belly with one hand and with the other, holding aloft a crescent-shaped bison horn, incised with the 13 days of the waxing moon and the 13 months of the lunar year. As above, so below, the figure indicates, as the moon waxes, wanes and is born anew, again and again, so is all life.

The painted myth of the hunter is about taking life as a ritual act in order to live; the sculpted myth of the goddess is about transformation, rebirth and life in all its aspects. To a modern mind, the two instincts seem antithetical, the one about separation and survival, the other about relationship and meaning. How can Buffy both be a hunter, a Slayer, and live within the everyday relationality of her family and friends? Why does the First Slayer tell her, 'Death is your gift'?

To live only within the myth of the hunter is to live for survival, in time, where death is final and the experience of life is despair. It is Angel's tragedy that after leaving Buffy, denying their relationality, his sensibility is reduced to that. To return to her is to return to the sacred feminine, the Palaeolithic goddess that links the First Slayer with the last, through a myth which contains that of the hunter and places it in the larger continuum of relationship, an eternal image of recurrence, of the whole.

When one Slayer dies, another is called: when one moon goes into darkness, another becomes. Inanna's journey to Ereshkigal is re-enacted time and again, the necessary death and concomitant new life, transliterated into the Christian religion as the festival of the new child at winter solstice, darkness turning light, and as death at Easter, the pagan festival of fertility goddess Eostre, at the equinox where winter turns to spring.

The myth of the goddess contains the myth of the hunter, but the myth of the hunter cannot contain the myth of the goddess. Death is Buffy's gift in time when, as the Slayer, she hunts vampires for survival: but to stay there would be to share Angel's now tragic existence. Death becomes her gift in eternity, as the deepest part of her – the First Slayer – already knows, when she realizes that, as mother, she must go into the darkness to save Dawn, now her child, as Demeter did Persephone, as eternity must always redeem time. Together, Buffy and Angel rise again, made anew, as the moon does, as we all do, bound into a participative consciousness from the time of the First Slayer, a sense of eternity which vampires, those creatures caught in time, may disturb, but cannot end.

Inanna and Ereshkigal are sisters: they are part and parcel of each other – the dark of the moon is still the moon. It will be interesting to see what is made of Buffy's next resurrection – the wonderful *noli me tangere* of the Christian myth or the terrible pursuit of the Assyrian? And what of her sex and sexuality, always something that becomes liminal in these circumstances? I think the aesthetic is pushing towards something simple and homely – not the Glory/God/Wonder Woman, so much as living eternity in time, Zen without the moral ambiguity.

Postscript Two - Looking Backwards from the Year 2003

A lesbian is the rage of all women condensed
to the point of explosion.

Radicalesbians, *The Woman Identified Woman*, c.1970

The essential myth of the moon is the myth of transformation.

Jules Cashford, *The Moon: Myth and Image*, 2002

Seasons Six and Seven of *Buffy the Vampire Slayer* operate as two aspects
of a single movement. The emotional keynotes of Season Six are
isolation, loss, despair, emptiness, loneliness and the impossibility,
for the Scoobies, of finding a way in which life can be tolerable,
both in spite of and because of their mystical superpowers and
formerly close-knit set of friendships. They are, in short, inhabiting
the mythological area of the Wasteland, an emotional landscape of
futility, failure and fear, a dark night of the soul in which there are
no external signposts to say – in 'Once More With Feeling' (6.7) –
'Where do we go from here?'

Season Seven maps the struggles each of the Scoobies goes through
in their search for personal authenticity and a new way of being in
the world, an essentially interior journey counterpointed by the
external dissolution of the old order as, across the world, Watchers
and Slayers are attacked and slaughtered by the new Big Bad, which
is also the oldest evil, the First Evil in the world.

This brief commentary focuses on two levels, therefore, the personal
and the universal, and their integration into the single new worldview,
which the philosopher Owen Barfield described as 'final participation'.
At the same time, it also suggests the continuation of the interplay in
the series between the political and the personal, in the form of Willow's
lesbian identity and Buffy's role in the labour market.

At the personal level, the closeness felt by the Scoobies for each
other, their mutual interdependence, becomes eroded. Their magical

resurrection of Buffy from the dead is not technically an offence against the natural order, since it is the supernatural resurrection of someone who was killed by supernatural forces; but Willow's justification of her act is undercut by her decision to carry out the sacrifice of the fawn, which represents the 'blessed one', in isolation and her obvious distress at the act. Even though she completes the formal invocation in 'Bargaining' (6.1) – 'Accept our humble gratitude for your offering. In death you give life. May you find wings to the kingdom' – her breaking voice makes it clear that she is not being emotionally truthful to herself, but rather following accepted forms and patterns which go against the grain of her feeling.

This typifies the failure of all of the Scoobies, in one form or another: they obey convention, and thus dishonour their real feelings, forcing themselves into an impossible mode of life, a kind of emotional living death. Xander is unable to articulate his fear of marriage to Anya; beneath the running gag of an ex-vengeance demon turning into part of the retail industry, Anya is unable to conceptualize her and Xander's relationship outside the formalities of a consumer magazine 'ideal wedding'. Giles feels that he has no role and leaves for England. Dawn is unable to talk about her loneliness and isolation and turns to shoplifting and lying. Willow is too emotionally insecure in her relationship with Tara to work through their quarrels and so abuses magic to make Tara forget; Spike is tormented with desire for Buffy, to the extent of trying to rape her when she rejects him. Buffy, torn from heaven by her resurrection, feels unable to tell her friends what they have done and how – 'After Life' (6.3). She finds life in the world 'hard and bright and violent'; alternately, she compensates by having sex with Spike (which she is equally unable to tell her friends about) and then hates herself for using him. Small wonder that all this false saccharine behaviour brings forth a demon ironically named Sweet ('Once More With Feeling') who obliges everyone to sing aloud their actions and feelings – 'I'm just going through the motions', 'I'll never tell' – in a dance of death.

Their quest is inward and, archetypally, the Scoobies are engaged on the Grail quest described in Europe's Middle Ages by Wolfram von Essenbach's *Parzival*. Contemporary mythologist Jules Cashford, commenting on Joseph Campbell's interpretation of *Parzival*, points out that in honouring the knightly code he was taught, Parzival dishonours his heart; out of this comes his failure, and the continuation of the world in a Wasteland. She says:

> Only the Grail can redeem the Wasteland... but what is the Wasteland? For Campbell it is simply the inauthentic life, a state of being which is barren of the truth of who you are... In practice, this means that you put what (you think) is expected or required of you (the social 'ought') before the impulse of your own heart, wherever it may lead... the often beguilingly reasonable claims of the society are never valid, Campbell insists. To be persuaded that they are is the third temptation of the Buddha – 'Perform your Duty to Society'. Your duty to society is no good, he insists, unless it is you. First, you have to be an individual, and it takes a hero to be one.

Parzival redeems himself and the world through his compassionate question to the Fisher King, 'What ails thou?' – 'the spontaneous *natural* impulse of a noble heart', as Cashford puts it – just as Xander saves the world and Willow by reiterating his simple, unconditional love for her. The authentic life, the Grail, redemption are sought and found by each of the Scoobies, not always in a single act – Spike's regaining of his soul is only the start of his process of reintegration – but always by refusing to prefer social mores over the human spirit.

The Grail myth is essentially a lunar myth, with the Grail as cup being symbolically transparent to the crescent New Moon, or (when it is a stone as in *Parzival*) to the Full Moon. The links to the myth of Inanna and to Gnostic thought, which the *Buffy* series makes so powerfully, also testify to this lunar inheritance, which underlies both of those traditions. With fortunate synchronicity, as Season Seven comes to its closure, a new, pivotal work on lunar mythology, *The Moon: Myth and Image*, has been published, which will be important for all those who wish to explore the archetypal structuring of *Buffy* or, perhaps, alternative ways of being in and seeing the world. In this lunar sensibility, the movement from the Wasteland's desolation of the heart to a new life is reflected by the cycle of the moon, from waning, through the three days of darkness, to the birth of the New Moon. The apocalypses which (almost) end each season of *Buffy* are thus transparent to:

> the idea of archaic apocalypses, such as flood or deluge, where the old is obliterated to make way for the new, [which] can be traced to the lunar model of cyclical renewal which gives meaning to catastrophe... It is an optimistic vision because, just as the disappearance of the Moon is not final, so the disappearance of human beings is not final either, neither individually nor as a race: they have a history beyond time.

The Moon in its phases – Waxing, Full, Waning – represents time: but the Moon in its cycle of birth, growth, decline, death and rebirth, represents eternity. The world of vampires, time-bound creatures, is one of perpetuity, an infinite multiplication of moments of time, which stands in relation to eternity as temporal life (*bios* in the Greek) stands in relation to eternity (*zoe*): *zoe* contains and transcends *bios*, eternity contains time, but *bios* can never contain *zoe*. The crescent New Moon, which has stood as a symbol for regeneration from the fifth millennium BC to present-day symbolism in Islam and orthodox Christianity, is both the product of the death of the old order and the initiation of the new: the Moon is 'the destroyer of barren and outworn forms *in order that* new forms may emerge'. The first shadow-caster used in 'Get It Done' (7.15) places the crescent Moon above a rocky Earth, as 'Creation' and, in the series finale, Buffy draws from a stone a mystic scythe, wavy-edged with the crescents of both New and Waning Moons – a lunar analogue for eternity conquering time, used by Druids before orthodox Christianity turned Death's sickle into a metaphor for fear rather than a symbol of transformation. Buffy as Artemis – sharing the root of the name, *Art*, with the hero Arthur and 'King Arthuring' the scythe from the stone – appears here in her aspect as 'the gentle Bear Mother who guards her young [the Potential Slayers] with the ferocity of a hunter' and in so doing, from the same etymological root, bears, gives birth to, a new order. The error of the 'three wise men' (*three*? *wise*? *men*? as the old lesbian joke goes) was to imbue the First Slayer with the demon, to turn *zoe* over to *bios*, as a projection of their own fear and weakness. Buffy rightly refuses this violation, as Parzival rejects the idea of God and the dualities of good and evil, right and wrong, which it represents, and in so doing, reaches for a new way of being. For, as von Essenbach says, 'Every act has both good and evil results' and the Moon contains in its cycle newness, fullness, dissolution and death: darkness devours the Moon, as Ereshkigal devours Inanna, yet both are reborn, in a qualitative view of time, at 'the right time'. Similarly, Spike's 'right time' has not yet come, yet he will recognize it instinctively when it arrives.

Willow flays Warren in a literal act of madness, but a symbolic act of removing his temporal bounds – the skin that locates him in a particular time and place – as Ereshkigal flays Inanna, and as the snake sheds its skin to be born again, as life to the world, in the Sumerian *Epic of Gilgamesh*. Warren is released to eternity, as a manifestation of the One, the oldest evil, the darkness which attends the Moon's death. The rage which inspires Willow to this is caused by his unintentional murder of her partner, Tara, and the powerful magic which she imbibes, which makes her feel all the suffering of the world and decide to end it by ending the world. Mythologically, her anger is transparent to the rage of Demeter, in *The Homeric Hymns*, who refuses to let the Earth yield or life continue, in her grief at her loss of Persephone, raped to the underworld, just as the First Slayer has been by her three Watchers, or as Sweet threatens to take Dawn ('Once More With Feeling'). Demeter's and Willow's acts are 'lunar-cy', arising from a fusion of rational mind and feeling, as in the dictum of the Aitareya Upanishad that 'the Moon became mind and entered the heart'. Only equivalent feeling will assuage them: the starving to death of 'the mortal race of human beings' (as a new Penguin edition of *The Homeric Hymns* puts it) in Demeter's case or the potential destruction of the world in Willow's. Xander is the Wise Fool who provides Willow with an alternative viewpoint, the unexpected, unnumbered, linking card of the Tarot Major Arcana, and who allows her to understand the 'Great Web of Life' (another lunar quality) as complete interconnectedness, beyond the dualities of suffering and pleasure.

Politically, this may be understood as a progression from the separatist radical lesbian agenda of the 1970s, to a different sensibility, which accepts the possibility of other modes of being, while nevertheless refusing simple assimilation. When Anya turns to Tara and Willow as the likely source of a curse for Xander, since they are lesbians and he is a man – 'Entropy' (6.18) – they shrug and accept men as likeable people although not desirable partners. Willow's fight against the seductive power of magic parallels popular representations of lesbians from the 1950s onwards (such as Ann Bannon's pulp fiction and films like *The Killing of Sister George*) as doomed to misery through taking to drink; however, as self-harm it operates as a symbol of her offence against her own sense of right action, in killing the fawn and is thus a portal of discovery, as much as an error. The interconnection of sisterhood between Willow and heterosexual Buffy is made clear by the forgiveness which is extended to Willow, and which is resented by Amy – 'The Killer Inside Me' (7.13) – 'she almost destroyed the world and everyone keeps loving her'. In the same episode, Willow's guilt-driven transformation into the male Warren does not alienate her new female partner, Kennedy, who transforms her back to her female form with a fairy-tale kiss, indicating a loving acceptance of her that goes beyond the transitorily physical.

At another level, Willow is politically linked to Buffy through their workplace identities. Buffy continues to represent the unacknowledged labour of reproduction, as the bank manager tells her that 'You have no income. No job' – 'Flooded'(6.4) – and she discovers that she cannot be paid for slaying. Her paid employment potential – 'Doublemeat Palace' (6.12) – means that, as Dawn says, 'She's gonna have crap jobs her entire life, right? Minimum wage stuff', immediately reminiscent, in the UK at least, of the unequal position that women still occupy in the labour market, and especially lesbian women, who have no substantive employment rights as well as lower wages and poorer career prospects than men.

The overall process, and the focus of the episodes, is for the Scoobies gradually to develop a new consciousness, as they follow through their individual quests. Sometimes this is expressed in starkly psychoanalytic terms: Spike and Principal Wood are linked by their focus on their mothers, Spike through a classic Oedipal relationship with his mother, enacted by his 'siring' her in a displaced act of penetration when he bites her to make her a vampire, to give her eternal life so that they can always be together; in her new-found power, she rejects and humiliates him. For Buffy and Willow, it is expressed by their need to break through what Northrop Frye calls 'mythological conditioning', the process of questioning the assumptions about the universe on which their interpretations are founded. This requires a leap of faith, the combined need and self-belief that enables Parzival to seek out new ways of being, beyond conventional wisdom or action. In universal terms, the thrust is towards a new way of understanding and living in our world.

Lunar myth was supplanted by solar myth – the myth of the warrior-hero – by the patriarchal, conquering tribes of the Iron Age in Old Europe. A consciousness of eternity, relationality and transformation was submerged by one of the lone hero, pitting the force of his short life against the natural world to try to conquer it, as in the *Epic of Gilgamesh*, the earliest of these tales. Nature and Spirit were divorced, and life was found wanting, since 'the further away the Sun, Moon, goddesses and gods went, the more human beings became alone'. That sense of loneliness, with no way of assuaging it, is the despair which 'devours from below' and which the series finale sets out to conquer. The last Guardian represents the unbroken lunar tradition, dying as Waning Moon (or Crone, in Wiccan tradition) and passing her inheritance to Buffy, whose role as Slayer ends, and role as Guardian begins (New Moon, Wiccan Maiden, Christian Virgin), as Buffy acknowledges in her description of herself as 'cookie dough... I'm not finished'.

Crucially, though, the series finale operates not through conflict between lunar and solar myth, but by their resolution. This has been the coherent theme of the whole series, since the meeting between Giles and Buffy in the first episode: Giles, as Watcher, is inheritor of the 'Shadow-Men' who enslaved the first girl-Slayer to work against her instinct, and thus is representative of solar myth, since 'sun-worship is essentially a *learned* cult... it had to be calculated'. However, breaking all the rules, he and Buffy work together, in functional partnership rather than hierarchical line management, to a shared end. This reinstatement of the lunar into relationality with the solar is the constant mythopoeia of the series, a reconciliation of opposites and redemption of Nature and Spirit, *bios* and *zoe*, time and eternity, which lies at the heart of the mystery traditions of Eleusis, of Dionysus, and of Gnostic Christianity, and which alchemists call the 'sacred marriage' of 'Sol and Luna'.

Literally, 'when the Moon is closely lined up with the Sun at New Moon and Full Moon, their tidal forces accumulate, causing bigger bulges [in the Earth's surface] and larger tides'. Alchemically, the *coniunctio* of Sol and Luna provides 'a structure of transformation in which the individual dies to the old self and is reborn into a new mode of being'. Sacred marriages take place between Faith and Wood as sexual coupling and subsequent friendly banter; between Angel and Buffy, when they kiss and she 'basks' in his presence; between

Willow and Kennedy as their continued relationship; between Buffy and Faith, when Buffy gives Faith the scythe and Faith returns it; between Andrew and Anya when he tells her 'You are the perfect woman' and they wheelchair-fight; between solar-Giles and the Moon when he bites into a Jaffa Cake, in reference to the TV advert which makes the lunar-Jaffa analogy; between solar-Anya and the Moon through her hatred of 'bunnies', since the 'rabbit in the Moon' is flung there in punishment in many myths; between solar-Xander and the Moon, since his blinded eye is analogous with the left eye of Horus in Egyptian myth, which was plucked out in battle with the dark god Seth and became the 'Wejdat Eye', which, as Full Moon, was restored by Thoth, guardian of time and timelessness; and crucially, between Sol-Spike, who bursts with burning brightness and Luna-Buffy, as she and he reconcile their troubled physical relationship through love at the emotional, symbolic level: 'I love you.' – 'No you don't. But thanks for saying it.'

With a brief glance to *Angel*, one might note the difference between this sensibility and the tragic/pathetic arc of Cordelia, whose lunar process/progress ends in her entire betrayal by the Powers and, first through possession by Jasmine, her Dark Half, and then by her coma, her becoming frozen as the Dark Moon. *Angel* operates consistently to a solar mythology which places dark and light perpetually at war with each other, which makes death final and tragic, and which falls into all of Parzival's early errors of perception and action; transformation through shared human feeling and instinct, rather than rigorous self-sacrifice to social duty, awaits a future season.

The presiding political principle is that of reconciliation of the individual and the community, through a valorization of lunar qualities. Dark Willow's hopeless rage at the pointless, random violence of the solar patriarchy is truly the rage of all women condensed to boiling point. It is 'the darkest place that I've ever been', but her fear that 'what lies beyond that' may be deeper darkness is unfounded: beyond the Dark Moon lies the New Moon, and her spell to 'use the essence of this scythe to change our destiny' suffuses her with moonlight, as White Willow, in a moving image of personal redemption. Lesbian Willow is 'more powerful than all of them [the "powerful men"] combined', as Buffy tells the Potentials ('some thirty-odd pimply girls', the number of days in the Moon's cycle and its marked face) and is able to release both herself and the rest of the world from the constrictions of the patriarchy simply because she links with all the other Wiccans in the world so that the scythe-Moon-Grail's power may be shared. The Guardian – who was once 'one of many' and is now 'alone in the world' – has her communal identity recreated, as Slayer-Buffy, 'one girl alone'. She deliberately ensures that 'my power is our power', so that 'any girl in the world who might be a Slayer, will be a Slayer', wonderfully giving birth to a new community of 'Slayers, every one of us', while at the same time losing her isolated position so that now, at long last, redemptively, she can find her own humanity, and 'live like a person'.

Finding the Grail ends the Wasteland and restores everyone: Parzival, the Fisher-King, and the kingdom. Contemporaneously, at the level of the physical world, the thrust is towards new views such as James Lovelock's *Gaia*, which offers a scientific vision of the interconnectedness of the Earth and Moon, which Willow and Buffy experience so strongly. At the level of the imagination, the requirement is for what Barfield, in *Saving the Appearances*, calls 'Final Participation', described by Cashford as 'a return to the old participative relation to nature, not in the old, original way – which is in any case impossible, consciousness inevitably moving on – but at a new *level*, through the Imagination'. This involves a relation in which we experience Nature as separate from us, but in which we create a new poetic union by participating with the natural world, consciously and imaginatively. In this vision, it is through the imagination that we will be redeemed, as it is through her creative, imaginative leap – 'we change the rules' – that Buffy redeems the world, transforming hopeless odds and an impossible situation, by an act of felt autonomy, as unexpected and unforeseen as all acts of artistry. In offering this viewpoint, the series not only provides redemption to Sunnydale's world, but extends a similar possibility to viewers, who may feel the resonance of its archetypes, and perhaps will be moved by them to wonder more about their own ways of being: after all, as Rilke says in the *Duino Elegies*: 'O Earth: invisible! What, if not transformation, is your urgent command?'

the only thing better than killing a slayer

heterosexuality and sex
in BUFFY THE VAMPIRE SLAYER

justine larbalestier

This is a musing about heterosexuality and sex in *Buffy the Vampire Slayer*, focusing on the relationship between Buffy and Spike. Their relationship is the longest-running sexually tinged relationship the show has seen, lasting six seasons. They hated, fought, taunted, desired, teased, fucked and loved each other for a long time.

The complexities of the Spike and Buffy relationship allow me to consider many aspects of heterosexual relationships between men and women, vampires and Slayers. In some respects Spike is a mixture of elements from all Buffy's previous love interests. He's Angel: the brooding demon lover with a soul; he's Parker Abrams: callous and mean to women; he's Riley: consumed by unrequited love.

We are led to believe that Angel is the only vampire who can fall in love, then along comes Spike. Spike's evil, Spike's soft, Spike's a devoted lover, Spike's a demon in the sack, Spike's a rapist. Spike's good – the saviour of the world. Buffy and Spike have casual, killer one-night stands; Spike and Buffy have an unequal relationship – he loves and she uses; Buffy and Spike have an abusive relationship; Spike and Buffy have an undying love between equals to conquer the ages. Buffy and Spike have it all.

Heterosexuality

The way I pronounce it, het-tra-sex-u-al-it-y, is a seven-syllable word. That's a mouthful. Doesn't exactly trip off the tongue. The term came into being, as 'homosexuality' did, at the beginning of the shift from a procreation ethic to one of sexual pleasure and did not stabilize its current meaning until the 1920s. (Katz 1995) Until that shift, sex acts that did not result in children within wedlock were considered perversions and punishable by law. It was wrong for a man to have sex with a man, not because he was a man and that made it unnatural, but because it could not result in a child and *that* made it unnatural. Presumably sex with a vampire (Angel and Darla's child aside) would be unnatural and wrong for the same reason.

It has been argued that 'heterosexuality' is a back formation, that *homo*sexuality came first. Whether or not this claim holds up, until very recently 'homosexuality' has been by far the more used, the more debated and argued-about term. There were histories of homosexuality long before the first history of heterosexuality was published. What is the need to discuss, problematize or argue about the natural state of things? As Anya points out, heterosexuality is, par excellence, viewed as natural: '[I]t's ludicrous,' she tells Xander, 'to have these interlocking bodies and not... interlock' – 'The Harsh Light of Day' (4.3).

Except that interlocking is sex, not heterosexuality. There's plenty of interlocking (kissing, anal sex, etc.) that works fine for heterosexual and non-heterosexuals alike. As Kathy Albury points out, 'there's more to heterosexuality than a dud root in the missionary position'. (Albury 2002: vii) Considerably more: heterosexuality is the default mode of sexual being and sexual desire of us all, that constrains how we exist even if we are not heterosexual.

> [E]ven a lesbian/feminist identity is produced within hegemonic norms... However... this is also true of hetero-sexuality. That is to say, far from begin a natural expression of

gender and sexuality, heterosexuality is always in the process
of being produced. (Richardson 2000: 250)

It's simply that for the vast majority of people that production is
invisible.

When it became clear that there was a mutual sexual attraction
between a more-than-200-year-old walking dead man (ewww!) and
a 16-year-old girl, there were no cries of protest; when it became
clear that there was a mutual sexual attraction between two young
women over the age of consent (and neither undead) there was a
good deal of consternation and debate. Showing romance and sex
between two women is still daring and controversial in a way that
showing the same between a woman and a man is not (that is if they're
both the same race and class, if the girl isn't too much taller than the
boy and if the age or ability gap is not too risible). Walking down the
street with your same-sex lover can be life-threatening even in Sydney,
London or New York City. That's normativity for you.

Heterosexuality has been a sticking point in feminist theory since
the 1970s, when 'some feminists argued that, if heterosexuality is
key to male dominance, feminists should reject sexual relationships
with men'. (Richardson 2000: 20–21) Feminists began to question
their desires rather than accepting them as natural. Are heterosexual
feminists complicit in their own domination? How should
heterosexual feminists deal with the sometimes 'acute disjunction
between [their] feminist politics and [their] heterosexual practice
and experience'? (Jackson 1999: 3) How do they deal with that
disjunction in a world where rape affects so many (mostly) women's
lives? Are men the enemy?

In Buffy's case, these issues are literalized: Spike really is the
enemy. He has fangs and claws and it's Buffy's job to kill him. She's
a Slayer and he's a vampire without (until the last minutes of Season
Six) a soul. Buffy is fucking the enemy, thus leaving herself open to
being fucked over by the enemy. Spike has attempted to kill her
many times and did indeed try to rape her in 'Seeing Red' (6.19).

It's not just the male and female bodies whose interlocking is 'natural', so too are the discourses around that interlocking. Romance and love legitimate heterosexuality, and all three are founded upon myths about sex. True happiness happens when you meet The One: you fall in love, have wonderful orgasmic sex and get married (though not always in that order). It's natural.

Heterosexuality depends on a coherently gendered world. To be straight you must first be a man or a woman. Foucault argues that you have to be gendered in order to *be* at all. As Anya, always insightful about the constructedness of identity, says to Dawn, 'you make a very pretty little girl' – 'Blood Ties' (5.13).

Anya would know. She has been performing American femaleness since the third season: 'For a thousand years I wielded the powers of The Wish... I was feared and worshipped across the mortal globe. And now I'm stuck at Sunnydale High. Mortal. Child. And I'm flunking math.' – 'Doppelgangland' (3.16). Anya has to learn to be mortal, child, girl. Her literal-mindedness in that learning process exposes the constructedness of being all these things and of heterosexuality. She exposes how unnatural sex and dating are:

Anya	Where is our relationship going?
Xander	Our what? Our who?
Anya	Relationship. What kind do we have? And what is it progressing toward?
Xander	I... Uh... We have a relationship?
Anya	Yeah. We went to the prom.
Xander	Yeah. On our one and only date. Second date called on account of snake, remember? And the whole... you used to be a man-killing demon thing. Which, to be fair, is as much my issue as it is yours.
Anya	I can't stop thinking about you. Sometimes in my dreams, you're all naked.

Xander	Really. You know if I'm in the checkout line at the Wal-Mart I've had the same one.
Anya	So I can assume a standing Friday night date and a mutual recognition of Prom night as our dating anniversary.
Xander	Anya. Slow down there. In fact, come to a screeching halt. See these things kind of have to develop on their own.
Anya	Okay. How?
Xander	I don't know. It just... happens.

'The Harsh Light of Day'

Xander's discomfort is not just with Anya's blunt forwardness, but also with her denaturalization of romance. She has exposed the rules ('a standing Friday night date') of dating and relationships, undercutting Xander's understanding of them as things that 'just happen'. As Xander observes ('still more romantic than Faith') there is little romance in Anya's understanding of relations between heterosexual men and women.

And yet Anya embraces conventional gender expectations and the related practices, rules and rituals of heterosexual love, sex and marriage as enthusiastically as she did those of a vengeance demon. She will wear white in a church, be a wife and take Xander's name – 'Mrs Anya lame-ass-made-up-maiden-name Harris' – 'Selfless' (7.5). They will be together forever. When these sites of ritual practice are wrenched from her in the aptly named episode 'Selfless', she feels her sense of identity and self dissolve.

Judith Butler has convincingly argued that we are all – not just globs of energy like Dawn, or ex-vengeance demons like Anya – performing our gender, our sexuality. Granted, we're not free to perform as we wish; our gender is not a mask that can be taken on and off at will. We are all of us, from George W. Bush to a Baghdad shoeshine boy, circumscribed within narratives, discourses, stories.

Even *Buffy the Vampire Slayer* is circumscribed, written and shot within a set amount of time, cut down to fit advertisements, bound by what can and can't be shown.

While our performances of gender, sexuality, etc. are constrained by these discourses, our performances also create the discourses, narratives, stories, create our performances. None of them, not the performances or the discourses, is entirely fixed. So even the most 'normal' (i.e. straight) people harbour anxieties about how they've performed maleness or femaleness: too girlie, too butch? 'I wonder what went wrong. Were you too strong? Did you bruise the boy?' asks Spike, right on target, hitting all Buffy's anxieties about being a normal girl – 'The Harsh Light of Day'.

Buffy's own anxieties about her performance of gender, of heterosexuality, are a running theme in the series, summed up in her desire to 'just… have a life' and 'do something normal' – 'The Witch' (1.3). It is very unlikely Buffy will get married or bear children or, indeed, live past the age of 25. Slayers don't have normal lives. Until Buffy, they didn't even have friends.

Buffy's sense of herself as normal is contingent on her ability to separate the Slayer from Buffy Summers: 'Accelerated healing powers come with the Slayer package. And the boyfriend who comes complete with combat medical training? That's just a Buffy Summers bonus' – 'Fool For Love' (5.7). It's an unstable separation, the further she gets from high school and college and the role of Buffy-the-student, the more untenable it becomes. One of the many dangerous consequences of her sexual relationships with Angel and Spike is that it makes that separation impossible. She spends her time off in the arms of the darkness she should be fighting. Normal girls have boyfriends; normal girls don't have boyfriends who are the evil dead.

In 'Normal Again' (6.17), Buffy's battle for normality is foregrounded. She is caught in a set of hallucinations (or are they?): she's not the Slayer, her parents never divorced, she never moved to Sunnydale, never fell in love with any vampires, never had a sister, never saved the world – even once. The episode's title is deeply ironic. Buffy is not normal: she's either a schizophrenic in a mental asylum who fantasises about being the Slayer; or she *is* the Slayer. The quest for normality, it seems, was doomed from the beginning.

Sex

What kind of heterosexuals are Buffy and Spike? Because there's straight and then there's *straight*. Together, Buffy and Spike most definitely aren't straight. Spike never was, but what about Buffy? Spike thinks she's no more straight than he is: 'The girl needs some monster in her man' – 'Into the Woods' (5.10). Buffy seems to agree: '[I]sn't that where the fire comes from? Can a nice, safe relationship be that intense? I know it's nuts, but part of me believes that real love and passion have to go hand in hand with pain and fighting' – 'Something Blue' (4.9).

Buffy started as a good girl. Until Spike, sex for Buffy (unlike the bad-girl Slayer, Faith) was not casual, not merely a means to let off steam; Faith, though, touching Xander lasciviously, says: 'A fight like that and no kill… I'm about ready to pop' – 'The Zeppo' (3.13). In contemporary western cultures to be a good heterosexual girl you have to be a certain kind of girl desiring a certain kind of boy, doing certain kinds of sexual acts with him. Sex is definitely okay if you're bonking as part of a committed monogamous relationship, such as Buffy had with Angel and with Riley.

But what kind of sex? 'Real' sex is heterosexual, penetrative sex. It begins with the entrance of the penis into the vagina and ends when the man climaxes. It's all about what Annie Potts calls the coital and orgasm imperatives. (Potts 2002: 8) And at the centre is the penis. The importance of penile penetration is such that men are almost secondary to their penises. There is:

> a synechdochal relationship between the man and his penis
> whereby the penis is discursively constructed as an entity –
> a self – in its own right; it is depicted as separate from the

man, with its own peculiar carnal intelligence that operates outside the man's rational cerebral thought... this popular portrayal of the penis permits individual men to use their penis-selves as alibis for riskier and coercive heterosexual behaviours. (Potts 2002: 9)

Or, as Xander would say: 'Nothing can defeat the penis!' – 'Beer Bad' (4.5).

(i) Tame the cruller and respect the donut

Heterosex being 'real' sex made sense under the procreative ethic: until recently it was the only way a woman could conceive. Doing it the first time was a cultural and sexual milestone: you could now make babies. Even though contemporary sex is focused on orgasms (which women rarely achieve from penetrative sex), first penetrative sex is still a huge deal, typically viewed as 'an achievement for men, and a loss of sorts for women'. (Potts 2002: 198)

Certainly, losing their virginity is a milestone for the three Scoobies: Buffy, Xander and Willow. This even though they were all sexually active as 'virgins': Willow fooled around with Xander and Oz; Xander with Willow and Cordelia; and Buffy with Angel. However, none of the three Scoobies' loss of virginity quite fits that typical story of male accomplishment and female diminishment.

For a heterosexual woman, the point is not just first sex, but first-sex-with-the-man-you-love. For Buffy (and Willow) the decision to become sexually active is huge and is made in the context of a monogamous relationship. When Buffy explains her decision to sleep with Angel, she is full of anticipation and nervousness, but also resolute. She's ready. She wants to not just because Angel's a hottie, or because she's sexually curious, but because of her feelings for him:

> *Willow*   'I like you at bedtime?' You actually said that?
>
> [...]
>
> *Buffy*   Totally unplanned. It just... came out.

Willow	And he was into it? I mean, he wants to see you at bedtime, too?
Buffy	Yeah, I, I think he does. Well, I, I mean he's cool about it.

[...]

Buffy	Will, what am I gonna do?
Willow	What do you wanna do?
Buffy	I don't know. I mean, want isn't always the right thing to do. To act on want can be wrong.
Willow	True.
Buffy	But to not act on want. What if I never feel this way again?
Willow	Carpe diem. You told me that once.

[...]

Buffy	Right. I, I think we're going to. Seize it. Once you get to a certain point, then seizing is sort of inevitable.
Willow	Wow.
Buffy	Yeah.
Willow	Wow.

'Surprise' (2.13).

Angel and Buffy do not discuss whether they're going to have sex or not; they just do it when the moment is right. That moment turns out to be after an escape from near death (the libidinous excitement of not dying is a common thread in first-sex experience for the Scooby gang). First they tell each other, 'I love you', then they kiss. Angel starts to say that maybe they shouldn't, but Buffy stops him: 'Just kiss me.' Their faces descend out of frame, cut to white out. Their first (and only) sex together is depicted as loving and consensual. Neither is using the other.

It is not until the next morning (and the next episode) that Angel becomes monstrous, that Buffy finds herself in the narrative of the good girl betrayed: Buffy has 'given' herself to her man and he has changed. He does not respect Buffy. But her narrative is a little different. Buffy may have lost her virginity, but Angel's loss is much bigger: his soul. His civilized veneer is stripped away; he has become the brutish demon that we are taught lies at the heart of all men. They are animals, who will do whatever they can to get what they want. For the rest of Season Two, the shadow of Angel's violence hangs over Buffy. The unspoken fear is not whether he will kill her, but whether he will rape her.

Being a virgin becomes shaming for a man much earlier than it does for a woman. At 16, Xander's virginity is an embarrassment. Buffy and Willow are also virgins, but no one's laughing. Xander's virginity is not only risible, it's dangerous: it makes him prey for a mantis-demon who eats male virgins in 'Teacher's Pet' (1.4). The demon 'knows' who's a virgin and who's not. This conceit is not confined to the *Buffy*verse. There is an expectation that a boy will be transformed by having penetrative sex for the first time. He will gain a surety he did not have. Boys will become men.

When Xander become a 'man' it is with Faith, who seduces him while hardly seeming to register who he is. Xander doesn't initiate the sexual encounter and has no say in when it begins or ends: 'That was great,' says Faith, throwing him out. 'I gotta take a shower'. Although music wells up during the sex act and there is a moment of tenderness when it's over, for Faith it's all about sex, not about any potential relationship with Xander. He may feel used ('still more romantic than Faith') but he also feels like he's become a man.

Or at least Xander knows he *should* feel that way. After Faith throws him out, his confusion about what's happened, how he's supposed to react is plain: he's bewildered. Should he swagger? Punch the air? Be hurt? He doesn't know what he's feeling: 'I can't believe I had sex.' 'The Zeppo' ends with a confident Xander, but his poise has more to do with solving problems on his own (defeating dead guys with bombs), than it does with his first penetrative root.

The narratives available for Xander's first heterosex differ to those available for Willow and Buffy. Yet he doesn't take them up. He doesn't swagger or boast about his 'conquest' of Faith. His reading is more romantic than that. He believes he is now 'connected' to Faith. A belief that Buffy squashes: Faith 'doesn't take the guys that she has a connection with very seriously. They're kind of a big joke to her. No offence'. But Xander is offended and hurt. The embarrassment felt by all during this scene is palpable – 'Consequences' (3.15). Sex is meant to mean something in the *Buffy*verse, even for boys (and, eventually, even for Faith).

When Willow attempts to engineer the popping of her cherry with Oz, she deploys every romantic scenario cliché there is: she wears a low-cut, tight red dress, the lights are low, there are lots of candles and Barry White is 'working for [her]'. 'I want to be with you,' she tells Oz, 'first.' He turns her down, not because he wants it to occur more 'naturally' but because he wants them to 'need it to for the same reason' – 'Amends' (3.10).

At the end of Season Three, facing the prospect of death, they find a shared reason: panic. Afterwards, they lie wrapped in each other's arms (a contrast to Buffy finding herself alone and Xander being thrown out) and Willow's assessment is that she 'feels different'. She's smiling; it's a good kind of different, not a loss. She raises the possibility that Oz might also be feeling different and then dismisses it because he wasn't a virgin. But Oz tells her that 'everything feels different' – 'Graduation Day Part One' (3.21). Having penetrative sex has transformed their relationship. They are serious now. It's real.

Contrast this with Anya's first heterosex after becoming human. Like Willow, she tries to initiate proceedings, though, unlike Willow, Anya is successful. Their modes are entirely different. Anya denaturalizes sex. There's no Barry White, candles or tight red dress (there's no dress at all – Anya opts for the naked approach). She neither stammers nor averts her gaze. She uses the language not of romance but of business and negotiation: 'At which point the matter is brought to a conclusion with both parties satisfied and able to move on with their separate lives and interests. To sum up, I think it's a workable plan' – 'The Harsh Light of Day'. She's also more direct: 'sexual intercourse, I've said it like a dozen times', compared to Willow's 'I'm ready to… with you' – 'Amends'. Anya describes how she'd like them to proceed: 'I'm thinking face to face for the actual event itself.'

Anya robs Xander not only of the initiative (as Faith did), she also unmans him ('I'm actually turning into a woman as I say this'), leaving him stammering, dealing with 'hysterical deafness' and struggling to steer things on to more normal narrative paths:

> It's just we hardly know each other. I mean I like you. And you have a certain directness that I admire. But sexual interc – What you're talking about, well, and I'm actually turning into a woman as I say this, but it's about expressing something. And accepting consequences. –
>
> 'The Harsh Light of Day'

His second experience of penetrative sex leaves Xander as uncomfortable and confused as his first. Anya understands sex from the vantage point of someone who is just learning social mores (or rather, late adolescent white Californian social mores). She has not learned all the codes, so when she undertakes acts such as sexual intercourse her unfamiliarity with them reveals those acts as unnatural and learned.

Buffy is a show that both embraces and critiques romance. Standard romantic scenarios, like the loss of virginity, are set up and then undone. Willow's *naïveté*, Xander's haplessness, Anya's unsocialized-demon viewpoint all expose the underpinnings of romance. But at the same time love and romance drive the show. Sex with them is more fulfilling than without.

(ii) Acts of nakedness

Not a lot of sex is actually shown on *Buffy the Vampire Slayer*. Until the fourth season, the only glimpse of lovemaking is a split second of Faith and Xander fully covered by sheets, in a distorted reflection in a TV set. Oz and Willow start kissing – cut to another scene – when next seen they are in post-coital bliss – 'Graduation Day Part One'. But there is a lot of implied sex.

First a brief detour away from heterosex: the depiction of Tara and Willow's sex life demonstrates that implied sex does not mean lame sex. Willow and Tara do not fall into the 'primarily acts of affection and not really sex at all' category which is a typical caricature of lesbian relationships. (Richardson 2000: 25) While there were times when their relationship resembled that of Buffy and Angel in Season Three (looking, but not a whole lot of touching), Tara and Willow have always been represented as intensely sexual: the unbelievably sexy spell of 'Who Are You?' (4.16), Tara's thumb to Willow's forehead, chanting, heavy breathing, glistening with sweat, half-closed eyes, a circle of light rising around them, Willow falls back gasping; and the 'You Make Me Complete' scene from 'Once More With Feeling' (6.7), which begins with Xander commenting on the 'get-a-room-iness of them' and ends with Willow going down on Tara as she sings: 'Lost in ecstasy/Spread beneath my Willow tree/You make me com... -plete.'

In the *Buffy*verse there are two kinds of sex: human (vanilla) and vampire (BD/SM). Normative, heterosexual sex is vanilla. Kath Albury describes vanilla sex as a 'loose catch-all descriptive term for sex which is non-fetishistic, or non-BD/SM', noting that '[i]t can be used as a slur, however I like the implication that sex comes in many flavours'. (Albury 2002: 76) All of Buffy's sexual experiences before Spike centre around the coital and orgasmic imperatives; they are also very vanilla.

Buffy's first sexual encounter after Angel is with mildly (hasn't killed or tortured anyone and no game face) bad-boy Parker Abrams pretending to be a good boy (as opposed to good-boy Angel *becoming* a bad boy). He exploits and parodies the romantic notion of the sensitive straight guy, with his 'gentle eyes', 'shy smile' and 'ability to talk openly', who only wants to meet the right girl who will truly understand him – 'Beer Bad'. He is exactly the kind of guy good girls are warned about. Buffy's one night with Angel is the metaphorical version of that narrative; her one night with Parker is the real thing.

When Buffy and Parker have heterosex, they are shown wrapped in sheets, holding each other and kissing with music swelling up. Together they are the cliché: 'heterosexual men will fuck anything that moves' and heterosexual women will put up with anything 'because they just want to be held'. (Albury 2002: vi–vii) Sex is important to a woman because of who she is fucking, for the tenderness and love that will result; sex is everything to the man – that narrative goes – it doesn't matter who it's with.[1] The next morning, once again, Buffy finds herself naked and alone in bed: 'Sleep with a guy and he goes all evil' – 'The Harsh Light of Day'.

Buffy's first sexual relationship when her lover is still there in the morning is with her psych tutor (despite the massive ethical problem, never touched on by the show, that he's her *tutor*!). Buffy and Riley are *straight*. Her desire for Riley with his college boy clothes – no black anywhere in sight – and his muscular, corn-fed Iowa body makes her wholesome. Their sex is almost always in bed, and for the first time Buffy is shown in bed naked doing things with another naked person. Instead of a fade out, there's rolling around in sheets in missionary position (standard and reverse) and lots of kissing. Very vanilla.

Or is it? Their sex may not destroy buildings or leave marks on their skin, but it *is* fuelled by violence. The montage sequence from 'The I in Team' (4.13) alternates between lovemaking and battles with demons. Images of penetrating enemies with weapons are contrasted with images of them penetrating each other. In 'Where the Wild Things Are' (4.18), Buffy and Riley are so turned on by the slaying they have to shag: they're both about 'ready to pop'.

The Buffy of Buffy and Riley is a good girl, parodied by Faith in the following exchange:

Spike	You know why I really hate you, Summers?
Faith-as-Buffy	Cause I'm a stuck-up tight-arse with no sense of fun?
Spike	Well. Yeah. That covers a lot of it.
Faith-as-Buffy	Cause I could do anything I want and yet I choose to pout and whine and feel the burden of Slayerness? I could be rich. I could be famous. I could have anything. Anyone. Even you, Spike. I could ride you at a gallop until your legs buckled and your eyes rolled up. I've got muscles you've never even dreamed of. I could squeeze you until you pop like warm champagne. And you'd beg me to hurt you just a little bit more. And you know why I don't? Because it's wrong. *[laughs]*
Spike	I get this chip out. You and me are going to have a confrontation.
Faith-as-Buffy	Count on it.

'Who Are You?'[2]

Good girls don't enjoy that kind of sex. They don't use people. They don't have sex without love.

Not long after this exchange with Spike, Faith-as-Buffy decides to ride Buffy's boyfriend, Riley. She leaves the door to his room open and proceeds to climb onto his lap. He, being a good boy, doesn't like to be watched, and is put off by her directness. He takes the sexual initiative and insists that sex is natural, not a game:

Faith-as-Buffy	So, how do you want me?
Riley	How do I…?

Faith-as-Buffy	Yeah. What do you wanna do with this body? What nasty little desire have you been itching to try out? Am I a bad girl? Do you wanna hurt me?
Riley	What are we playing at here?
Faith-as-Buffy	I'm Buffy.
Riley	Okay. Then I'll be Riley.
Faith-as-Buffy	Well, if you don't wanna play…
Riley	Right. I don't wanna play.

'Who Are You?'

Riley doesn't want to play: He wants to have real sex, which begins with kissing and doesn't involve anyone playing at being anyone else. Faith freaks when he says 'I love you', insisting that 'This is meaningless'.[3] But for Riley and Buffy it isn't.

Or is it? It eventually becomes clear that Buffy is not in love with Riley, that she's *playing* at being normal with her normal boyfriend. And Riley is so locked into a good boy/good girl sex dynamic that he is unable to work out his masochist desires with Buffy. He has to go elsewhere to get 'suck jobs from two-bit vampire trulls' – 'Into the Woods'. Good girls don't do *that*; good boys don't want that. Buffy, according to Riley, has turned him and given him masochistic desires. Because Buffy needs 'some monster in her man' – 'Into the Woods'. Buffy's ultimate bad-girl perversion is in fucking Riley but not loving him.

(iii) You make it hurt in all the wrong places

If human sex is vanilla, swelling music, glistening bodies and lots of kissing, then vampire sex is all about leather, face-licking and pain: bondage and discipline; sadism and masochism. Vampire sex is often on the verge of breaking the bounds of consent.

The first time we see Spike and Drusilla, she is cutting his face with her fingernail and licking the blood. Vamp Willow likes to torture unconsenting victims and Vamp Xander likes to watch. Even Harmony, who as a human was a vanilla pin-up girl, has violent vampire sex with Spike:

Spike	We've got an extra set of chains.
Harmony	Eww. Just because Dorkus went in for that.
Spike	Drusilla.
Harmony	Whatever.
Spike	Say her name.
Harmony	Dorkus.
Spike	Bite your tongue.
Harmony	Do it for me.

'The Harsh Light of Day'

Riley and his random prostitute vampires are dealing in blood and pain (what looks like blood-soaked fellatio).

Unsurprisingly, vampires eroticize blood and pain, their own as well as that of their human victims. They get off on hurting one another, giving and receiving sexual pain. For obvious (American prime-time TV) reasons, we don't see a whole lot of this; instead there are gestures of deviance, props (chains, leather etc.) and behaviours that suggest these activities. There is face-licking: Vamp Willow licking Willow is a splendidly perverse suggestion of lesbian fetishistic sex *and* of onanism. And there's talk. Vampire sex seems to be about talking as much as it is about pain.

However, vampires are not the only ones in the *Buffy*verse who engage in fetishistic sex or BD/SM. Anya makes numerous announcements about the adventurousness of her sex life with Xander: 'Yes, we've enjoyed spanking' – 'The I in Team'. However, Xander and Anya's activities are portrayed as amusingly cute and cuddly, not dangerous or violent. There's also a moment when Xander and Buffy imagine Willow and Oz doing the kinds of things Vamp Willow revels in:

Willow	Oh, right. Me and Oz play 'Mistress of Pain' every night.
Xander	Did anyone else just go to a scary visual place?
Buffy	Oh, yeah.

'Doppelgangland'

When Anya and the other Scoobies talk about SM/BD, it's not vampire sex; it's comedy. Faith, however, doesn't just play at it. One of the many hints that something is up with her, that the bad-girl Slayer may have crossed the line, is her attitude to sex and sexual practices. It is constantly implied that she has nasty, dangerous sex. This is mostly demonstrated by her initiating sex – with Xander in 'The Zeppo', and with Robin Wood in 'Touched'. However, in 'Consequences', she sexually attacks Xander, taunting him and then throttling him until he passes out.

Perhaps one of Buffy's fears in the midst of her affair with Spike is that she will become like Faith – only capable of loveless sex that blurs the boundaries between being the Slayer and being Buffy and that she will no longer be able to police herself. Her brutal beating of Spike in 'Dead Things' (6.13) sees her at once venting her anger on someone who can't fight back (at least as far as she's aware) and transferring her desire for him into violence.

That desire lets her professional life – according to Dracula the darkness *is* Buffy's true nature, 'Buffy vs. Dracula' (5.1) – into her personal life. Perhaps Spike is right when he tells her not to 'get prim and proper', that he 'know[s] what kind of a girl [she] really' is – 'Smashed' (6.9). Perhaps death is her gift in the sack as well as out of it.

Spike and Buffy definitely have vampire sex.[4] Their bonking is neither normal nor natural. It consumes them. It hurts them:

| Spike | You were amazing. |
| Buffy | You get the job done yourself. |

Spike	I was just trying to keep up. The things you do. The way you make it hurt in all the wrong places. I've never been with such an animal.
Buffy	I'm not an animal.
Spike	You want to see the bite marks?

'Dead Things'

Buffy and Spike's fornicating leaves visible traces on their skin. They have to keep their sleeves down. They are marked.

Buffy's fear that she came back 'wrong' encapsulates her disgust with herself, not only for engaging in vampire sex, but for enjoying it. Buffy is fucking the darkness instead of fighting it. As Spike observes during the fight that segues into their first bonk: 'Hello? Vampire. Supposed to be treading the dark side. What's your excuse?' – 'Smashed'.

The sex she has with Spike renders her monstrous; it does not make him more human. This is both the opposite of her sex with Angel, which makes him monstrous, and of her love for Angel, which makes him more human. If she continues to have vampire sex with Spike and enjoy it, she will lose her ability to even play at being normal. Spike explicitly wants to end her attempts at normality: 'good way to drive yourself crazy that is' – 'Doublemeat Palace' (6.12). He is releasing her from her good-girl human bonds. To make things worse, she initiated the process.

Buffy and Spike's first fuck in 'Smashed' is a gorgeously choreographed fight that literally brings the house down. They beat the crap out of each other, insulting each other as they do it. She hurls him into a wall, and then instead of hitting him again, she shuts up his taunt by kissing him. Next, in the most explicit depiction of sex shown on *Buffy*, she pushes him violently into a wall, straddles him, opens his fly, and mounts him.

It's compulsive and out of control. It fills Buffy with horror at the thought of being discovered. Their sex is a thing to take place in darkness, in crypts, behind trees, metaphorically and literally, because Buffy is ashamed:

Buffy	He's everything I hate. He's everything that I'm supposed to be against. But the only time that I ever feel anything is when... Don't tell anyone, please.
Tara	I won't.
Buffy	The way they would look at me. I just couldn't.

'Dead Things'

Yet fucking Spike is something she wants to do. When Buffy becomes invisible, for the first time she goes to Spike for sex rather than him pursuing her. It's perfect. She can fuck Spike, tear apart his crypt, and no one's the wiser – 'Gone' (6.11). But just as the Troika's ray gun made her disappear, sex with Spike is erasing her connection to her friends and eroding her chances of successfully playing at being normal.

Throughout Season Six, Buffy is unable to come to terms with her desire for Spike. Ultimately she chooses abstinence to manage it. Spike does not accept her decision and attempts to rape her – 'Seeing Red'. The implication is that vampire sex is always on the brink of turning into rape.

(iv) You think we're dancing?

Let's imagine sex as a continuum of desire beginning with seeing, looking, flirting and ending with naked bodies interlocking. There's a reason there are so many Buffy and Spike shippers and have been since 'School Hard' (2.3). Spike and Buffy have been dancing along that continuum since they first met. In 'Fool For Love' Spike says of his fight with an earlier Slayer: 'I could've danced all night with that one.' 'You think we're dancing?' asks Buffy, disgusted. 'That's all we've ever done,' says Spike. He's right.

In 'School Hard', Spike's very first episode, Buffy and Spike are already subtly sexually linked. Spike's lover Drusilla cuts his face with her fingernail, creating a blood smear. A little later Buffy paints the sign for parent-teacher night; she has a smear of red paint on the same cheek. Spike first sees the Slayer at the Bronze, he watches from the shadows as Buffy dances. She is caught in his gaze, prefiguring his later lovelorn stalking. The song playing in the background features the lyrics 'One step away from crashing to my knees'. Spike is more than one step (several seasons, in fact) from crashing, but his journey towards desiring the Slayer has begun.

Spike continues stalking the Slayer in 'Halloween' (2.6); this time he has minions with a video camera. He is appreciative of the resulting footage: 'Baby likes to play.' 'Once I know her I can kill her,' he tells Drusilla. But the better he knows Buffy, the less likely that becomes. In the climactic fight of 'What's My Line? Part Two' (2.10), Kendra and Buffy switch so Buffy can go up against Spike. 'I'd rather fight you anyway,' says Spike. 'Mutual,' replies Buffy.

Spike's desire for Buffy is evident when he encounters Faith-as-Buffy in the scene quoted above. Throughout, Spike looks as if he'd be quite happy to be ridden until his legs buckled – 'Who Are You?' Indeed, this is probably where Spike's insistence that Buffy has a dark side originates. Perhaps it's also where his desire for Buffy first becomes lodged inside him, though he doesn't realize it until his erotic dream about her in 'Out of My Mind' (5.4).

Even before he realizes he loves her, Spike speaks about Buffy as though they're dating. He announces to Initiative scientific staff just before killing them: 'Sorry. Can't stay. Got to go see a girl.' After finding Buffy's name in a list of student accommodation, he leans back and says, 'Hello, gorgeous' – 'The Initiative' (4.7). Buffy stakes Spike when he is invulnerable and he says, 'Oh. Do it again' – 'The Harsh Light of Day'. 'She is cute when she is hurting, isn't she?' Spike says to Angel – 'In the Dark' (A1.3).

They are also linked by others: Parker asks Buffy if she and Spike used to date in 'The Harsh Light of Day'; Willow offhandedly wishes that the two of them would get married – 'Something Blue'; Glory calls Spike Buffy's boyfriend – 'Blood Ties'; and Drusilla's visions reveal that Spike is in love with Buffy: 'I knew... before you did. I knew you loved the Slayer. The pixies in my head whispered it to me' – 'Crush' (5.14).

Their dance ceases to be fighting-as-dancing and becomes a literal dance in 'Once More With Feeling'; and, like a traditional musical, it ends with a kiss. That kiss, however, does not mark the beginning (or the end) of their relationship. We have seen them kiss before: 'Something Blue' and 'Out of My Mind'. But it is a kiss – as is the one they share at the end of 'Tabula Rasa' (6.8) – into which Spike insists on reading romance and desire for more: 'We kissed, you and me. All *Gone With The Wind*, with the rising music, and the rising… music, and what was that, Buffy?' – 'Tabula Rasa'.

The Curtains Close

Put baldly, in the *Buffy*verse sex in the context of a loving relationship is good, and sex that is not about love is bad, or at the very least, empty. It's love that allows Angel, a vampire, to have human sex with Buffy. It's the absence of love (and the commercial transaction) that defines what Riley does with two-bit vampire trulls as vampire sex.

Spike doesn't have a soul, he's in love only with pain, that's why Spike and Buffy's relationship can't work and why, though their sex may be earth-shattering (or, rather, *house*-shattering), it's not enough. Indeed its very violence is part of the reason why it can't be love. When there *is* love they don't have sex at all:

Spike   Yeah, I hear you say it but I've lived for soddin' ever, Buffy. I've done everything. I've done things with you I can't spell but I've never been close to anyone. Least of all you. Until last night. All I did was hold you, watch you sleep and it was the best night of my life. So yeah, I'm terrified.

'End of Days' (7.21)

With a soul, Spike doesn't need to have sex with Buffy; holding her through the night is enough. With a soul, what Spike feels for Buffy has become sanctified (complete with golden glowing light). So much so that when they at last have sex in the final episode it's off-screen. They are not even shown kissing.

And yet. The three couples who bonk in 'Touched' (7.20) are not all in love. Faith and Robin aren't (at least not yet); Xander and Anya aren't entirely sure; Kennedy might be, but Willow is still uncertain. However, the sex between all three couples is shown as loving and necessary,[5] not empty at all.

Then there's Buffy and Spike, with their holy love, spending that same night just holding each other. But is their love holy? That's merely Spike's take on his feelings for her. Does Buffy see him as her one true love? Probably not. Buffy's approach to Spike in Season Seven is strongly reminiscent of a recovering alcoholic determined to abstain from the demon booze. Buffy avoids touching Spike; early on in the season, she has difficulty even making eye contact. Viewed this way, her night of having Spike 'just hold her' seems masochistic.

Buffy's final declaration about her future does not concern who her great love will turn out to be; it concerns who *she* will turn out to be:

> *Buffy*   I'm cookie dough. I'm not done baking. I'm not
> finished becoming whoever the hell it is I'm going
> to turn out to be. I make it through this and the
> next thing and the next thing and maybe one day I
> turn around and realize I'm ready. I'm cookies. And
> then, you know, if I want someone to eat me, or
> enjoy warm, delicious cookie-me, then that's fine.
> That'll be then. When I'm done.
>
> 'Chosen'

The very last episode of *Buffy the Vampire Slayer* does not end with Buffy united with her one true love (whether it be Angel, Spike, or some other vampire with a soul); nor does it end with the various

Scoobies grouped with their boy or girl friend; it ends with the Slayer surrounded by her friends. Sex, romantic love, whatever – in the *Buffy*verse it is friendships that are key.

Notes

1. Faith is a bad girl precisely because she falls down on the male side of this equation, wanting sex, not intimacy. Part of the recuperation of her character in Season Seven – which allows Faith to be a goodie again – is the possibility of a romance between her and Robin Wood – 'Touched' (7.20) and 'Chosen' (7.22).

2. Deliciously, in the Sixth Season Buffy-as-Buffy does Spike exactly as Faith-as-Buffy describes.

3. A belief that her Season Seven relationship with Robin Wood begins to erode.

4. Though not all of Spike's sex is – his tryst with Anya is much less violent – 'Entropy'.

5. And possibly not entirely vanilla, what with Willow's comment about girlfriends with pierced tongues – 'Chosen'.

Works cited

Albury, Kathy, *Yes Means Yes: Getting Explicit About Heterosex* (Sydney, Australia: Allen and Unwin, 2002)

Jackson, Stevi, *Heterosexuality in Question* (London: Sage Publications, 1999)

Katz, Jonathan Ned, *The Invention of Heterosexuality* (New York: Dutton, 1995)

Larbalestier, Justine, *The Battle of The Sexes In Science Fiction* (Hanover, New Hampshire and London: Wesleyan University Press, 2002)

Martin, Emily, 'The Egg and the Sperm: How Science Has Constructed a Romance Based on Stereotypically Male-Female Sex Roles', *Signs: Journal of Women in Culture and Society*, 16 (3), 485–501, 1991

Potts, Annie, *The Science/Fiction of Sex: Feminist Deconstruction and the Vocabularies of Heterosex* (London and New York: Routledge, 2002)

Richardson, Diane, *Rethinking Sexuality* (London: Sage Publications, 2000)

URLS

The Buffy Dialogue Database:
        http://vrya.net/bdb/
BtVS Episode Guides and Transcripts:
        http://ww3.buffy-vs-angel.com/guide.shtml

blood and choice

the theory and practice of family in AΠGEL

jennifer stoy

Defining and maintaining a family unit has been one of, if not *the* pre-eminent concern in Joss Whedon's fictional universes. The bonds formed by affinity, blood, choice, love, loss and a number of other factors are constantly explored, analysed, deconstructed and evolved in *Buffy the Vampire Slayer*, *Angel* and *Firefly*. Rarely is a family unit based on the traditional, genetic/blood definition; instead, various individuals form bonds, often under metaphorical or literal fire. For example, in *Firefly*, Mal and Zoe fought together on the losing side in a civil war; in *Buffy*, one of the ways in which the Scoobies have self-selected is by fighting evil together.

These chosen families become the centre of the characters' lives. Even under less apocalyptic conditions, such as the ones where Angel and Cordelia meet up in Los Angeles, non-traditional family structures are the norm.

Of the three series, however, the creation and evolution of family has had the largest philosophical and narrative impact on *Angel*, where not only the emotional and psychological impact of family, but also the responsibility and ethics of a self-defined, dynamic family unit have been the primary focus. As with many of the symbolic and narrative concepts of the show, *Angel*'s family paradigm borrows a great deal from its parent show, but comes to different conclusions.

For instance, where *Buffy* has held that Buffy herself is ultimately the central figure of responsibility in the fight for the world (though recently this assumption has been strongly challenged by the series finale, 'Chosen' (7.22), when Buffy chose to share her powers as a Slayer with every girl in the world who had that potential), *Angel* diffuses that duty throughout the family unit and shows the dissolution of the family as a disaster with severe repercussions for the mission and the hopeless they seek to help. Family has evolved into the core image and problematic of *Angel*, and it is necessary to analyse the series' paradigm of family to understand its narrative and ethical arc.

To that end, three important questions emerge. One, how is the family constituted as a unit on *Angel*? Two, what is the narrative work being done by the disintegration of Angel's family and its literally apocalyptic fallout? And three, what do the differences between the family paradigms in *Buffy* and *Angel* mean for the similar concepts and metaphors on the two shows?

'Evil right down to her Mary Janes - but family, what are you gonna do?' Finding Family's Boundaries

Amidst the shifting definitions, practices and alliances between friends, lovers and blood relatives, deciding who exactly 'counts' as family at Angel Investigations is a complicated undertaking. Strangely, it is through the death of long-time arch-nemesis Lilah Morgan in 'Calvary' (A4.12) that these borders become more evident for viewers. Lilah's murder at the hands of a possessed Cordelia Chase, revealed at that precise moment as the evil mastermind behind the Apocalypse engulfing Los Angeles, is a watershed moment for the series and its family paradigm. It forces us to ask why Lilah has never worked as part of the family, if the family can recover from Cordelia's descent; and why Lilah is the villain to receive such a personalized and vicious slaying from not one, but all three core characters of the series: after her murder, Lilah's corpse is drained by Angelus and is finally beheaded by her former lover, Wesley, to prevent her rising as a vampire.

In answer to the first question, what would seem to be obvious bars to family membership for Lilah – an overt allegiance to evil, constant disagreement with Angel – are in fact characteristics that define family members more often than not. In fact, one of the recurring tropes of *Buffy* is that characters such as Riley and Spike have been recruited into the family from inimical structures. This perhaps explains why Lilah is such an effective nemesis. Violence, dissonance and personal betrayal are earmarks of family relationships on *Angel*, from Connor sending Angel to the bottom of the ocean, the evil that Cordelia wreaks while under the control of her mystical 'child', Jasmine, to Angel's sacrifice of his son to secure Connor a new and better life. Even such 'innocents' as Fred are guilty of planning and abetting cold-blooded murder, as happened in 'Supersymmetry' (A4.5).

Meanwhile, disagreements about the working direction of the family have been an overt topic of discussion since early in the second season, with episodes such as 'Reunion' (A2.10) proving the rule and not the exception. None of these preclude family bonds; as Angel's fantasy day sequence in 'Awakening' (A4.10) shows, Angel regards the three people who have betrayed him the most – Wesley, Connor, and Cordelia – as his nearest and dearest. In short, evil and betrayal do not in any way preclude familial bonds.

Lilah's status as non-family is further complicated by her personal relationships with the group, particularly Angel and Wesley. Previously, in 'Billy' (A3.6), she has prevented Cordelia from shedding human blood, and her occasional willingness to provide Angel useful information is a narrative recurrence that stretches from 'Carpe Noctem' (A3.4) to 'Home' (A4.22). In fact, Lilah has often helped Angel achieve his goals more fully than his friends, particularly in 'Forgiving' (A3.17), 'Ground State' (A4.2), 'Apocalypse, Nowish' (A4.7), and 'Home', episodes where Lilah's intervention or assistance has been key in moving the narrative forward. This tendency toward strategic alliance also explains why the character is one of the most successful of Whedon's villains and why events relating to the character have signalled paradigm shifts on the series.

Lilah comprehends the value of understanding and even empathizing with her enemies – obliquely referenced by Cordelia's claim in 'Billy' that she 'was [Lilah], with better shoes' – and exploits that knowledge in a creative, flexible way. A signal of Lilah's effectiveness is the terror in which the family holds her; in 'Calvary' a wounded and dishevelled Lilah elicits as much suspicion as a caged Angelus. At the same time, the family concept is powerful enough to affect the ruthless lawyer; her involvement goes from mimicking the personal to becoming actually personal, a final character arc which begins with Lilah and Angel's actions in 'Forgiving'. Yet Lilah's constant justification that she's 'just doing her job' is only a partial explanation of why Lilah can never be family.

While she understands and even eventually wants the family paradigm that Angel Investigations establishes, her personal motivations for wanting to be family preclude this. Lilah might want to be family, but only because of her relationship with Wesley, and that's inadequate. One has to want to be part of the ethical mission of family to ever have a chance at being family.

Meanwhile, Wesley and Lilah's affair provides further insight into the boundaries of making Angel's family. The relationship between the two has most often been analysed as a more intense version of the relationship between Buffy and Spike in *Buffy* Seasons Five and Six; however, the more important connection is the way romantic partners are treated by the family on *Angel*, in contrast to their treatment in *Buffy*. Romantic relationships in *Buffy* have often served as a way of introducing new members into the group, who are often legitimized as family members, as happens with Tara in the aptly-named 'Family' (5.6). This has never been the case in *Angel*; outside romances have never legitimated new family members.

In fact, as *Angel* has progressed, the family unit has become figuratively and literally incestuous, with Connor and Cordelia's sexual relationship providing a phantasmic end through their daughter Jasmine – who psychically makes everyone part of 'the body Jasmine' – from an arc of relationships that began with Darla and Angel's one-night stand in 'Reprise' (A2.15). The hotbed of family romance and the *Buffy* paradigm of allowing lovers to have a place within the family are denied and, as we will see, this is a major reason why the family unit goes to hell on *Angel*.

So by looking at trends through the unusual situation of Lilah – a character who can have personal relationships with Angel, Wesley and Cordelia without being part of the family – we get a better idea of where the boundaries of family lie. First and foremost, there is an absolute boundary concerning desire/choice and joining the family. To be family, one must want to be family despite personal animosity, the threat of betrayal and constant ethical fiction. A proof of this is the limited status and effectiveness of the family since two of its central figures, Wesley and Cordelia, have emphatically not chosen or desired to be part of the family, instead eschewing it because of its conflicts with their personal wants.

Secondly, the family requires personal commitment not only to the group and its flaws, but also to its ethical mission. This differs from *Buffy*, where personal commitment to a core family member is enough to guarantee partial family membership. While *Angel*'s paradigm guarantees a higher level of efficiency in crisis and as a day-to-day organization, the perils of family romance far outweigh the benefits. However, the difference from the *Buffy* paradigm of family also allows us to see the third crucial component in constituting the *Angel* family: the importance of believing in the ethical crusade that is commonly called 'the mission'.

In this case, it is the fate of Angel's mystical and ill-starred son, Connor, which provides us with the critical lens for understanding this concept. Connor's narrative arc has concentrated on his finding a purpose in a world that he does not understand or accept. Many of the apocalyptic events have been caused or catalysed by Connor, including the very nadir of the family by helping to separate all its members. The Season Three finale, 'Tomorrow' (A3.22), shows us an Angel Investigations which has almost entirely renounced the mission and the family, and finds itself separated and alone, wondering 'where did everyone go?' Despite the various attempts to create and recreate new family units throughout Season Four, without the mission, these attempts fail. In the end, not even blood can prevent these failures, as evidenced by Wesley's inability to save Lilah from her perpetual Wolfram and Hart contract and Connor's death at his father's hands in 'Home'.

(Connor's death is not, technically, a death, as he is reconfigured into a new life and family by the deal Angel makes with Wolfram and Hart. However, as Tim Minear makes clear in postings on the Buffistas.org message board, the prophesy that 'The father will kill the son' came true in 'Home'.)

Angel is finally forced to kill Connor when it is clear that Connor cannot cope with the multiple compromises and fictions that make up life in Los Angeles, a tragic yet seemingly inevitable outcome for the character. Meanwhile, Wesley, distressed at his dead lover's post mortem servitude, attempts to 'free' her by burning her contract, something that fails miserably. Lilah, who has already been party to Angel's deal with Wolfram and Hart that will allow him to erase Connor's life and give him a new, more normal one, attempts to comfort Wesley by telling him 'it means something that you tried'. Yet her oblique tolerance of Wesley's failure to save her from Hell reminds us that without all three of these defining parameters, the family on *Angel* becomes a crippled, dangerous agent that destroys not only its internal members, but also those it is tasked to protect.

'I don't wanna use the words 'tragic farce' but...' The Apocalyptic Disintegration of Angel's Family

Dysfunctional families, as such, are nothing new to Whedon's universe. Episodes such as 'I've Got You Under My Skin' (A1.14), 'Family', 'Untouched' (A2.4), 'Gingerbread' (3.11) and 'Lies My Parents Told Me' (7.17), as well as a number of shorter scenes in other episodes, set the precedent that blood family is a fractious, often unpleasant institution. Traditional families are more often than not abusive families, and even the best of parents, such as Joyce Summers, are never extraordinarily competent. Most blood relatives are never seen, or make appearances at their worst moments, with 'Gingerbread' and 'Hell's Bells' (6.16) examples of this in *Buffy*.

The other kind of 'traditional' family, that of the blood bonds created between vampires, also tends toward terror, though paradoxically it can also be the most stable of family bonds. The relationship between Darla, Angelus, Spike and Drusilla gives us a compelling vision of just how perverse a loving family can be, with decades of murder, mayhem and terrorizing balanced by long-term loyalty and dedication to the concept of family. In short, most representations of family in *Buffy* and *Angel* are of dysfunctional, unstable families, or of stable families held together by blood. The most recent breakdown of the family in *Angel,* however, is more significant than the usual painful interfamily conflict in Whedon's universe. The disintegration of the unit signifies nothing less than the end of the world.

The almost catastrophic set of events during Season Four of *Angel*, where the sun has been blacked out and an apparently omnipotent Beast stalks Los Angeles, starting such apocalyptic events as a rain of fire and the complete destruction of long-time Angel Invest-igations foe Wolfram and Hart, is directly linked to the breakdown at 'Angel, Inc' and to the seemingly impossible double bind that Angel and Wesley have put Cordelia in with the actions of 'Sleep Tight' (A3.16) and 'Forgiving'. Historically, Cordelia has served as a mediatrix between Angel and Wesley and their conflicting roles in maintaining the family. The inevitable conflict between the personal loyalty and leadership of Angel and Wesley's sometimes ruthless devotion to the mission has always been channelled into an effective family unit by Cordelia's balancing of these two sides.

One of the ways to read the kidnapping of Connor in 'Sleep Tight' is as the natural, if personally agonizing, end of the stances Angel and Wesley hold about family and mission. Unfortunately, thanks to the added supernatural element of Jasmine, the conflict never reaches resolution; Cordelia's true choice in this conflict is to avoid it and fail in her role. This leads to the forcing of an evolution of the family dynamic, but not before cataclysmic destruction, the birth and supplanting of a new goddess and the end of world peace.

What are the material results of this original failure? Most obviously, it leads to Cordelia having an insufficient support system for dealing with her new, part-demon nature and making the choice to become a higher being. While perhaps having Wesley around to investigate her demon abilities wouldn't have changed Cordelia's decision, it would perhaps have been more informed. Also, the disunity and separation of the group gives Connor the opportunity to send Angel to the bottom of the ocean, which further isolates Wesley from returning to the group, as Fred and Gunn are less connected and inexplicably less sympathetic to Wesley after the kidnapping than Angel ultimately proves to be. Most unnervingly, Cordelia's choice, which is one that seems to be made to the best of her abilities, is apparently a terrible mistake.

The Cordelia that returns at the end of 'The House Always Wins' (A4.3) is now a vehicle to bring about a new world order and continue the estrangement of the core group at Angel Investigations. Notably, despite the prominent placement of a group photograph of Wesley, Angel and Cordelia in episodes throughout the season, the family as it stood is not restored to its previous form. Despite Angel's 'retarded fantasy' in 'Awakening', it is not a return, but an evolution of the family – one that puts Angel in charge of Wolfram and Hart and is termed by Lilah as being 'grown-up'.

So what is the message being sent by this 'tragic farce' of familial disintegration and estrangement? What does it tell us about family? First, the disintegration of Angel Investigations, particularly the core group, is about the dangers of letting personal pride get in the way of the group's mission. Angel, Wesley and Cordelia each fail to make the choice to involve the family's mission in their decision-making.

Angel is so delighted to be a father that he refuses to consider the larger implications of Connor's existence until he has no other choice; Wesley is so heartbroken at Fred choosing Gunn that he fails to share the prophecy with the group; and Cordelia's romantic feelings for Angel overshadow her responsibility to mediate between the personal and the mission in the group.

All three of them then share the blame for the breakdown; they pursue their selfish interests while the family and the mission go to hell and, worse yet, blame each other for losing the mission. The hypocrisy, when placed with the failure to communicate and compromise, is the catalyst for the loss of faith that the entire group suffers throughout Season Four. Worse still, when prior personal connections begin begetting Apocalyptic consequences (Angel's fling with Darla in 'Reprise' leading to Connor and the Beast-connection, Cordelia's one-night stand with Connor proving to be caused by controlling forces, Wesley's trust of Lilah leading her to harm Lorne), there is no support structure to turn to. Instead, until 'Salvage' (A4.13), these disasters lead to more recrimination and bitterness within the group.

This all serves to reinforce that the family unit is necessary as an emotional, personal structure, but also that the family in *Angel* is not only the primary unit for self-esteem – an attribute it shares with *Buffy*'s family unit – but is also a unit for action, both positive and negative. To dissolve or weaken the family is to weaken its members' ability to be the champions their larger sphere needs them to be, and this is its primary duty and its primary difference from the family paradigm of *Buffy*.

'I have a right to it.' - 'Not in my city.' Critical Differences Between the Family Paradigms of *Buffy* and *Angel*

One of the narrative tendencies of *Angel* has been its reworking of previous arcs, both character and storyline, and symbolic motifs of

Buffy. From relationships like Wesley and Lilah's to the Connor character providing an exact inverse to Dawn Summers, *Angel* has often not only reinterpreted its parent show, but also expanded upon it. In the case of family, *Angel* has reinterpreted *Buffy* and taken that concept into a direction that *Buffy* could not, allowing for series evolution.

Family has typically been examined more consistently in *Angel*, even as it has based its examinations on *Buffy*. In fact, the family concept has often been contradictory and underused in *Buffy*. While Buffy and *Buffy* may pay lip service to the idea of the self-selected family unit and the importance of her group relations in her fight, *Buffy* as a series is about Buffy Summers' inner strength, her ability to win battles by understanding the nature of power, be it as part of a group, by herself, or by diffusing her power as is seen in 'Chosen'. The exchange between Buffy and Angelus in 'Becoming Part Two' (2.22) remains paradigmatic for the series: 'Take it all away, and what's left?' 'Me.' Given the focus on Buffy, it's almost ironic that the series ended with a reified importance on the core family group and belonging to a group (a more typically *Angel* message), whereas the new family dynamic in *Angel* leads to the possibility of a less centralized unit.

Yet the similarities of family – at least in the organization of the core family group – are similar in both shows. Metaphorical families created by characters in both *Buffy* and *Angel* have become the stable units of interpersonal relationships in both shows because of the fraught dynamics of friendship and romance in the *Buffy*verse; as one fan asks of Wesley and Gunn in a discussion of that relationship: 'Is it at all possible to depict m[ale]/m[ale] friendship that the slasher community does NOT consider to be subtextual?' The line between friendship and romance is extremely permeable and unstable, as is most recently demonstrated by Willow and Fred in 'Orpheus' (A4.15), where Fred's enthusiasm for having another science-loving smart woman around the hotel is read by Willow as Fred making a pass at her, causing an unnerved Willow to stammer, 'I'm seeing someone'. Pairs of friends in *Angel* (and in *Buffy*) tend to behave like lovers, which is attested to by the continuing vitality and variety of the *Buffy* fan fiction and slash communities.

In contrast, the bonds between the three primary characters in both shows have provided the emotional and metaphorical touchstone for each other, the secondary characters and the viewers. As evidenced by the trinity of Buffy / Xander / Willow in *Buffy* and Angel / Cordelia / Wesley in *Angel*, the relationships between these trios have been the focus of many of the most successful storylines in both shows. However, while the finale of *Buffy* can be seen to re-signify the importance of the trio (Buffy, Willow, and Xander all leave Sunnydale alive), the opposite proves true in *Angel*. 'Home' seems to suggest the end of the trio as focus: Angel has isolated himself through his choice to remove Connor from everyone's memories; Cordelia is in a coma; and Wesley's obsession with saving Lilah is foregrounded, suggesting that the three characters will no longer provide the show's focus.

The similarities between the trios do remain vital: in both shows, tensions between the central trio have caused chaos in the greater, perpetually apocalyptic sphere that each trio inhabits. However, the differences in these breakdowns are more significant than the similarities would suggest. *Buffy*'s trio find themselves distanced from each other thanks to the inevitable pressures of 'growing up', going to college, finding new romantic relationships, and so on. In many ways, this distancing fits very naturally into Mutant Enemy's habit of literalizing metaphors about adolescence and post-adolescence.

In contrast, the long decay of the family in *Angel* is the cause and not the effect of external chaos. For this group, new romances are not a sign of maturity, but of trouble within the group that endangers their bond and the world around them. Two unstable romantic triangles replace the stable family trinity and lead to the implosion of Angel Investigations as a unit, reaching its nadir as a process in 'Tomorrow', which ends with Angel, Wesley and Cordelia as physically and emotionally removed from each other as possible. Notably, each one is also completely alone at the end of the episode, isolated from not only each other, but also from the rest of the world.

The impossibility of making things right between the three, due to internal and external events, seems to suggest that rather than recreating the perfect family portrait, which is what happens with the *Buffy* trio, *Angel* as a series has chosen to allow change and evolution in the family, because while it is true that things are not the same between Angel, Wesley and Cordelia, part of the emotional journey of the past season has been to heal the wounds. What is significant about the evolving family paradigm in *Angel*, as compared to *Buffy*, is that healing does not necessarily mean a return. Even as the three perhaps wish for things to be as they were, their actions suggest they understand they can't go home again and that to be faithful to their concept of family, they must move beyond its previous configuration.

These tendencies all tend to point towards the philosophical import of these two differing family paradigms. In *Buffy*, the greatest ethical duty of the family is to act as an emotional anchor. Spike points this out in 'Fool For Love' (5.7), claiming that it's Buffy's emotional ties to her family that make her as successful as she is. External forces tend to have the most effect in both weakening and strengthening the Scooby family; it is axiomatic that the Scooby gang cares about each other and that love is an emotional touchstone in times of trouble. The work of this kind of family is support and acceptance, which allows it to be more forgiving of the lovers and friends of its members and give them at least limited space in the group.

In *Angel*, however, the family is a unit of constant action. While personal bonds are undeniably important, the family in *Angel* has never truly outgrown its original pattern of its members fighting united (in purpose, if not always in loyalty) to help those in need. Without a clear sense of mission and an affirmation about the importance if not always the constancy of personal loyalty, the family in *Angel* quickly becomes a monstrous entity that can end the world in its dissolution. It is not as concerned with being an emotional anchor, and thus the family can occasionally fail in its secondary work of supporting its members, as it fails Wesley in 'Forgiving'.

Ultimately, the differences between family in the two series reinforce the communal responsibility of the group to the world that characterizes *Angel*; the nature of its family is another outgrowth of the ethical message of the series, which is that in a flawed, inherently corrupt world everyone is in need, everyone is culpable and everyone needs to be a hero. The rejection of *Buffy*'s family paradigm and the development of the unique and much less personally fulfilling family unit of *Angel* typify the spin-off's differing ethical universe. Once again, *Angel* re-appropriates an aspect of its parent show and takes it in an entirely new direction. In short, as we slowly start to understand the family dynamic in *Angel* and its relationship to that of *Buffy*, we understand the greater philosophical and narrative bent of the series.

they always mistake me for the character i play!

transformation, identity and role-playing in the BUFFYverse (and a defence of fine acting)

ian shuttleworth

There's a particular astigmatism of mainstream critical perspective, certainly within the United Kingdom, which the more catholic among us find intensely frustrating. It is that, in certain areas, notions of genre obscure those of quality. A depressingly high proportion of generalist critics – in whatever medium: film, theatre, book reviewing – continue to cling to the notion that certain genres of work attract the kind of fans who gobble the stuff up indiscriminately. The leap of logic comes with the conclusion that, therefore, all work in a given genre is in effect pulp; there's no point in judging for such an audience, runs the reasoning (such as it is), therefore there's nothing to judge. The genres affected are, of course, principally SF, horror and fantasy.

This genre snobbery extends past the begetters of SF, fantasy and horror works – the writers, the directors – to, in appropriate media, performance. This is particularly annoying, as more often than not the demands of these genres call for greater complexity of performance than do more naturalistic dramas. Indeed, the very notions of performance and identity are more integral to the fabric of such works; granted, the appearance/reality *topos* has been common in drama since long before honest Iago and Shakespeare's other smiling, damnèd villains, but such *topoi* are matters of persona rather than person.

It is always more interesting for an audience to have to negotiate its own deals with and interpretations of identity, the identity of the viewpoint and other characters as it encounters forces which are more insidious than identifiably external baddies. And it's also more interesting to see performers negotiate *their* own deals with the characters they play as they undergo such narrative transformations.

This complexity of identity forms a major thread in the two *Buffy*-verse series. In fact, virtually every principal character in *Buffy the Vampire Slayer* in particular has undergone one or more major transformations, with the associated demands this makes on the actors concerned in terms of complexity of performance; in *Angel*, the continuities, divergences and tensions between 'Angel' and 'Angelus' are a primary basis of the drama, enacted once again in Season Four.

There have also been a number of instances in which the entire world is changed around, or sometimes with, the central characters, from the sinister – the *Crucible*-in-Sunnydale of 'Gingerbread' (3.11), and the 'Wish-verse' dealt with below – to the comic – nebbish Jonathan Levinson's apotheosis in 'Superstar' (4.17), which spills over from the storyline into the opening title montage – to the fundamental: when the reformed Faith returns to Sunnydale in 'Dirty Girls' (7.18), she appears to continue an established relationship of teasing banter with Buffy's younger sister Dawn. But Faith has never in fact met Dawn before, and her false memories of their past footing were created along with everyone else's when the mystical Key was given human form as Dawn Summers early in Season Five, when Faith was already in prison off-screen near Los Angeles. However, it is the instances of individual transmogrification that shed most light, both on some of the series' thematic concerns and on the acting abilities of those who depict them.

In a wholly naturalistic series, we can judge the quality of the players' performances by the skill and subtlety they bring to their portrayals of developments on-screen and the ramifications these may have with various back-stories, whether the latter have previously occurred on-screen or are simply implied or recounted. This has also been increasingly the case in *Buffy*, as the supernatural Big Bads in latter seasons became not just metaphors but to an extent pretexts for direct examination of character and relationships.

But in the *Buffy*verse we also have the opportunity to judge how the performers integrate their 'true' characters with the frequent changes wrought upon them. Every actor in any role is in a sense routinely being at once him- or herself and someone else; the players in *Buffy* and *Angel* are further called upon frequently to invest the characters themselves with such a dualism, and thus to cope with a second order of 'elseness'. Or sometimes even a third order: on various occasions, Sarah Michelle Gellar, Alyson Hannigan and David Boreanaz have each been asked not just to ring the changes on their own characters, but also to play their principal character *pretending* to be a secondary character. (Indeed, Boreanaz has in his time had it both ways, having played both Angel posing as Angelus and vice versa, as well as finding a middle ground in Season Two's 'dark Angel' phase – no pun intended.) Most prominently, in 'Who Are You?' (4.16), thanks to a magical body-swap, Gellar succeeds in playing Faith *pretending* to be Buffy, and pretending plausibly enough for those around her not to notice, but with enough discreet signals for the audience to be clear about the imposture; indeed, the body-swap is not even made verbally explicit when it takes place.

None of these twists and turns are revolutionary in themselves; indeed, as Shakespeare buff Joss Whedon is no doubt aware, one of their most famous antecedents is in *As You Like It*, when the exiled Rosalind, disguised as a young man, offers to 'pretend' to be Rosalind so that her suitor Orlando can 'woo' her/him/her. (A further gender-bend is added by the fact that Rosalind would originally have been played by a boy actor.) But the regularity with which they crop up in *Buffy*, and to a lesser extent in *Angel*, lifts matters onto another plane. Far from indicating a lack of ideas, with the same furrow being ploughed repeatedly, it demonstrates the very opposite: a deep and abiding preoccupation with senses of identity and role-playing as everyday parts of personality in all its forms. Just as palpably, this demands a range, precision and subtlety from actors which would astound most of the mainstream critics who automatically turn their noses up at genre works simply because they *are* genre works.

Xander seems exceptionally prone to refashioning, perhaps to compensate for his lack of a discernible individual 'shtick'; indeed, 'The Zeppo' (3.13) is concerned with his continuing attempts to define a role for himself in the Scooby gang. Xander's very ordinariness (as a friend remarked, 'In a Stephen King novel, he would be the boy who grew up to become the author'), and thus his greater potential for audience identification, makes his trans-formations implicitly more significant for the viewer. His possession by a hyena-spirit in 'The Pack' (1.6) is a hyper-exaggeration of the dangers of peer pressure within a closed group. When he becomes the 'army guy' of his fancy-dress costume in 'Halloween' (2.6), his coldness and control are not just a bleak gag for the single episode, but constitute the first manifestations of a hitherto latent side of his personality. After his reversion, Xander retains knowledge both of military hardware and of the layout of Sunnydale's army base, allowing him to raid its arsenal in 'Innocence' (2.14); more significantly for the character, though, he grows more fully into the 'heart' of the core Scooby quartet, becoming a confidant and voice of reason to both Riley and Buffy as their relationship begins to founder in Season Five.

Part of this development may have been dictated by the more visible ageing of actor Nicholas Brendon over the course of the series, becoming increasingly thickset of body and face, to the extent that in Seasons Six and Seven the wardrobe department noticeably began dressing him in ways that concealed his waistline. Brendon (who was aged 32 by the end of Season Seven's shoot) would be ever less plausible if his character continued to live in his parents' basement and generally be a menial-jobbing, early-twenties dork – hence in part the establishment both of a permanent job and a nice apartment for Xander in his own right and the de-emphasis of the character's actual age. (In much the same way, moving Cordelia to Los Angeles and away from her supposed contemporaries has allowed Charisma Carpenter, aged 28 by the first season of *Angel*, to escape the formal reminders of her character's relatively tender years and thus to be permitted to develop a more mature portrayal.) Xander's proposal to girlfriend Anya in 'The Gift' (5.22), and his subsequent agonized desertion of her at the altar in 'Hell's Bells' (6.16) and its aftermath over the subsequent season and more, set the seal on the character's full adulthood at a time when it increasingly stretched plausibility to have Brendon continually playing a post-adolescent.

More immediately evident, though, is the simple fact that Brendon is in unobtrusive possession of the acting skills to carry such a progressively more rounded character. Consummate as he is with the delivery and timing of the one-liners which were for much of the time Xander's forte, he is also capable of the increasingly greater range demanded of him. The younger Brendon's brooding menace can just about stand comparison with David Boreanaz's Olympic standards thereof when Xander is reinvented as the Master's vampiric lieutenant in a Sunnydale without Buffy in 'The Wish' (3.9); later, when split into two opposing personalities in 'The Replacement' (5.3), he can portray both 'Lame Xander' and 'Suave Xander' without ever approaching the crass eye-rolling of William Shatner's James T. Kirk in the similarly plotted *Star Trek* episode 'The Enemy Within'. (Brendon's twin brother Kelly Donovan – each twin uses his middle name as a professional surname – plays 'Suave Xander' only in shots in which both 'halves' are on-screen.)

Xander's continuing tutelage of Anya following her own transformation from vengeance demon at the end of 'The Wish', as she re-learns what it is to be a mortal human, and even during and after her enraged re-demonization in the wake of the wedding upset, is often sardonic and sometimes candidly remonstrative but above all loving. This is another demonstration of Xander's role as the 'heart' of the Scooby gang, which is made explicit when the core quartet's qualities are combined to form a 'super-Buffy' in the Season Four climax 'Primeval' (4.21). During this final phase, the role settles on him of non-superpowered, compassionate human insight – 'the one who sees' (formally acknowledged with the brutality of Caleb's half-blinding of him in 'Dirty Girls' – also, it has been pointed out, a faint echo of Xander's appearance in the Sunnydale High talent show performing an extract from *Oedipus Rex* with Buffy and Willow in 'The Puppet Show', 1.9). In short, Xander possesses a blend of humour and percipience, which makes him a direct, non-emerald-skinned counterpart to Lorne in *Angel*.

The explicit comedy in Xander's character often belies an essential modesty in Brendon's acting style, which enables him to continue contributing even when given perhaps less than his fair share of screen focus: this is one of the hallmarks of a valuable ensemble actor. Watch his responses and reactions, even with little or no dialogue, in the final season or two: Brendon, as Xander, may not be at the forefront, but he is always there, observing and engaged.

Joss Whedon, in his audio commentary to the DVD release of 'Welcome To The Hellmouth' (1.1) and 'The Harvest' (1.2), has rhapsodized about Alyson Hannigan's qualities of luminosity as an actress and her astonishing ability to command audience sympathy and even empathy in the role of Willow. As with Xander, most of Willow's transformations play against the primary type of her character. She is likewise 'turned into' her costume – a ghost – in 'Halloween', but this merely affects her corporeal solidity rather than her personality. What is notable, though, is that her clothing beneath the spectral sheet, her original choice of get-up (albeit at Buffy's instigation, to help Willow get Xander's attention), is unwontedly sexy. Whilst the character is plainly uncomfortable with trying to be so openly alluring, this appearance sows the seeds of her next metamorphosis in 'Bewitched, Bothered and Bewildered' (2.16), in which (in common with every other woman in Sunnydale) she develops a spellbound, outright predatory lust for Xander.

This in turn reaches full bloom when Willow, like Xander, is vamped in 'The Wish', and more so when Vamp Willow returns in 'Doppel-gangland' (3.16), having been accidentally summoned to Sunnydale proper to exist in parallel with the 'real' Willow. The remarks made in this episode about the polymorphously perverse proclivities of Vamp Willow (says 'real' Willow: 'so evil and skanky… and I think I'm kind of gay') and their possible basis in the character of the normally demure Ms Rosenberg are put into some perspective by Willow's com-portment under previous transformations. While much heat and little light has been expended in various discussion fora about whether Willow is 'truly' gay by dint of her subsequent (and obviously committed) relationship with Tara, the more obvious point is that, however permanent her shift in sexual *orientation*, there have by now been numerous signs that in terms of her sexual *conduct* she can be both a kitten and a panther as the occasion seems to her to demand.

Willow's nadir and zenith of self-assurance are almost simultaneous in Season Six, as her magical confidence comes to compensate for her personal insecurity, and ultimately becomes a form of addiction. Her Wiccan errors are almost always related to her feelings for Tara, from her readiness to resort to various forgetfulness spells in 'All the Way' (6.6) and 'Tabula Rasa' (6.8), through her addictive phase after their break-up, culminating in 'Wrecked' (6.10), and her climactic grief-driven journey to the veiny, raven-haired dark side in the final phase of the season, after Tara's shooting. In her dark phase, Willow possesses a Mephisto-phelean ability to articulate others' own doubts and fears, comparable to that of Angelus in mid Season Four of *Angel*. However, even at such an extreme, her natural compassion remains. Her deter-mination to destroy the world is not directly fuelled by an excess of revanchism, but rather by a misplaced kind of messianic fervour: dark Willow, having for a moment empathized with the everyday agonies of everyone on the planet, genuinely believes she's acting in everyone's best interests and that we'd all be better off dead.

Her greater diffidence in her final-season dealings with Kennedy can be ascribed to a number of factors. Principal among these is a carry-over from her caution in matters magical after the previous season's personal corruption. Her subconscious choice of self-punishment after her first kiss with Kennedy in 'The Killer Inside Me' (7.13) – assuming the appearance and increasingly the temperament of her beloved's killer and her own victim, Warren – is another example of Tara-related turmoil. It also perfectly dramatizes her paradoxical apprehensions about involvement with Kennedy: fear that it will be the same as with Tara, and equally that it won't, and in either case that this will be a betrayal of her heart's past. Nor, despite UPN's greater liberality on that score than the WB network on which the first five seasons were screened in the USA, should we ignore the potential dubiousness of a lesbian Willow 'in the market' in a house full of Potential Slayers, most of whom are under the Californian age of consent (indeed, the fact of Kennedy's being 19 years old disappeared during script revisions, and is never explicitly established on-screen).

More practically, though, there is a component of deliberate rowing back on Whedon's part, partly in order to reinforce the sense that the final season is, as he announced beforehand that it would be, in many ways a return to 'Buffy, Year One'. This is more problematic in the case of Willow than with almost any other character: 'buying' (in Whedon's preferred term) her return to emotional home base after her stint as the Big Bad is a transaction that calls for skilful negotiation, particularly after the single most grievous misjudgement of the entire series, 'Wrecked', in which writer (and, by then, show-runner) Marti Noxon indulges in a catastrophic ad hoc blurring of models of psychological dependency and of physical addiction which reduce Willow for the duration of the episode to a caricature junkie, little better than an ephemerally convenient plot-device. Buying her character back plausibly and meaningfully from such a disaster is no easy matter. The 'it's about power' motif, one of the threads running through Season Seven (in this case, from the very first line of the season) helps by placing Willow's journey in a more pervasive context.

(On a tangential note, I cannot help lamenting a missed opportunity for a potentially delicious passing joke in 'Older and Far Away' (6.14). When Willow mentions 'the whole Spellcasters Anonymous thing', she is clearly alluding to a 12-step-type recovery programme. One characteristic of such methods is that those involved explicitly draw strength from a 'higher power' of their own choice… so, er, how exactly would that work with a recovering magic addict?)

The 'teeth' that Willow occasionally shows, and the arc of her self-confidence, give depth to the aforementioned luminosity of Alyson Hannigan's characterization. Xander may be the metaphysical heart of the Scoobies, but Willow more regularly commands the hearts of the audience for the majority of the seven seasons. Whedon himself is evidently not immune from this captivation, as indicated on his Season One DVD audio commentary, when he describes Hannigan as:

> King of Pain – when anybody attacks [Willow], we learned early on, it opens up your heart… She's so good playing that vulnerability… She brings so much light and so much tenderness to the role, it's kind of extraordinary… I knew that [viewers] would respond to her on a level that they couldn't even respond to Buffy…

This last remark clearly refers not simply to the character of Willow, but to Hannigan's characterization of her; a perusal of the 24-minute demo reel-cum-pilot of *Buffy* shot to hawk the idea of the series around production companies (never officially made available, but circulating freely on the internet), in which Willow is played by Riff Regan, confirms the extent to which Hannigan's performance fits the character and reveals the qualities with which she imbues Willow. At the other end of the series, it is of course one more testimony to Hannigan's acting abilities that she largely succeeds in eradicating the stain of 'Wrecked' over the subsequent season and a half, by consistently playing power and timidity alike from the heart of Willow.

Hannigan can play on audience heartstrings like a concert harpist, as Willow undergoes her succession of emotional travails: her unrequited love for Xander, her romantic and moral torments during and after her clandestine affair with him in Season Three, when each is already in a steady relationship, and the protracted, several-step break-up with her lycanthrope boyfriend Oz, before the loss of Tara and the cautious linkage with Kennedy, finally consummated, in traditional fashion, on the very eve of doom. As an actress, she is a perfect interpreter in particular of the bare emotional directness which is the speciality of Noxon on form.

Writing and performance in this vein mesh most completely in 'New Moon Rising' (4.19), in which Oz's return to Sunnydale throws into question Willow's deepening relationship with fellow witch Tara and impales her on the horns of a bisexual dilemma. The final-scene Tara/Willow exchange – 'I understand: you have to be with the person you love'/'I am' – has a supreme truthfulness and economy and is the precise moment at which Willow's transition of sexual orientation is simply but definitively completed for any viewer not in denial. It is, I maintain, no exaggeration to say that the final movement of 'New Moon Rising' can look the corresponding segment of *Casablanca* in the face without shame. (In contrast, another example of Noxon overplaying her heart-on-the-sleeve predilection is the final act of 'Into the Woods' (5.10), which does not so much look *Casablanca* in the face as dress up in its clothes.)

Moreover, when she begins to lose direct audience sympathies in Season Six, the torch is passed to her other half, Tara, maintaining the focus of heartbreak *on* though no longer *in* Willow. And some time after Tara's demise, the climax of 'The Killer Inside Me' is another moment of exquisite agony; although the episode necessarily intercuts footage of Hannigan and Adam Busch playing the Warren-possessed Willow, it is clearly Hannigan who makes the emotional running throughout. (Indeed, Busch's own strongest scene in the episode, a walking duologue with Kennedy, is given when I suspect he had a master shot of Hannigan to refer to in order to pin down his Willow characterization, something he was probably lacking in other scenes due to the way they were shot.)

It is convenient, though unfair, to consider Oz in this context as an adjunct to Willow. His werewolf nature, uncovered in 'Phases' (2.15), particularly as regards his attraction to the likewise anthropically challenged Veruca, culminating in 'Wild At Heart' (4.6), is an obvious metaphor for adolescent and young-adult coming to terms with 'the beast within' (a far simpler, far less theologically convoluted version of Angel's relationship with his vampirism), but its portrayal is strengthened by actor Seth Green's mastery of laconicism. When one watches the series as a whole, Whedon and his writing team are revealed to have gradually distilled Oz's initially general quirkiness down to a wryly sparing way with words and deadpan facial looks, in order to exploit Green's playing strength in this area.

The fact that, when the character is fully evolved, Oz never wastes a syllable is again utilized by writers when putting him into serious emotional situations; the knowledge that every word counts lends his utterances, in Green's performance, an unfussy heft. This is of course shown powerfully in 'New Moon Rising', but the necessity of plot exposition here renders Oz uncharacteristically garrulous (in relative terms) for much of the episode until its climax; possibly a better example is the aftermath of the discovery of Willow and Xander's liaison in 'Lover's Walk' (3.8) until Oz and Willow's reunion in 'Amends' (3.10): there is simply no inclination to talk around the central issues.

Giles has at different points undergone both psychological and physical metamorphoses. The former occurs in 'Band Candy' (3.6), in which the adult population of Sunnydale is magicked by some evil chocolate back to their respective teenage selves. While Joyce

Summers and Principal Snyder are revealed with differing degrees of sympathy as fundamentally lame teens desperate to find a way into the in-crowd, Giles becomes his earlier 'Ripper' self, described by Buffy as 'Less "together guy", more "bad magic, hates the world, ticking time-bomb guy"'. Conversely, the extent to which Giles has consciously mastered his Ripperish impulses and reinvented himself is discreetly underscored in 'A New Man' (4.12), in which, even though physically transformed into a particularly thuggish demon, he remains (barely) on top of the growing appetite for violence which his new physiology brings (with the delicious exception of taking a minute out to chase, growling, his sinister rival for the role of mentor to Buffy, Professor Maggie Walsh).

The Giles persona that we principally know is kept in place by force of constant will. There is little danger that Ripper will ever regain the upper hand, although the deliberate suffocation of Ben in 'The Gift' is, as it were, an invocation of Ripper for the purposes of good. However, on a number of occasions Giles has taken to the bottle as the only practical means of escape from the doubts or griefs that assail him. Rather than stoop to the level of making his drinking an issue in itself (a depth only plumbed with Willow in 'Wrecked' – sorry to harp on about it), Whedon and Co. use it to signal unassumingly that Giles, too, realizes he is fulfilling a role, but one which sometimes grows too much for him in terms of its internal rather than external obligations.

The single most succinct example of this is in 'Forever' (5.17): a brief, wordless scene, the day after Joyce Summers' funeral, shows Giles at home, obviously drinking heavily and listening to one of his old rock albums. Nothing is said; actor Anthony Stewart Head is all but motionless (a contrast all the more telling for his fondness, remarked on by Whedon in a Season Six DVD commentary, for 'fiddling' business); the significance and potency lie in the numbness being depicted, and in Head letting the soundtrack make the message explicit... for the song is Cream's 'Tales Of Brave Ulysses', the same track which his and Joyce's *faux*-teenage selves had listened to in 'Band Candy'.

Head – naturally, as the oldest of the principal actors by a couple of decades – has the longest and most varied dramatic *curriculum vitae* of the company, ranging from the romantic serial played out over several seminal television commercials for Nescafé Gold Blend (Taster's Choice in the USA) to a UK national tour as Frank N. Furter in *The Rocky Horror Show*. His performance encompasses the strengths of several of the other players: like Hannigan, he quickly demonstrates the resources to sustain a character far more complex than the initial quaint Britisher of early Season One episodes (Alfred the butler, almost, with the library of Sunnydale High as the Batcave). His skill with the dryly English one-liners complements Brendon's with the wacky ones; his precision of emotional nuance may have rubbed off to an extent on Sarah Michelle Gellar over the seasons, as she has acquired an eye for underplaying feelings to match the technical abilities she always possessed. Nor is all that fiddling and trademark spectacles-polishing a way of upstaging his colleagues, but rather a component of naturalistic acting; whatever he may be busying himself with, it never obtrudes, and sets an example of ensemble acting for others to follow.

Giles's dramatic function is less as a protagonist or agent in himself than as someone who reacts to and supports developments around him. Head has nevertheless found in this essentially secondary role a current and eloquence of its own, particularly through the second half of Season Three and in Season Four. Deprived first of his formal position as Watcher by the Watcher's Council, in 'Helpless' (3.12), and then of any purpose whatsoever for being in Sunnydale, as his librarian's cover job disappears with the destruction of Sunnydale High and his position as informal mentor to Buffy is threatened by her new milieu at university and specifically by Maggie Walsh, Giles flounders – but does so, in Head's portrayal, quietly and discreetly. Without ever stealing the thunder of Buffy and her younger associates, Head builds up an aggregation of little signals that underline and extend the central metaphor of the series as a whole.

Buffy is, it has been said often enough, really about growing up and negotiating one's way in a world which persists in putting knotty and seemingly unnatural problems in one's way. Head's Giles, more even than the explicit allusions in the character of Joyce Summers, reminds us that the difficulties of growing up are not experienced solely by those who do the growing, but also leave their mark on those whose nests they fly. In this phase, Giles, like Xander, needs to find a definition for himself; unlike the younger man, though, Giles does not even pretend to know how to fashion one, and privately comes close to despair until a series of events over the first half of Season Five – Buffy's request that he resume as her de facto Watcher, his purchase of the magic shop and finally his formal reinstatement by the Council – cumulatively offer him the salvation of a full role again, and grimly exceed it as his surrogate-father status becomes more and more necessary through Joyce's illness and eventual death. Thereafter, in thinking the unthinkable with regard to preventing Glory's plan to merge dimensions – that it might be necessary to kill Dawn – he makes the transition from the suffering of the abandoned parent to that of the involved and loving parent amid horrific life complexities.

When he, in turn, leaves Sunnydale since Buffy cannot (a decision explained in the series by the wonderful number 'Standing' in the musical episode 'Once More With Feeling' (6.7), and in real life by Head's own contrasting familial desire to be at home in England with his growing daughters), the absence of Giles in the second half of Season Six is palpable. His magnificent, Sergio Leone-style return at the cliffhanger ending of 'Two To Go' (6.21) is glorious not simply as a moment in itself but because the visuals contrast with the typical understated Giles of the words: in response to Willow's 'There's no one in the world with the power to stop me now', he merely remarks, 'I'd like to test that theory'. Blackout; end credits. In Season Seven, he again assumes a pastoral and educative role, this time to the brigade of Potentials; however, by 'Lies My Parents Told Me' (7.17), with its well-intentioned but wrong-headed plot against

Spike, it has become apparent once again that knowledge in itself is not enough. It's about power. And also about the different quality of wisdom, about which more anon.

A slew of supporting characters have their roles modified through transformation. Oz has already been mentioned; Cordelia's former Valley-bitch sidekick Harmony, following her vampification, attempts and fails derisorily to recreate herself as Buffy's arch-nemesis; Jonathan likewise tries without success to magick a valued identity for himself in 'Superstar', before experiencing his own mini-Willow arc towards darkness and back as one of Season Six's trio of geeks.

This is a useful point at which to note Whedon and Co.'s readiness to respond to the fortuitous discovery of talented players. Danny Strong as Jonathan is a case in point: his first appearance in the series, as a near-victim of the 'Inca Mummy Girl' (2.4), is fleeting, and in the couple after that his character does not even have a name, but having spotted his potential, the writing team first expand him to all-purpose class nebbish, then give form to his suffering with his thwarted suicide attempt in 'Earshot' (3.18) and his status as representative of all those saved by Buffy when he presents her with the Class Protector award in 'The Prom' (3.20), before imbuing him with an interest in magic which drives 'Superstar' and his subsequent status as the boy with the magic bone in Season Six. Similarly with his Trio comrades: Adam Busch as Warren showed that his original adolescent sexbot-building saddo could be expanded into a disconcerting misogynist and general sociopath to stand as alpha geek; Tom Lenk first appears in another role, as Cyrus, one of Harmony's vamp minions in 'Real Me' (5.2), before being cast as Andrew and proving so engaging that he returns to be slowly rehabilitated in Season Seven, a counterpart in various aspects to Willow, Xander and Spike and arguably a personification of that final season's interest in classic modes of narrative (again, see below).

Anya, too, was originally a one-off character: scarcely even a 'Monster of the Week' in her own right so much as a means of bringing Mark Metcalf back as the Master and allowing the team to ring the changes by playing a vampiric Xander and Willow and a hard-bitten Buffy newly arrived from Cleveland (location, as we are reminded, in the final minute of 'Chosen', of another Hellmouth). However, Emma Caulfield embodied that reviewers' cliché, quirkiness, to inspire Anya's return as a human and subsequent awkward coming to terms with mortality; indeed, by the end of the series, we have seen her in two separate phases of demonhood and two of humanity – three, if you count the 'origin of Anyanka' flashbacks in 'Selfless' (7.5), when her original Norse name Aud is mispronounced in order – I assume – to enable her to apparently and succinctly declare, 'I am odd'. Among the main players, Caulfield elicits perhaps the most repeated spontaneous praise in DVD commentaries, for her skill at putting left-hand spin on the most banal remarks to show Anya as at once part of and apart from the core group and their various life issues.

It is of course true that fandom can be as prescriptive and as rigidly prejudiced as those outside the genre whom I mentioned at the beginning of this essay. I've already alluded to the debate about which sexuality label should be hung on Willow. Dawn comes in for particular stick from many diehard fans. Whedon's motives are suspected: Dawn was written in, say some, perhaps at the network's request to appeal to a more youthful demographic. To which the succinct response is, do the maths: by Season Six, Dawn is no younger than Buffy was when called to Slayerhood pre-Season One, or in the semi-canonical 1992 movie. Moreover, run the accusations, this 14-year-old (on her first appearance) is annoyingly one-note and whiny. To which the succinct response is: 'Well, *duh!*'

However, a more detailed response is called for, which is that such accusations increasingly fly in the face of Michelle Trachtenberg's performance. When Dawn learns that her entire existence rests upon an act of magic which has incarnated the unspecified but crucial Key as a 14-year-old girl, Trachtenberg finds an intensity and truth in her character, as 'Blood Ties' (5.13) and 'Forever' amply demonstrate. In Season Six, her skill at playing wordless reactions is such that she gives arguably the most consistently nuanced performances over much of the season, and the following year shows in 'Potential' (7.12) that Dawn has both team spirit and the insight to step back from attempting to grab the glory. She isn't anyone's token youngster.

(Such complaints are rather more justified in the case of her counterpart in *Angel*, Connor. Vincent Kartheiser seems perhaps a slightly less adept and thoughtful actor, but more to the point, the writing team have never really found a firm slot for his character beyond that of all-purpose gadfly, complication and turncoat in whatever way occasion demands. One or two unkind parties in British fandom have taken to referring to Connor as 'Kevin', after comedian Harry Enfield's surly teenager character, a view given unintentional backing when Kartheiser's screen test – included as an extra on the *Angel* Season Three DVD set – includes the classic Kevin line, 'This is *so unfair!*' The apparent writing-out of Connor at the end of Season Four can be seen as a tacit acknowledgement that the character never really bedded down.)

Cordelia and Wesley do not experience such literal changes until relatively late in the game – we can discount transitory instances such as Cordy's temporary demonic-pregnancy-dementia in 'Expecting' (A1.12) – and indeed, in 'The Wish', Cordy remains ineluctably herself as the entire world around her changes. It could be argued that the development of Cordy and Wesley as characters after they are spun off to the Los Angeles of *Angel* is a metamorphosis of a sort, but this is more usefully seen within the context of the growing 'complexification' of narrative and characterization, which is both a characteristic of the form of the two series and a major strand of their thematic concern with coming to terms with a life which is always fluid in its rules and markers, even in everyday life, never mind when one's role in it is battling against infernal evils.

However, when first Cordy and then her Angel associates are transported to yet another world, Lorne's home of Pylaea, in the final four episodes of *Angel* Season Two, this new environment sees the first of a series of major transitions for both her and Wesley. Cordy's dream of success and status is given the greatest possible realization by her installation as queen of Pylaea, but of course turns out to be no kind of solution to her LA frustrations. Nor, though, is it the simple opposite, an unambiguous curse (although it is the 'curse' of her visions which confirms her on the throne); rather, it is simply the case that all the usual complexities of emotion, power structures and the inevitable villainies simply continue under a different sun (well, pair of suns). It may be a hard decision for her to return through the dimensional portal with her comrades, but fundamentally there is no wrench of lifestyle involved. Wesley, meanwhile, finds in his explicit recognition by the Pylaean rebels as their new general a validation of his current status as the man in charge of things; he no longer suffers when such validation is unforthcoming from his father, as evidenced in the phone call home in 'Belonging' (A2.19).

The Pylaea mini-arc heralds more lasting transformations for each character. Cordy gets a second shot at wish-fulfilment in 'Birthday' (A3.11), being given the life of stardom which would have been hers but for meeting Angel and succeeding Doyle as the vessel of early-warning visions. However, she finds that by now her sense of duty to the good fight is so ingrained that she insists on returning to the 'real' world, albeit as an undefined and only sporadically manifested strain of demon. Her apparent reward at the end of Season Three leaves her with an even more vague, and apparently sinecure, angelic status, sitting on a cloud somewhere (possibly eating Philadelphia cream cheese), before being returned to the mortal plane with a view to ultimately being revealed as Season Four's Big Bad.

At this point, it looks as if pure ill fortune struck the series. Charisma Carpenter's pregnancy meant that she was unable to play the full part apparently first envisaged for Cordy in *Angel* Season Four, so the plan was changed to make her instead merely the semi-possessed vessel of the Big Bad. Far more tellingly, though, the pregnancy may have taken its toll on Carpenter's energies as an actor; as both actor and character grow closer to term, she seems visibly unable to make the effort required to play Cordy as increasingly and believably sinister, a transformation which Carpenter would have had little problem with in other circumstances. The season as realized on-screen is a tribute to Mutant Enemy's and Carpenter's commitment to each other, but appears undeniably compromised in both direction and quality by the (literally) growing biological demands made on the actress.

Much more compellingly enacted is Wesley's metamorphosis, a kind of ongoing version of Season Two's 'dark Angel' arc, which divests Alexis Denisof of the last vestiges of tweediness as Giles's former Mini-Me and sees him incarnated as precisely what Wesley claimed to be on his first leather-clad appearance in *Angel*: 'a rogue demon-hunter' – 'Parting Gifts' (A1.10). (And, even to this straight male essayist, downright sexy with it.) The explanation is simple and brutally succinct: when Gunn asks what changed him so, Wesley replies, 'I had my throat cut and all my friends abandoned me' – 'Spin the Bottle' (A4.6). There is never any prospect of an explicit rapprochement outside of Angel's happy-family fantasies in 'Deep Down' (A4.1) and again in 'Awakening' (A.4.10); as with Buffy's return after temporary exile from Revello Drive in 'End of Days' (7.21), there is merely a coalescence of forces in the face of pressing circumstance. Wesley is no longer a sidekick, or a surrogate leader as during the 'dark Angel' phase; he has acquired an individuality, a selfhood.

Here's an indicator both of how fluid *Buffy*verse events can be and of the universality of this 'rite of transformation' in *Buffy*: when I began writing this essay for the first edition, I noted that the sole unambiguous exception to the rule is Tara, who is nevertheless revealed in 'Family' (5.6) as *believing that she is about to* undergo such a metamorphosis when she comes of age and her alleged demon-nature asserts itself (as it did, we learn in the back-story of *Angel* Season One, with the similarly half-human, half-demon Doyle at a similar point). However, as with Cordy and Wesley, Tara's identity grows and deepens on a purely human level through her association with Willow and thus the other Scoobies.

The week of the completion of my draft, however, saw the US and UK broadcast of 'Tough Love' (5.19), in which Tara, in Benson's words, 'suffers some brain suckage' by Glory. Amber Benson rises to the ongoing challenges and opportunities offered overall by the role of Tara fully and admirably. During her season of mindlessness she finds a continuity of character even after a mapping which is the opposite of that normally undergone by figures in the *Buffy*verse. Where, for instance, Spike (and in many ways even the extreme example of Angel/Angelus) experiences transitions of temperament whilst retaining a relatively linear, if not fully fixed, sense of self, Tara loses her very identity for the better part of four episodes; yet Benson invests Tara's post-mindwipe witterings with the same range of moods and quirks as her previous lucid remarks. Even though Tara in this phase cannot recognize herself, the way that the remains of her mind work indicate a continuing, albeit thoroughly ravaged, personality until her cure by Willow in 'The Gift'.

In Season Six, as Willow's predilection for magic takes hold, Tara takes over the role of 'King of Pain': it is her heartache we see at a loved one going wrong, to the point of breaking up the relationship. It is interesting to note that, in Season Seven of *Buffy*, the addiction motif is discreetly underpinned by a number of uses of the word 'intervention' – the jargon term for the collective ultimatum given to an addict by their loved ones to address their problem. The word is scarcely ever used in direct relation to Willow; it simply adds to the atmosphere. Of course, in this particular case, Tara's intervention, rather than setting Willow on the path to recovery, drives her to rock bottom.

Benson's skill, like Hannigan's (and perhaps by this point even exceeding it), in playing to and from the heart allows Tara also to become the 'den mother' for the Scoobies, a successor to Joyce, as indirectly pointed up by her post-breakup day with Dawn in 'Smashed' (6.9). Following Joyce's death, Buffy and the other

Scoobies have to address the worldly problems of adulthood in 'life is the Big Bad' Season Six, but it is following Tara's death that the personal, individual burdens of adulthood are brought home to them. And in addition to her dramatic abilities, 'Once More With Feeling' reveals Benson to have the sweetest singing voice of all the lead players, a gift to which Whedon responded by writing for her the at once heavenly and salacious number 'Under Your Spell'; again, Tara takes the burden from the much more apprehensive and tremulous-voiced Hannigan as Willow.

Riley's innate nature is overridden both by the diet of chemicals fed to him and by the chip embedded in his torso. The chip business is frankly superficial, little more than a plot device, but the cumulative effect of the removal both of these additives and of his association with the Initiative is to make him another character in search of a role by which he can define himself. If he is to be more than an appendage to Buffy, he feels he requires some kind of experiential knowledge of the darker world she inhabits; this, even more than the issues he undoubtedly has about her former relationship with Angel, is behind his flirtation with vamp-victimhood. In the end, of course, he fails to find any such niche (as either the writers and Marc Blucas fail to find a sufficient distinctiveness for him or it becomes apparent that he was never intended to be a major locus of audience sympathy), and off he flies back to the uniformed bosom of Uncle Sam, where it is easier to slot into a team than to stand as an individual. His fleeting return in 'As You Were' (6.14) is no more than the dramatic equivalent of Xander and Anya's break-up sex a season later; not even a newly acquired facial scar can give Riley's character serious shadows.

Faith's entire life, we learn from bits and pieces of back-story, has been a battle against those who would ignore or deny her the opportunity to find a place for herself, and an increasingly resentful and aggressive battle. She cannot properly complement Buffy, and so feels on some level that she has no alternative but to become her opposite. The extent to which she is living out a role she has assigned to herself is finally revealed by her breakdown during the climactic fight with Angel in 'Five by Five' (A1.18), and her realization that she can rewrite her own script at the end of 'Sanctuary' (A1.19) is the beginning of her redemption and thus of her retrieval of self-definition. Eliza Dushku brings to the role a combination of breezy nonchalance and equally insouciant callousness, with insights into Faith's disturbing self-loathing.

Just as interesting is the challenge posed by Faith's return on the side of good, first to Los Angeles in 'Salvage' (A4.13) and then on to Sunnydale in 'Dirty Girls'. Dushku takes a short while to find her feet again after a two-year sabbatical, but is shortly back on top – where Faith likes to be ('Just like ridin' a biker') – and blending the old no-bullshit mordancy with a new conscientiousness, whether it be backing Buffy up or as genuinely reluctant commander-in-chief after the *putsch* in 'Empty Places' (7.19). Dushku turns in especially fine performances in Faith's duologues with Spike and Principal Wood. (D.B. Woodside, like a number of supporting players, deserves lengthier praise for his considered performance than space permits here; brief acknowledgement, too, to the ensemble abilities of Indigo as Rona and in particular of Felicia Day as Vi – I for one would not be surprised if Angel Investigations get a visit in the future from Vi the Vampire Slayer.)

This strength of identity, whether it be rooted in a fixed sense of self or an impassioned quest for it, may also go some way towards explaining why many viewers feel that the Big Bads of Seasons Four and Seven don't quite cut the mustard. All the other principal season villains show a certain flair in their self-allotted roles, which the respective actors utilize: Mark Metcalf with the Master's subterranean stratagems in Season One; David Boreanaz as the newly liberated Angelus in Season Two; Harry Groener's gleeful mixture of homespun folksiness and demonic plotting as the Mayor in Season Three ('There's more than one way to skin a cat... and I happen to know that's factually true'); Clare Kramer's revelling in Glory's consumer-frenzied near-omnipotence in Season Five (not just divine but a diva – if the painting on her apartment wall is intended to be an original Tamara de Lempicka, this puts Glory in the company of the artist's best-known collector, Madonna Ciccone Penn Ritchie); and the dynamic of the Trio, and Warren in particular, in Season Six, followed by the chilling assurance of Dark Willow.

Put bluntly, neither Maggie Walsh nor Adam in Season Four has such a hook. Lindsey Crouse takes a dry pleasure in Professor Walsh's above-ground role as the assured bitch-queen of UC Sunnydale (giving lectures which I suspect are consciously written in a pastiche of the style of Crouse's ex-husband David Mamet); however, for the Initiative-supremo side of her character, Crouse limited herself to playing mainly on Maggie's repressed quasi-incestuous feelings for Riley, and the problem with such a decision is that there has to be a sufficiently solid surface layer for this repression to abrade against. As Adam, George Hertzberg – perhaps constrained by his various prostheses leaving him only half a face to act with – is reduced to telling us that he is a super-bad assemblage of human, demon and machine, without being able often enough to *show* us in his own portrayal, rather than simply in terms of the atrocities we see Adam has committed. Moments such as the chilling gleam in Adam's eye (singular) at the end of the 'Frankenstein in the woods' scene in 'Goodbye Iowa' (4.14) are all too rare.

Both Maggie and Adam are little more than plot functions which happen to overlay people who neither are, nor are seen to be striving to be, sufficiently defined as individuals. Conversely, Kramer's Glory shows that even Big Bads can suffer meaningful identity crises; the psychological and emotional confusion of the increasingly frequent spontaneous metamorphoses between Glory and Ben would not work at all if Glory in particular were not invested, through Kramer's performance, with a firmly grounded identity in the first place.

And if Maggie and Adam fail to find a persona, how much more difficult is it in the case of the First Evil in Season Seven, which doesn't even have a fixed personal form in which to appear and is, moreover, incorporeal. It makes for a wonderful spine-chilling cliffhanger at the end of 'Lessons' (7.1) when we see half-mad Spike being lectured in turn by the likenesses of Warren, Glory, Adam, the Mayor, Drusilla, the Master and finally the twice-dead Buffy herself. But what film director John Carpenter refers to as 'left-wing' horror, the 'it could be any one of us' school of spooky villainy – fans still debate whether Dawn's vision of Joyce in 'Conversations With Dead People' (7.7) was or was not the First, despite writer Jane Espenson's unambiguous declaration that it was – begins as a strength yet comes as the season progresses to hamper the sense of an almighty set-to which will take the series out on a high.

I yield to none in my admiration of the final clutch of episodes in Season Seven: the dramatic craft, in writing and performance alike, for my money just overtakes even the dizzying climax of Season Five. However, a part of me also identifies with those who remark that not even a Hellmouth full of Turok-Han Ubervamps can fill the gap left by the absence of a single, personally whackable Big Bad.

The introduction of Caleb as the First's lieutenant is, I think, an acknowledgement of this (as well as an obligation Whedon felt he owed to actor Nathan Fillion after the mid season cancellation of his space-western, *Firefly*, in which Fillion starred). More explicit still, and almost a little rueful, is the pre-emptive criticism put into Buffy's mouth that a more appropriate and 'cool' name for the First would be 'the Taunter'. The same problem, to a lesser extent, handicaps Season Four of *Angel*: Cordelia is the vessel of the Big Bad rather than the thing itself and, as mentioned above, Charisma Carpenter appears unable to give sufficient force to the instances when Cordy does act directly. And the same partial workaround is adopted, with the casting of Gina Torres, who had played Fillion's lieutenant in *Firefly*, as Jasmine.

Probably the most interesting of the non-Buffy identity-seekers and role-players, though – and possibly, by the final seasons, even more fascinating than the protagonist herself – is Spike. In one phase he, like Harmony, revels in his self-proclaimed status as 'the Big Bad', and (after an initial bout of success on Spike's part in Season

Two) we snigger at the bollix he makes of it. In the next, inhibited from harming humans by an Initiative brain-chip implanted in 'The Initiative' (4.7), he tries to reconcile his confused and confusing hybrid status: barely tolerated but never accepted by the Scoobies, still hungering after their downfall but unable to do more than sow seeds of disharmony among them, and yet also paradoxically eager to join them on demon-hunts once he finds that his chip permits him to indulge his fondness for ultra-violence as long as it is perpetrated on inhuman creatures.

This taste for a good ruck is itself an invented part of Spike's self-definition, part of the new character he fashioned for himself after being vamped by Drusilla. 'Fool For Love' (5.7) reveals both this and the delightful if heavy-handed truth about his human existence as 'William the Bloody', putting his frequent incompetence as an evil-doer into perspective and once again emphasizing that the reality of *Buffy*verse identity is more complicated than Buffy's specious reassurance to Willow in 'Doppelgangland' that a vampire's personality 'has nothing to do with the person it was'.

Much of this saga, even when Spike is at his most insidious, as in 'The Yoko Factor' (4.20), is superior comedy – the behavioural irony of Spike finding himself impelled, as T.S. Eliot put it, 'To do the right deed for the wrong reason' – and James Marsters is a superior comedian of the sort required; it's a gentle modulation from the black acerbity of early Spike in his Season Two double-act with Drusilla. However, both Spike's character and Marsters' growing intuitive command of it, nurtured by the ongoing requirements of the series, take off with his realization in Season Five that his obsession with Buffy is rooted in a desire to get on top of her in an altogether more horizontal context, and that his previous lovey-dovey episode with her when a spell of Willow's goes awry in 'Something Blue' (4.9) is less a wild aberration than a pre-echo of a strain that has always been present in his personality.

Spike's admission of this, first to himself and subsequently to Buffy, the aid and protection he offers Dawn and his genuine mourning for

Joyce as he acknowledges a collective and heartfelt regard for 'Summers women', constitute a further and almost conscious level of synthesis between his pre- and post-vamp senses of himself, and generate some passages of acting on Marsters' part which are quite as heart-rending as Alyson Hannigan in full spate, such as the final scene of 'Intervention' (5.8) – a less defined pre-echo of the later uses of the term. By the climax of Season Five, Spike seems to have implicitly completed this aspect of his journey and become a fully fledged member of the Scoobies; this is evidenced not so much by the overt action of Buffy re-inviting him into her home as by the casual comradeship of his exchanges with Giles and Xander, such as the 'Crispin's Day' allusion to *Henry V* which the two English characters grimly share on their way to the final showdown.

It doesn't last, of course. Buffy's growing realization that she reciprocates his feelings on some level, albeit tangled, is dramatically more effective if Spike is once again put at some distance from the Scoobies, so the combination of attraction and repulsion means that she begins to respond explicitly to him only outside the core knot of relationships. 'Outside', and also 'as an alternative to', violent, passionate sex with Spike (which literally brings the house down in 'Smashed') is both an escape from and a catharsis of the life problems which pervade the season – the resurrected Buffy is on one level responding to Spike's very un-alive-ness, that which separates him from her world but which in some senses he and she now have in common. Only on breaking up with him in the final moments of 'As You Were' can she show the tenderness of using his human name of William and acknowledging that this side of his nature persists.

The end of the brief affair – and his remorse at his subsequent attempted rape of Buffy in 'Seeing Red' (6.19), undeniably wrong, but equally undeniably motivated by his human rather than his demonic side, precipitates Spike's greatest identity crisis. Again, our expectations are subverted: we finally learn that he has undergone a series of tests to earn a boon not for purposes of revenge but of self-improvement – giving Buffy 'what she deserves' is to be not

Spike the chip-free berserker, 'the [undead] man I was' to whom he refers when pining for Drusilla in 'Lover's Walk', but Spike the ensouled, more nearly 'what I was' [before he was vamped] as he says in 'Grave' (6.22). He has so many 'wases' to choose from, but in fact what he becomes is something else still.

For in yet another reverse, our first glimpse in Season Seven is not of a noble, resolute quester, but a lank, gibbering wreck. Marsters is superb in his portrayal both of gaga Spike and of his erratic, two-steps-forward-one-step-back recovery: trying to right himself from the outside in by donning the 'costume' of a cool fighter, in 'Beneath You' (7.2), and muttering allusions both lateral and back in time: 'What's a word means glowing?' he rambles in 'Same Time, Same Place' (7.3), continuing, 'Gotta rhyme' – the word, of course, is 'effulgent', from William the bloody awful poet's verse in 'Fool For Love'.

Only in this distrait condition could Spike now become a sleeper agent for the First, and his horror at recalling his under-the-influence murders is genuine and powerful. When Buffy asks him, in 'Beneath You', 'Since when did you become the champion of the people?' – recalling the description of Buffy herself as 'the warrior of the people' in Willow's resurrection invocation in 'Bargaining Part One' (6.1) – he replies, 'I didn't', but ultimately he does, albeit on a far from grandiose route. Nor, even now with a soul and the burden of remorse, is his journey straight or his past record expunged; when he finally frees himself from the weight of his mother-loving memories in 'The Killer Inside Me', he tells Wood, 'I don't give a piss about [having killed] your mum', and it's not just for effect. He, too, has found a selfhood, free of fixation on either William's mother or Spike's sire, Drusilla, and he embraces it, contradictions and all.

The complexities of this Spike, and the skill and success of Marsters' portrayal of him, are perhaps best evidenced by the fact that crucial climactic moments in 'Chosen' can be read in differing ways, and work equally well either way within the emotional journey. If Buffy and Spike did make love during their final night in the basement of Revello Drive, it's proper consummation at last, and it *is* making love rather than the previous season's desperation-sex; if not, the night's chastity fits the increasing nobility of Spike. When she finally declares to the semi-transcendent Spike in the Hellmouth, 'I love you' and he replies, 'No you don't. But thanks for saying it', then if he is telling true, it's a final and definitive acceptance of the multi-layered reality of their relationship; if she is, and the flame which surrounds their clasped hands is the real consummation, then he is with equal bravery offering what they both know in their hearts is a face-saving fiction even at the very end.

Marsters' off-screen attitude to his role has often been blithe: 'What, are you kidding? He's *evil!*' was the gist of one answer in a convention Q and A session in the hiatus after Season Five. Increasingly, though, his performance has grown along with the writing of Spike, and even outstripped it, so that ultimately he succeeds in simultaneously playing every possibility and yet leaving room for the viewer's interpretation. Those who bewail the Spike strand as usurping the allegedly rightful Buffy-centrism of the series, such as Jaime J. Weinman in a remarkable polemic in the online magazine salon.com (and, I must admit, I was sceptical myself when I heard about Spike's final journey in prospect), have only to watch with open, unblinkered eyes to see that it works, and that what makes it work is Marsters' performance.

For as with all of the principal players Whedon has assembled, it is not just a matter of being able to portray explicit suffering but of knowing when to *stop* performing, when to let camera and context do the work, even with a shot as prosaic as a pile of cigarette butts under the tree where Buffy has discovered Spike lurking in 'No Place Like Home' (5.5). The cast and creators of the *Buffy*verse series rapidly evolved their approach to a stage where they realized they could trust the audience; they know that it is better to show than to tell, and also know that showing two points is enough for the viewer not just to infer a line between them, but also to extrapolate it beyond those points. This is, in turn, exploited through subversion, by throwing curves into the narrative line when we least expect them. Viewers of *Buffy* and *Angel* are gently but insistently asked not simply to be consumers, but to take an active part in a process closer to theatrical transactions of character and identity, to work *with* the players and characters as both the scope and the limitations of identity and role continue in dynamic flux.

As is natural in such a mode of operation, this is nowhere more apparent or indeed more necessary than in the case of the Slayer herself. 'The Slayer' is a distinct concept from 'Buffy Anne Summers', and indeed the meat of the underlying drama lies in her attempts to reconcile the two elements of the series title, or to find an accommodation with both in the world. In Buffy more than anywhere else, the fact that identity is a matter both of person and of role is constantly apparent – often implicit, but increasingly overt as she moves away from the structures first of formal schooling and then of a parental framework. The Season Four finale, 'Restless' (4.22), is more than an amusing coda to the previous episode's climactic battle with Adam and the invocation of a 'Super-Slayer' drawing both on the qualities inherent in Giles, Willow and Xander and upon a link to the primal well of Slayer-power. In Buffy's dream-confrontation with the First Slayer, it also lays the foundations for the following season's explicit quest by Buffy for a path by which she can be sufficiently true both to her human desires and obligations and to the duties and impulses of the Slayer.

Again, the metaphor for adolescence and young adulthood, with its conflicts of independence and bonds and its needs to define a self capable of dealing with such conflicts, does not need labouring. In Buffy's case, the process explicitly begins only a little while after physical puberty, with Slayerdom foisted upon her at the age (one infers) of 15, and just keeps growing from there on in, until at 20 she finds herself on the one hand able to dictate terms to the Watcher's Council – 'Checkpoint' (5.12) – and on the other suddenly the head of the family, with both human and supernatural obligations to her sister, Dawn.

During the high-school phase, it is possible to discern passages in which, although each insists on interfering with the other, either the Buffy or the Slayer element is foregrounded for an episode or so. Indeed, much of Season Three is a see-saw between the two. Buffy *qua* Buffy attempts a normal high-school life by running for Homecoming Queen, in 'Homecoming' (3.5), or flees Sunnydale altogether in a bootless attempt to shun her Slayer obligations, with which even her first name seems so bound up that she temporarily discards it – 'Anne' (3.1). Conversely, Buffy *qua* Slayer is given the grim surprise that attaining her majority means an increase in formal Slayer demands and severance from the surrogate fatherhood of Giles ('Helpless'), or experiences the temptation personified by Faith to set herself above the law by virtue of her Slayerness – 'Bad Girls' (3.14). One side or the other keeps gaining the upper hand.

Increasingly in Season Five, though, both sides of the teeter-totter are simultaneously weighed down, and Buffy's challenge is to bear the loads, always and together, without breaking at the fulcrum which is her sense of self. There is simply no let-up as these demands grow equally and oppositely intense; another attempt at flight, this time into herself in a state of catatonia, fails, and finally – like heroes and messiahs down the fictional and mythological ages, and also like a number of historical figures (consider Yukio Mishima as a bizarre example) – she is forced to the realization that the only resolution lies in consummating both strands of obligation at once in a noble death.

On her return from beyond in Season Six, her sense of identity is largely fixed, and it is a case of finding a path for her known self through an always too unknown and mutable world. She lies for a while about the nature of her afterlife, not for her own advantage, but to save her friends' guilt at having recalled her from heaven, while she comes to terms all over again with the fact that 'The hardest thing in this world is to live in it'. She does so only partially – see my remarks above about sex with Spike as an escape from the living world.

And the single greatest challenge to her path – the demon-venom-provoked delusions of 'Normal Again' (6.17) – is presented in effect not as a change to her body chemistry, but to everything else around her: is she really the Slayer, or have the past six years been the delusion of a schizophrenic in an LA mental hospital? This sense that it is the world rather than Buffy which has changed is reinforced by a clutch of what would otherwise be 'cheats', non-point-of-view shots of the hospital (including the episode's closing homage to Terry Gilliam's cinematic masterpiece, *Brazil*). In the end, it is her integrated sense of self which grimly triumphs: she is Buffy, but she is also the Vampire Slayer – her world, and thus ours as viewers, is Sunnydale. Nor does the end of Season Six offer her even a temporary respite or a step on the way to resolution; having thwarted the Troika, she is in many ways a bystander, at best a more than averagely useful soldier, in the matter of dark Willow, which is resolved by Xander's faith and love rather than any Slayerly skills.

Season Seven once again sets the see-saw swaying, with Buffy finding herself responsible not just to herself, her family and regular associates and to the world of humanity in general, but increasingly to the growing band of Potential Slayers under her roof. This time the crises are not those of personal duty or comradely leadership, but of conventional vertical command. When the flashpoint comes in 'Empty Places', Buffy does not flee as before, to LA or into catatonia: she is ejected, because she must follow her Slayer's conviction rather than subordinate it to the reservations of those around her. And the ultimate solution is to sacrifice neither her personality nor her status. She remains who she is, and remains perched on the see-saw; what breaks is the fulcrum, and the ground beneath it. And that fulcrum is, as is the nature of fulcra, a tiny point: 'The' – definite article, singular. She remains Buffy, she remains Vampire Slayer; what she rejects is her place (notwithstanding Kendra and then Faith) as *the* Vampire Slayer. Her final anticipatory half-smile at the end of 'Chosen' is not that of someone who is triumphant; it is that of someone who for the first time, in herself and in the world, simply *is*.

Whedon's and others' DVD commentaries, and frequent reported remarks from her acting colleagues, acknowledge and praise Sarah

Michelle Gellar's technical prowess in the mechanics of screen acting right from the first episode, whether it be her ability to eat a cocktail cherry at exactly the same moment for a series of re-shot masters and cutaways or her skill at mutely speaking volumes in the prolonged reaction shots during her first interview with Principal Flutie. As the series progresses, though, Gellar swiftly finds the core of Buffy, such that she can adroitly act on a number of levels at once. She can indicate the repressed fears beneath the flinty exterior in 'Anne' or 'I Only Have Eyes For You' (2.19) without recourse to quivering lips or frightened eye movements for only the camera to see. Of course, any actor must be able to play subtext, but it is in practice rather more rare to find one – let alone an entire cast – who can consistently do so without the subtext, in Giles's words in 'Ted' (2.11), 'rapidly becoming text'. Indeed, in 'Hush' (4.10), the central company play for half an hour or so without any verbal text at all, after a group of demons steal the voices of the Sunnydale population.

Most impressively, Gellar can take on board the entire body language of another person, whether as the Buffybot in 'Intervention' or as Faith-in-Buffy's-body in 'Who Are You?', without veering into gross parody. (Eliza Dushku is almost as impressive as Buffy-in-Faith, but more of her screen time here is combat of one kind or another rather than character work.) It is also telling that, even when her body is inhabited by someone else, the outward figure of Buffy Summers cannot escape the ineluctable role of the Slayer: the Buffybot also engages in Slaying combat, most gloriously (no pun intended) in 'The Gift', when she engages in the kind of banter which the fleshly Buffy is now too tired and burdened to maintain; and Faith-as-Buffy ultimately resigns herself to the Slayer's obligation to save a church congregation held hostage by vampires.

But more than offering multi-layered performances, Gellar comes to show a kind of Zen acting power in making herself a *tabula rasa* (once again, no pun intended) for the camera and/or the audience to work on. It is tempting to speak of a Beckettian minimalism in her – and the entire ensemble's – performance in 'The Body' (5.16), but to take such a cerebral stance on the episode is to do it a gross injustice. It is simply one of the finest pieces of television drama, and the single finest depiction of bereavement in any medium, that I have ever seen. It achieves this phenomenal power by demanding of the cast that they simply go numbly through the motions in dealing with the death of Joyce, not even explicating their numbness but letting the gaping void at the heart of matters come through un-modulated even by so much as a note of incidental music. Any sneerer at either *Buffy* in particular or genre work in general should simply be sat down in front of a television and told to shut up for three-quarters of an hour while they are shown 'The Body'; their awestruck silence afterwards may be taken as recantation and apology.

Still more complex than the figurative curse of Slayerdom upon a young woman in a natural search for a selfhood she can feel comfortable with is the literal curse upon the person of Angel. The double-edged malediction – first, that while remaining a vampire his soul be restored to him; second, that he live in constant peril of losing it for a moment's true happiness (however 'boinkily' that happiness may be defined) – is at every moment Angel's overriding motivation and self-definition.

His vampiric sire, Darla, granted a similar (though not identical) possibility of redemption when restored to humanity, first tries to deny this change of identity by continuing on a path as evil as that of her vampire incarnation, and ultimately seeks to renounce it and return to the reassuringly known selfhood of centuries past by begging that Angel re-vamp her. (The fact that her eventual reclamation by Drusilla was performed by force is incidental; vamp-Darla clearly welcomes the return to what, by now, she identifies as her true self.) But Angel embodies a paradox: while his condition is the central plank of his current identity, he seeks redemption, and thus true embodiment as a whole person, through devoting himself to the rescue of others and thus engaging in the most profound kind of self-denial.

All this is despite the certain knowledge that, to put it bluntly, vamps have more fun. The vampire Angelus is clearly far more comfortable with himself and his role – he has a flamboyance in word and deed which comes with complete self-assurance, and in his caged speeches in 'Soulless' (A4.11) and 'Calvary' (A4.12) the malign form of an insight lacking or suppressed in his ensouled alter ego. This assurance is not just conscious, but moral... within a soulless, vampiric morality. Angel, on the other hand, labours hard and painfully along his chosen (rather than predetermined) path. Even when he dismisses his associates Wesley, Cordy and Gunn in 'Reunion' (A2.10) and embarks on a renegade crusade against Darla, Dru and Wolfram and Hart, 'dark Angel' carries a continuing awareness that he *is* renegade, that he *has* abjured the way of light. His suffering even as he rampages is reminiscent of the Catholic teaching that the greatest torment of the damned in Hell is the knowledge that they are denied heaven. (In this respect, note too that Angel's moral horror is almost greater still on discovering the utterly amoral atavism that his fully demonic side can manifest in Pylaea.) His fervour to be a good, instructive, corrective father to Connor is partly a manifestation of this notion of redemption through good works... redemption in his own eyes if not those of the cosmos.

Where *Buffy* is at heart a human drama, *Angel* targets a slightly older audience demographic in part by being more theologically complicated. However it may be populated by Powers That Be, Oracles and various species of demon, and however the 'hell' of Wolfram and Hart's home office may be revealed as this world – 'Reprise' (A2.15) – rather than the nether dimension to which Angel has previously been dispatched at the end of Season Two of *Buffy* – 'Becoming Part Two' (2.22) – the cosmos of *Angel* is governed by forms of Judaeo-Christian, and specifically Catholic, concepts such as redemption through good works. (In detail, of course, it's even more closely akin to certain Catholic heresies, but that's another subject.) Angel's rejection of the Gem of Amara – 'In the Dark' (A1.3) – can be seen as denying himself an unearned (or not yet earned) illusion only of redemption, a kind of spurious indulgence. Angel is not noticeably a theist, but he bases his function, and his notions of both his past and his future transformations, his current and his ultimate hoped-for identities, on concepts of divinity and damnation.

The word almost invariably used (and this essay is no exception) to describe Angel's usual mood and David Boreanaz's performance is 'brooding'. To be sure, the role certainly calls for one hell of a lot of it, but 'twas not ever thus. In his early appearances in *Buffy* Season One, Angel is positively playful, more like a vastly attenuated Angelus (and, indeed, in the first phase of his brief appearance in Sunnydale in 'Chosen', his exchanges with Buffy perhaps deliberately strike the same note… until mention is made of Spike). This may be partly because at first the viewer knows him simply as someone who appears periodically to Buffy to give her little pointers, and Whedon does not wish to make the truth too obvious too soon (although he professes surprise that so few viewers worked it out in advance of the revelation). On his debut appearance, he describes himself simply as 'a friend', and in this phase functions more or less like Hal Holbrook's character in the film of *All The President's Men* – as a kind of 'Deep Fang'. He is revealed to be a vampire only in the episode entitled 'Angel' (1.7).

Thereafter, he darkens rapidly, so that by 'School Hard' (2.3), it is not implausible when the newly arrived and at this point seriously menacing Spike says to him, 'You were my sire, man, my Yoda'. (In one of the series' most famous 'retcons' – retrospective continuity changes – this is later glossed as a metaphorical statement, since Angel is in fact Spike's grandsire.) By this stage, though, Angel is becoming a more imposing physical presence as well, probably due in part to Boreanaz's by now regular workout regime: his body and jaw-line have beefed up so that he cuts a significantly more impressive figure when standing ominous in dim light.

Boreanaz has also gained command of the role of Angel to the extent that, when he reverts to Angelus following his 'moment of true happiness' with Buffy – 'Surprise' (2.13)/'Innocence' (2.14) – the actor can retain strands of continuity with the ensouled Angel as well as introducing diabolical contrasts. However, it is his season in Hell between the end of *Buffy* Season Two and his return in 'Faith, Hope and Trick' (3.3) that fully creates the character we subsequently come to know. The reminder of what Angel has to lose banishes the last vestiges of levity from his sense of himself. He may continue to crack deadpan one-liners – such as 'You can go to *hell*.' / 'Been there, done that' in 'Lonely Heart' (A1.2), or 'I thought I knew eternity' when watching Cordelia's supremely atrocious performance as Ibsen's Nora Helmer in 'Eternity' (A1.17) – but they are always tempered by the consciousness of who he is at root and what he must transcend. Boreanaz develops a seemingly throwaway delivery for such lines, whereby Angel seems to disregard them but is in fact showing loathing of this half of his identity, as is made clear when he lends the same delivery to virtually every line Angel utters during his dark phase in *Angel* Season Two. Even after he returns to his senses, it is clear that (to paraphrase Geno Washington) it is not just the blues that walk with him, but the downright midnight blacks.

Having established this palette, Boreanaz does not, to be honest, vary it much in the subsequent two seasons. His responses to Darla's pregnancy, to the first newborn then teenaged Connor and to the will-they-won't-they courtship dance with Cordy in the latter part of Season Three, all take place within known parameters of character. It is really only the verbal machinations of the caged Angelus in mid Season Four that push the envelope; we have seen this kind of insidious malice before, in *Buffy* Season Two, but with Angelus largely deprived of the ability to back up his words with deeds, our attention necessarily becomes much more tightly concentrated on his devilishly silver tongue.

This sense of treading water (no 'Deep Down' pun intended) also limits the characters around Angel. Amy Acker, who as Fred promised for a while to become the Willow of *Angel* – hence perhaps, in part, that affinity the two of them half-find in 'Orpheus' (A4.15) – recovers too quickly and completely from her Pylaean stir-craziness; Andy Hallett as the delicious Lorne is by Season Four largely reduced to gulping Sea Breezes and wondering why his empathic mojo isn't working. In particular, the more than capable J. August Richards as Gunn finds himself too frequently reduced to token brother-isms and the tangle of relationships that he describes in 'Players' (A4.16), in what is clearly another moment of pre-emptive self-deprecation on the writers' part, as 'a turgid supernatural soap opera'. Even the previously excellent Julie Benz, who compellingly navigates Darla through return as a mortal, re-vamping and the near-acquisition of a soul as her miraculous offspring grows inside her in Season Three, is on her ghostly return in 'Inside Out' (A4.17) little more than a mouthpiece for pious platitudes.

The darkly glittering exception to this tendency is Lilah, whom Stephanie Romanov broadens and deepens into the kind of multi-faceted villain her predecessor Lindsey seemed set to become, before his line-dance over and back across the boundary between good and evil and actor Christian Kane's final departure for a career in alt.country music. As per the standard Wolfram and Hart contract of employment, death shows little sign of curbing Lilah's complex magnetism as the Angel Investigations team take over the law firm's LA operation – a radical shake-up perhaps considered necessary after a couple of seasons which, though frequently powerful – e.g. much of Keith Szarabajka's portrayal of the zealous Holtz and individual episodes such as 'Waiting in the Wings' (A3.13) – feel overall more diffuse and directionless than their main narrative arcs ought to have permitted.

There is ample evidence, then, that the major characters in *Buffy* and *Angel* are engaged in a constant process of negotiating identities and roles for themselves as each metamorphosis provides additional facets to their evolving personae. However, each series has also included a number of self-conscious, reflexive meditations on this process seldom seen outside postmodern comedies.

In *Angel*, 'Eternity' is superficially an opportunity for self-deprecating satire on the culture of TV series, as actress Rebecca Lowell finds herself a prisoner of her past long-time screen role. On a deeper level, though, what confines her is her status as an icon, her obligation to maintain *that* role (or at least its outward youthful trappings, by persuading Angel to vamp her) in order to hang on to her sense of who she is. Rebecca, like Angel, defines herself in terms of others, but of their perception rather than actual value to them; she has acquiesced in a self-definition that operates from the outside in. In many ways, Angel's temporary, drugged 'reversion' to Angelus operates the same way; as Wesley tries to point out to him, the Doximall in his champagne has given him only the *illusion* of happiness, but on some level Angel's identity sensors tell him that he is untroubled, therefore he must be evil, therefore he must be Angelus. It can also be argued that in the drug-dreams of 'Orpheus', Angelus's scathing commentary on moments from Angel's century of ensoulment, and Angel's face-to-face rebuttal of his own demonic persona, are an enactment not just of a divided personality but respectively of the cynical and the engaged viewer of a series based on this premise.

In *Buffy*, 'The Zeppo' revolves around Xander's quest for a role within the Scooby gang, which he can use as a source of self-esteem. The very title of the episode (in an epithet bestowed on Xander by Cordy) refers to the fourth Marx Brother, widely held to be redundant to the workings of the act. Xander attempts to carve a niche for himself as 'Car Guy', providing wheels for the gang; but when he drives up in his tacky Chevrolet BelAir and tells the girls, 'It's my "thing"', Buffy jumps pertly to another kind of identity prop altogether when she asks, 'Is this a penis metaphor?'

But it is not just Xander who is overtly conscious of playing, or needing to play, a defined role within the outfit. The motif is woven through the episode, not just on a structural level with our tantalizing side-glimpses of the other Scoobies toiling away in their allotted place at the Hellmouth, but with a number of reflexive remarks tossed out by them in passing. In the pre-title 'teaser', Willow notes the periodic subversion of her usual character by declaring, 'Occasionally I'm callous and strange'; on the most banal level of all, Giles defines himself in relation to the gang's doughnut purchases: 'I always have jelly; I'm always the one that says, "Let's have jelly in the mix".'

'Restless', too, is more than a kind of satyr-play to bring Season Four to an end and herald Buffy's search the following season for a personal synthesis between her human and Slayerly roles. In each of the three others' magical dreams, their subconsciouses riff on their senses of self, past, present and potential: Giles's appearance on the stage of the Bronze, delivering his instructions to the others in song; Willow not only experiencing the classic actor's nightmare but also indicating how precarious her growing self-confidence is by imagining herself before a high-school class in exactly the same costume she wore in 'Welcome To The Hellmouth'; Xander reprising his soldier bit one more time as Captain Willard to Snyder's Colonel Kurtz in a delicious recreation almost shot for shot of a scene from *Apocalypse Now*. Indeed, they even illuminate in passing the roles of others: Xander's vision of Spike training as a Watcher prefigures the blond vampire's gradual but distinct crossover to the forces of good in Season Five, and in Willow's surreal nightmare production of *Death Of A Salesman*, Riley proudly proclaims, 'I'm Cowboy Guy' – which, of course, he is: the nearest thing the series has ever had to an unambiguous white-hat.

The musical 'Once More With Feeling' is another such instance, in which characters regularly surprise themselves by bursting into song (and, in the case of demon Sweet's captured minion, surprises everyone else by not doing so). Characters are at once invested with self-consciousness as they look back on their own and others' musical performances (Anya classifying her and Xander's show-stopping number 'I'll Never Tell' as 'a retro pastiche that's never gonna be a breakaway pop hit' and Giles referring with characteristic deadpan wryness to the police 'taking witness arias'), and also liberated from it as they find themselves able to say in song what they could never say in speech. Giles could never confess to Buffy that he feels he's standing in her way, nor Xander and Anya come clean to each other about their pre-wedding fears, nor Buffy admit the true nature of the afterlife she had inhabited... and whatever Tara might say to Willow in off-screen pillow talk, she could certainly never say in front of us that 'You make me com...-plete'. Despite the inherent discipline of the musical form, this freedom extends even to the off-screen team, with writer David Fury making a cameo appearance as Mustard Man and Marti Noxon as Parking Ticket Woman.

And, of course, it also deserves saying at much greater length than I can do here that it's a damn fine musical in its own right. Although the songs span a number of genres, the guiding spirit remains that of Stephen Sondheim, from whose shows such as *Into The Woods* (after which a Season Five episode was named) Whedon has taken on board that happy-ever-after is a rule to be twisted and even trashed. Rather than a ringing affirmation in the final curtain, what we are given is the frank uncertainty of 'Where do we go from here?' This is also the sentiment of the final line of the entire series: 'What are we gonna do now?' But the lack of closure is here deliberate. With the liberation of uncounted no-longer-Potential Slayers, and thus of Buffy herself, this is a beginning at least as much as an ending.

For one of Season Seven's major themes is the getting of wisdom. Whedon's debt of gratitude to his mother as an educator, both professionally and in terms of the spirit she inculcated in him, has long been a matter of record; more recently he has also spoken warmly of the three years he spent at the leading English independent school, Winchester College, during his teens. *Buffy* in particular implicitly stresses throughout that 'learning' is a wider and deeper matter than 'being taught', and this reaches its culmination in the final season.

From Willow, in retreat with Giles (in scenes shot at Tony Head's own English West Country home) in the first episode, through to Buffy and Spike at the end, again and again we see people not graduating as in the Season Three metaphor, but finding themselves *in* themselves, as a precursor to events we will never be vouchsafed. When Buffy literally closes the door on Giles's Watcher schooling at the end of 'Lies My Parents Told Me', she is not declaring the end of her education, but its transition to another mode, that of her own thought and experience; she even dares to eschew conclusions, as in the case of her return to 1630 Revello and that closing moment itself. 'Chosen' is the end of a seven-year rite of passage, yet passage by its nature is not just from one state but to another.

The major coup of 'Chosen', too – its radical redistribution of the means of Slayage – is a moment of mass transformation into selfhood. Whedon has said 'I designed Buffy to be an icon', and a feminist subtext has always been present and thoughtfully advanced in the series. Some of the more explicit manifestations of this theme in Season Seven, such as the deprecatory edge to the repeated point that the Shadow Men who created the First Slayer are *men*, may be obtrusive and even a little clumsy. However, it is none the less possible (*pace* Zoe-Jane Playdon elsewhere in this volume) to read the effects of Willow's Scythe-related spell as propounding a more universal agenda. In this interpretation, the XX chromosomes of the liberated Potentials are almost incidental to the underlying message, which is that vast numbers of *people* have been freed of arbitrary burdens: the burden, for a handful, of later being *the* Slayer, and for the rest, the double-edged sword of Damocles which on the one hand threatens at any moment to foist this status on them and on the other prevents the unchosen majority from ever fully realizing themselves. The spell liberates numberless victims, all of whom are women, but it speaks of the liberation of all, of the vital importance of being permitted the opportunity to try to be everything we each can be. It's a form of the American Dream, but again in this formulation America, like womanhood, is merely an emblem for a desire and a moral principle common to all humanity.

More than this, however, Season Seven goes back beyond 'Buffy, Year One' to classical modes of storytelling. The season is jam-packed with 'callbacks'. Halfrek's admiring remark to Anya in 'Lessons' about her achievements as a vengeance demon, 'Do I have to mention Mrs Czolgosz?', refers to Anya's recollection in 'Superstar', on her past demonic career: 'I'd wish he was... in love with President McKinley or something.' (Leon Czolgosz was McKinley's assassin.) Faith's first reappearance to Buffy in 'Dirty Girls', borrowing her stake with a 'May I? Thanks', is a recapitulation of her original arrival in 'Faith, Hope And Trick'. Giles's remark in the school corridor in 'Chosen', 'The Earth is definitely doomed', echoes right back to the end of the Scoobies' very first adventure, in 'The Harvest', and in a scene cut before transmission, Dawn also recapitulates that season's 'Prophecy Girl' (1.12) climax, telling her listeners that it's romantic. Such verbal and narrative patterning is a feature of folk tales.

But the season displays much deeper roots even than this: I maintain that in it, the story itself in effect constitutes a self-conscious being commenting on its status within the series and within the world of stories. The main Willow plot strand of 'The Killer Inside Me' is about as direct an invocation as one can imagine of a classic narrative *topos*: what could be more archetypal than a wicked witch's curse on a well-beloved young woman, which is lifted by a kiss? (In this episode, too, actor Iyari Limon dispels accusations that her character Kennedy is so callow and immature as to be, for want of a less blunt term, a starfucker; she voices continuing scepticism about magic, but she still shows loving concern for Willow and ultimately redeems her, despite rather than because of Willow's Wiccan power.)

'Storyteller' (7.16) is of course a dramatization of Andrew's compulsive fabulism, showing him cack-handedly glamorizing his own and others' tales; beneath this, however, it enacts the *topos* of the unreliable narrator interfering with the story he or she tells. And on closer examination still, it can be seen that the really unreliable party here is Buffy, who lies to Andrew to manoeuvre him to the Seal of Danzalthar and lies again to elicit the tears that will close the Seal. Andrew may romanticize his narratives absurdly but, except where he has a direct stake in matters, he never once says anything that is outright untrue ('except for that possible... word misunderstanding' in 'Dirty Girls', where he misconstrues the term 'vulcanologist' and recounts that Faith once killed a kinsman of Mr Spock); his portraits of other characters and events are comically florid but fundamentally right. (I am unpersuaded that his praise of Anya to Xander at the end of 'Chosen' – 'She died saving my life' – is intended to be construed as factually untrue at all, let alone as either deliberately or culpably so.) His principal fidelity is to the language and forms of story; his sporadic covering of his own hide may come more easily to him this way, but it is a manifestation of his overall perspective rather than a reason for it. Hence my suggestion that he is in this respect the personification of the entire season.

As for the climax, consider Whedon's remark in his DVD commentary to 'The Harvest' that at the climactic moment he instructed the director to 'Give me the Spielberg'. 'Chosen' gives us the Spielberg in spades, again and again showing the kind of instinct for making the classic seem fresh which is that director's forte. It dares to go for the big, bold, majestic sweep, not because of a sense of obligation to top previous climaxes, but because this is the climax that *this* story demands. It dares to give us an almost unalloyed upbeat ending, notwithstanding the deaths of Anya and (it appears) Spike. It dares, time and again, to give us brink-of-death switchbacks. It even dares to have us sitting there mistakenly thinking, gosh, Whedon's really splashed out and hired John Williams for the score. And it all works.

Plus one more crucial reminder, just before the big finish, with the role-playing game scene the night before the final battle – Giles: 'I used to be a highly respected Watcher; now I'm a wounded dwarf with the mystical strength of a doily' – jogging us one last time that at bottom, all this supernatural stuff is just pretend, just something to which we give our time and enjoyment and participation as active, intelligent viewers. And we can know that and still give ourselves over to the exhilaration of that big finish. Because that's what the best stories do. And, of course, they explain us to ourselves in the process.

And it *is* just a story. A superb story: seven years of high wit and deep insight, of excitement, suspense, horror, amusement and unashamed tears; of tearing up the genre rulebook and time and again confounding expectations; of respecting its audience and asking us to work together with it; of top-notch acting and directing. But a story. Look again at that title: can all this emotional investment, not to mention all this chin-stroking and scholarly cogitation, really be justified over something called *Buffy the Vampire Slayer*?

Yes.

And what *are* we gonna do now?

After those seven years, we have at least an inkling.

Grrr. Arrg.

episode guide

BUFFY Season One

1.1 Welcome to the Hellmouth *by Joss Whedon*

Buffy and Joyce arrive in Sunnydale. Buffy befriends Willow, Jesse and Xander, rather than Cordelia, and tells Giles she is not interested in Slaying. Angel approaches her and is cryptic; Buffy saves Willow and Xander from the girlish vampire Darla and monstrous Luke, who are gathering food for the Master, who is trapped in the Hellmouth, but she fails to save Jesse.

1.2 The Harvest *by Joss Whedon*

Luke is to conduct a massacre at the Bronze to make possible the Master's escape from the field of force that traps him in the Hellmouth. Buffy tricks and dusts him, saving Cordelia; Xander dusts Jesse.

1.3 The Witch *by Dana Reston*

Buffy tries out for the cheerleader squad; various magical mishaps occur to other members – Cordelia goes blind. Amy, daughter of past cheerleader Catherine, finally makes the squad when Buffy is poisoned by a death spell. Amy is possessed by witch Catherine; the spell and possession are broken and Catherine trapped in her own trophy statuette.

1.4 Teacher's Pet *by David Greenwalt*

Xander fancies replacement biology teacher Miss French who is actually a virgin-eating giant mantis of whom even vampires are scared. Buffy rescues him from being eaten and disorients and destroys Miss French with a mixture of bat cries, bug spray and violence.

1.5 Never Kill a Boy on the First Date *by Rob Des Hotel & Dean Batali*

The Master organizes the creation of the Anointed One by the slaughter of a busload of people. Buffy's date with senior classman Owen turns into a battle in the mortuary with a religious psycho turned vampire whom she assumes to be the Anointed and kills. She dumps Owen for being an adrenalin junky. The Anointed is actually a small child.

1.6   The Pack *by Matt Kiene & Joe Reinkemeyer*

During a zoo trip, a clique of school bullies and Xander are possessed by hyena spirits. They eat the school's pig mascot and (while Xander is caged after attempting to seduce Buffy) Principal Flutie. Buffy breaks the spell, cast by an evil zoo-keeper, and throws him to his beasts.

1.7   Angel *by David Greenwalt*

Buffy is rescued by Angel from the Master's three assassins; she discovers Angel is a vampire, cursed with a soul and trying to atone. Darla, Angel's sire and ex-lover, frames him for an attack on Joyce; Buffy cannot bring herself to attack him. Darla attacks Buffy with guns and Angel dusts her.

1.8   I, Robot –You, Jane *by Ashley Gable & Thomas A. Swyden*

The scanning of Giles's rare occult volumes with help from technopagan computer teacher Jenny Calendar frees the demon Moloch to possess the net. He befriends and seduces various bright kids, including Willow, and builds a robot body for himself. Buffy traps him in this and destroys him.

1.9   The Puppet Show *by Rob Des Hotel & Dean Batali*

Principal Snyder makes Giles direct the school talent show. A dancer's heart is cut out, by a demon that needs this and a brain to retain human form. Buffy suspects Morgan, a genius, with an oddly animated ventriloquist's dummy, Sid. Morgan is killed; Sid turns out to be a transformed demon hunter. Sid and Buffy save Giles from the demon's guillotine. Sid dies.

1.10   Nightmares *teleplay by David Greenwalt, story by Joss Whedon*

Everyone's nightmares start to come true, including the death and vampirization of Buffy. She and the others manage to find the source of this, a child beaten into a coma by his baseball coach, and wake the child up.

1.11   Out of Mind, Out of Sight *teleplay by Ashley Gable & Thomas A. Swyden, story by Joss Whedon*

Mysterious attacks on the popular culminate in an attempt to disfigure Cordelia. Marcie, a nondescript schoolgirl, has been ignored so long she became invisible. Buffy defeats her and Marcie is abducted to become a government assassin.

1.12   Prophecy Girl *written & directed by Joss Whedon*

Buffy learns of the prophesy that she will be defeated and killed by the risen Master; she tries to walk away. Xander asks her out, and she rebuffs him. When she realizes that Giles plans to confront the Master in her place, she knocks him out, and goes, and dies. Xander finds her in time to resuscitate her and she kills the Master, closing the Hellmouth.

BUFFY Season Two

2.1   When She Was Bad *written & directed by Joss Whedon*

Buffy returns from vacation in bitch-mode, flirting with Xander and snubbing Angel to an extent that causes Cordelia to rebuke her. The Anointed One has his minions abduct Willow, Giles, Jenny and Cordelia, who were physically close to the Master's death, to his new factory lair so their blood may reanimate him. Buffy rescues them and smashes the Master's bones.

2.2   Some Assembly Required *by Ty King*

Bright Chris has raised his dead footballer brother, Darren, from the dead and is trying to create a perfect mate for him – Cordelia is abducted to provide the head for this patchwork girl and Buffy and Xander save her. Darren dies again trying to save his headless bride from the flames. Giles and Jenny go on a first date.

2.3   School Hard *teleplay by David Greenwalt, story by Joss Whedon*

Spike and Drusilla arrive in Sunnydale. Buffy is obliged by Snyder to cater a Parent-Teacher evening which Spike and the Anointed One's minions attack. Buffy fights them off; Snyder's hostile comments to Joyce are discounted because of Joyce's admiration for Buffy's courage. It becomes clear Snyder is part of the great Sunnydale cover-up. Spike kills the Anointed One.

2.4   Inca Mummy Girl *by Matt Kiene & Joe Reinkemeyer*

An expected male exchange student turns out to be female – actually, a mummified human sacrifice on show at the museum has risen and is buying herself life and beauty by sucking people dry. She falls for Xander, and cannot bring herself to kill him; Buffy, who feels empathy for her plight as a chosen sacrifice, destroys her.

2.5   Reptile Boy *written & directed by David Greenwalt*

Cordelia persuades Buffy to join her at an exclusive fraternity house party. Actually, the rich boys regularly sacrifice young girls to a reptilian demon for wealth and power; the killing of the demon by Buffy results in various alumni going bankrupt and to jail.

2.6   Halloween *by Carl Ellsworth*

Snyder conscripts the gang to chaperone young masqueraders; Buffy, Willow and Xander buy costumes from Ethan Rayne, which change their natures – Willow becomes a ghost, Xander a soldier, Buffy a drippy belle, various children monsters. Spike exploits the situation. Giles knows Ethan and smashes his Chaos idol returning things to normal. Oz notices Willow for the first time.

2.7   Lie To Me *written & directed by Joss Whedon*

Ford, a crush from Buffy's LA schooldays, arrives in Sunnydale; dying of cancer, he plans to betray Buffy and a crowd of vampire wannabes, including ditzy Chanterelle, to Spike to live forever as a vampire. Buffy outwits him and Spike and stakes him when he rises. Buffy learns of Drusilla's presence in Sunnydale and is jealous of Angel's past.

2.8   The Dark Age *by Rob Des Hotel & Dean Batali*

When young, Giles, Ethan and friends raised the demon Eyghon, possession by whom is a sexual high, and had to exorcize him. Eyghon returns seeking revenge – Ethan tattoos Buffy with Eyghon's mark, while Eyghon possesses Jenny. Eyghon is tricked into possessing Angel, whose own demon expels him. Jenny, by now in love with Giles, is alienated from him.

2.9   What's My Line? Part One *by Howard Gordon & Marti Noxon*

Spike plans to cure Drusilla and hires demonic assassins to kill Buffy, who has problems of her own – it is Career Week at school. Kendra, the Slayer created by Buffy's brief death, arrives in Sunnydale and attacks Angel, leaving him to burn in sunlight.

2.10   What's My Line? Part Two *by Marti Noxon*

Angel is saved by bar owner Willy and sold to Spike, who needs his blood to cure Drusilla, whom Angel sired. Kendra and Buffy bond. Besieged by a bug demon assassin, Xander and Cordelia bicker and then snog. Oz takes an assassin's bullet for Willow. Buffy rescues Angel and leaves Spike for dead. Drusilla rises renewed. Kendra leaves.

2.11 Ted *by David Greenwalt & Joss Whedon*

Joyce's forceful new suitor takes against his potential stepdaughter; they fight and she apparently kills him. He returns good as new and keen to kill her. Ted is actually a robot into whom his creator downloaded his mind and his fifties attitudes to women; Buffy and the gang rescue Joyce from him.

2.12 Bad Eggs *by Marti Noxon*

Buffy fights the Gorch brothers, cowboy vampires. In a child care exercise, pupils are given eggs to care for which are demonic and hatch spawn that possess everyone save Buffy and Xander. Buffy fights their progenitor, a Bezoar demon, which kills Tector Gorch.

2.13 Surprise *by Marti Noxon*

Spike, crippled in 2.10, gives Drusilla a celebratory present – parts of a demon, the Judge, who will burn all that is human. Willow starts dating Oz. Buffy and Angel steal the Judge's arm and Jenny, one of the gypsy tribe who cursed Angel, argues that Angel needs to take it far away. They lose it to vampires on the docks and end up having sex.

2.14 Innocence *written & directed by Joss Whedon*

The gypsy curse is broken by Angel's happiness and he becomes the demonic Angelus again, joining Spike and Drusilla in their apocalyptic plans. Buffy and Giles quarrel with Jenny; Willow finds out about Cordelia and Xander. Xander uses post-Halloween soldier memories to steal ordnance from an army base. Buffy blasts the Judge, invincible to any weapon forged, with a rocket launcher.

2.15 Phases *by Rob Des Hotel & Dean Batali*

Oz, bitten by a young cousin, becomes a werewolf and the prey of hunter Cain whom Buffy humiliates. Willow makes clear to Oz that his lycanthropy does not matter to her. Angelus starts his campaign of mocking cruelty against Buffy and her friends.

2.16 Bewitched, Bothered & Bewildered *by Marti Noxon*

Cordelia dumps Xander to regain her friends. He blackmails Amy into casting a love spell which misfires, making every woman in Sunnydale, including Joyce and Drusilla, proposition him. A besotted Amy turns Buffy into a rat. Giles makes Amy break the spells. Cordelia decides she will date Xander 'no matter how lame he is'. Angelus flirts with Drusilla.

2.17   Passion *by Ty King*

Partly forgiven by Buffy and Giles, Jenny reconstructs her ancestor's curse; warned by Drusilla, Angelus kills her before she can cast it, destroying her computer. He leaves her corpse in Giles's bed. Giles attacks him, setting fire to the factory, and Buffy has to rescue Giles.

2.18   Killed by Death *by Rob Des Hotel & Dean Batali*

Hospitalized with bad flu, Buffy has to confront her memories of a dead cousin and realizes that there is a demon, Der Kindermord, who preys on children. She deliberately makes herself ill enough to see and fight it. Angelus attacks her in the hospital and Xander confronts him.

2.19   I Only Have Eyes For You *by Marti Noxon*

Supernatural events at Sunnydale High are caused by ghosts of a student who shot his teacher lover and himself in the 50s – Giles briefly thinks the ghost is Jenny. Buffy learns forgiveness. The attempted exorcism culminates in Buffy's possession by the boy, Angelus's by the woman; Angelus's invulnerability to bullets breaks the cycle of repetition and frees the ghosts.

2.20   Go Fish *by David Fury & Elin Hampton*

Experiments by the school coach turn several of his star swim-team into aquatic monsters; the coach tries to kill Buffy when she finds out and she throws him to his creations. Xander goes undercover as a swimmer but is not affected enough to change.

2.21   Becoming Part One *written & directed by Joss Whedon*

Archaeologists uncover the entombed demon Acathla, which Angelus (whose turning by Darla, curse and falling for Buffy we see in flashbacks) steals in an attempt to wake Acathla and suck the world into Hell. Willow finds Jenny's backup disc; her recasting of the curse is interrupted by Drusilla who kills Kendra and abducts Giles for his knowledge of the Acathla ritual.

2.22   Becoming Part Two *written & directed by Joss Whedon*

Accused of Kendra's murder, Buffy is approached by Spike who offers help against Angelus in exchange for Drusilla's life. Giles resists torture, but under hypnosis tells Drusilla the ritual, thinking she is Jenny. Expelled from school by Snyder and thrown out by Joyce when she finds Buffy is the Slayer, Buffy fights Angelus as Acathla wakes. Willow's curse re-ensouls Angel. Buffy stabs him and sends him to Hell to save the world. Despairing, she leaves Sunnydale.

BUFFY Season Three

3.1 Anne *written & directed by Joss Whedon*
Waiting tables in LA, Buffy meets the former Chanterelle, now Lily, whose boyfriend is abducted by social worker Ken, actually a slaver from a factory-like Hell, and returned old and dying. Buffy follows Lily to Hell and raises the slaves in revolt. Buffy gives Lily her job and second name, Anne, and returns home. The gang have fought vampires in her absence.

3.2 Dead Man's Party *by Marti Noxon*
The gang and Joyce are still furious with Buffy for not contacting them; this erupts into bitter argument during a welcome back party and is resolved by an attack of zombies raised by an African mask from Joyce's art gallery.

3.3 Faith, Hope and Trick *by David Greenwalt*
Faith, Kendra's replacement, arrives in Sunnydale pursued by her enemy Kakistos and black techie vampire Trick; she and Buffy are prickly before bonding to defeat Kakistos. Giles persuades Buffy to talk – she admits that Angel was re-ensouled when she stabbed him; she leaves her ring in Angel's mansion and Angel reappears, out of his mind.

3.4 Beauty & the Beasts *by Marti Noxon*
Violent deaths leads to suspicion of Oz, who has escaped the cage he locks himself in three nights a month. Buffy suspects the returned, feral Angel she has found in the woods. In fact, a fellow-student with an abusive relationship with his girlfriend has taken a drug that changes him into the brute he thinks she wants. Angel kills him.

3.5 Homecoming *written & directed by David Greenwalt*
Trick sells tickets for a Slayer hunt. Buffy stands against Cordelia for Homecoming Queen and it is they, not Buffy and Faith, who are hunted and have to unite against their foes – a demon, the surviving Gorch, and twin assassins. Trick is recruited by the Mayor. Cordelia faces Gorch down with sarcasm. Neither Buffy nor Cordelia wins the election. Willow and Xander kiss.

3.6 Band Candy *by Jane Espenson*
To create a diversion while babies are fed to a demon he has debts to, the Mayor has Trick hire Ethan to sell candy bars that revert all adults to their

teens. Joyce and Giles make love, though Buffy thinks she has intervened in time. With help from a punk Giles and (briefly) a nerd Snyder, Buffy captures Rayne, saves the babies and kills the demon.

3.7   Revelations *by Doug Petrie*

Giles and the gang are furious that Buffy hid Angel's return. Faith's posh new Watcher, Gwen Post, warns of a magic artefact, the glove of Mynegin, and she and Xander incite Faith to attack Angel lest he misuse it. In fact, it is Gwen who uses it – she has been expelled from the Council. Buffy severs her arm. Faith feels her trust generally abused.

3.8   Lover's Walk *by Dan Vebber*

Spike arrives in Sunnydale, mad with grief that Drusilla has dumped him; he kidnaps Willow to make him a love spell and takes Xander hostage. Abandoned by him in the ruined factory, they are found making out by Oz and Cordelia; Cordelia is badly injured. The Mayor sends vampires to kill the disruptive Spike; Buffy and Angel help Spike and mocking them he decides to torture Drusilla into loving him again.

3.9   The Wish *by Marti Noxon*

Cordelia, humiliated by Harmony and unforgiving of Xander, makes a wish to vengeance demon Anyanka and finds herself in a world where Buffy never came to Sunnydale, the Master rose, and Xander and Willow are vampires. She is killed but not before she tells Giles what has happened. A harder Buffy arrives and dies fighting the Master; Giles smashes Anyanka's necklace power centre and returns things to normal.

3.10   Amends *written & directed by Joss Whedon*

Angel is tormented by visions of those he killed, notably Jenny, and told he is damned and must kill Buffy. Buffy realizes that the source of this is the First Evil, a corrupting force, and confronts and kills its priests. Angel tries to commit suicide by facing the dawn, but it snows in Sunnydale, indicating that someone powerful is looking out for him. Oz forgives Willow.

3.11   Gingerbread *teleplay by Jane Espenson, story by Jane Espenson & Thania St. John*

Haunting by apparently sacrificed children sends Joyce and Willow's mother on a rampage against occultism. Snyder seizes Giles's books for burning and

Buffy, Willow and Amy are condemned for witchcraft – Amy escapes by changing into a rat. Cordelia intervenes with a firehose and Buffy breaks the spell which enabled the demon to pose as the dead children.

3.12 Helpless *by David Fury*

After meditation sessions with Giles, Buffy finds her powers weakening; he is putting her through a test ordered by the Council where she has to defeat a vampire by intelligence. The vampire turns his Council minders and abducts Joyce; Buffy tricks and kills him, passing the test, but Council boss Quentin sacks Giles for caring too much.

3.13 The Zeppo *by Dan Vebber*

Sidelined from the struggle against another apocalypse – we see this semi-parodically in background shots – and mocked by a vengeful Cordelia, Xander is befriended by, and has to defeat, zombie delinquents who plan to blow up the school. Along the way, Faith casually seduces him. Cordelia mocks him again and Xander is smugly cool.

3.14 Bad Girls *by Doug Petrie*

Faith talks Buffy into doing things her way – neglecting school to burn out vampires, taking silly risks, stealing weapons from a store, mocking uptight cowardly new Watcher Wesley, dancing sexily together. The Mayor becomes invulnerable on schedule. Fighting the vampire minions of demon Balthazar, Faith accidentally kills Deputy Mayor Finch. Buffy is appalled. Faith does not care.

3.15 Consequences *by Marti Noxon*

Faith lies, blaming Buffy for Finch's death; Giles plans to deal with it quietly. Buffy and Faith see the Mayor with Trick; the Mayor realizes they know of his villainy. Xander reasons with Faith and she nearly kills him; Angel stops her and talks to her about bloodthirstiness. He is getting through when Wesley arrives with Council heavies, from whom Faith escapes to the docks. Buffy and she are attacked by Trick; Faith kills him, saving Buffy. Faith asks the Mayor for Trick's job.

3.16 Doppelgangland *written & directed by Joss Whedon*

Warned by Faith of Willow's hacking skills, the Mayor decides to kill her. Willow is tricked by Anya into helping retrieve Anyanka's necklace; Willow wrecks the spell; vamp Willow is brought to Sunnydale. She beats up the Mayor's assassins who attack the Bronze, where she kills Sandy; she tries to seduce Willow who overpowers her. They impersonate each other, confusingly. Vamp Willow is sent back and staked.

3.17   Enemies *by Doug Petrie*
Faith tries to seduce Angel, failing which she casts a spell to bring Angelus back as her lover and the Mayor's ally. They trick and capture Buffy, and Faith boasts of the Mayor's planned Ascension, before discovering that she has been tricked by Angel into blowing her cover.

3.18   Earshot *by Jane Espenson*
Contaminated by the ichor of a demon, Buffy acquires the power to read minds, which starts to drive her insane, but not before she learns someone plans mass murder at Sunnydale High. Angel saves her; the gang, including Cordelia, eliminate various suspects. Buffy thinks wimp Jonathan plans a shooting: in fact, he plans suicide and she stops him. Xander discovers it is the cook. Buffy learns Giles slept with Joyce.

3.19   Choices *by David Fury*
The Mayor receives a box of demon beetles he needs to eat for his Ascension; Buffy steals them from the town hall, but Willow is captured and threatened by Faith. The Mayor offers a swap which Buffy accepts against Wesley's orders. Faith loses her knife, the Mayor's gift.

3.20   The Prom *by Marti Noxon*
Xander discovers Cordelia's new poverty and pays for her Prom dress. Anya asks him to the Prom. Angel decides to leave town. Buffy saves her schoolfellows from Hellhounds raised and trained by a social reject; she is acknowledged as Class Protector. Everyone dances.

3.21   Graduation Day Part One *written & directed by Joss Whedon*
From Anya, they learn that Ascension means becoming a vast pure demon; the Mayor plans to speak at Graduation and eat the class. Faith poisons Angel with an arrow; Wesley forbids Buffy from seeking a cure and she mutinies. The cure is a Slayer's blood – Buffy fights Faith, whom she stabs with her own knife, but Faith throws herself from the building.

3.22   Graduation Day Part Two *written & directed by Joss Whedon*

Buffy makes Angel drink from her; in hospital, comatose, Faith tells her in a dream that the demon Mayor will be physically vulnerable and still have human emotions. Oz and Willow make love knowing they may die. At Graduation the Mayor turns, eating Snyder; the class fight back. Buffy taunts him with Faith's knife and he chases her into the library, which Giles blows up. Harmony is vamped. Angel leaves Sunnydale.

BUFFY Season Four

4.1   The Freshman *written & directed by Joss Whedon*

Buffy, Willow and Oz arrive at university, where Buffy feels at sea; she dislikes her control-freak roommate, Kathy. She meets her psychology professor, Maggie Walsh, and Maggie's TA, Riley. She is mocked and beaten by Sunday, a vampire whose band prey on unhappy students. Sunday steals her stuff, smashing the Class Protector parasol, and Buffy gets angry and kills her. There are commandos on campus tracking vampires.

4.2   Living Conditions *by Marti Noxon*

Everyone worries that Buffy is cracking up – her hostility to Kathy becomes unreasonable and deranged. In fact, her suspicions are right; Kathy is a demon who has been magically removing her soul in order that Buffy be dragged off when Kathy's father comes to take her home. Buffy's soul is restored; Kathy is taken; Willow moves into the room.

4.3   The Harsh Light of Day *by Jane Espenson*

Willow is attacked by Harmony, now a vampire and Spike's lover. He has returned to Sunnydale in search of the Ring of Amara, which renders vampires invulnerable to stakes and sunlight. Anya seduces Xander; Buffy sleeps with plausible Parker; Spike rejects Harmony when he finds the ring. Buffy defeats him and takes the ring. (See A1.3)

4.4   Fear, Itself *by David Fury*

The Scoobies attend a Halloween party; blood spilled on a mystic rune, part of decorations, evokes a fear demon. Buffy is dragged into the depths; Willow's spell goes wrong; Oz starts to change; Xander becomes invisible. Anya, who arrived late, fetches Giles. Buffy accidentally releases the fear demon, which is small, so she stomps on it.

4.5   Beer Bad *by Tracey Forbes*

Moping over Parker, Buffy takes to hanging out in the bar with poseurs who are rude to bar staff – including Xander. Oz is attracted to Verucca. Buffy and her new friends start to devolve – they into Neanderthals, Buffy into a fetchingly monosyllabic Cave-Buffy. Parker tries to seduce Willow who mocks him. The barman brewed magic beer – the bar catches fire and Cave-Buffy saves the day.

4.6   Wild at Heart *by Marti Noxon*

Oz escapes from his cage and meets another werewolf, the amoral musician Verucca. He locks her into his cage with him next night and Willow finds them together. Willow tries to curse Verucca, who arrives at sundown to kill her; Oz attacks Verucca as they both change, and kills her. Buffy overpowers him. Oz decides to leave town.

4.7   The Initiative *by Doug Petrie*

Spike is captured by the commandos – the Initiative, a military/research unit, commanded by Maggie Walsh. Riley is the commando leader – his friends Graham and Forrest his subordinates. Spike escapes to Buffy's room where he attacks Willow and discovers that a chip in his brain prevents him. Riley and other commandos try to seize Willow and Buffy fights them off.

4.8   Pangs *by Jane Espenson*

Work on a new cultural centre uncovers the lost Sunnydale mission, where local Indians were imprisoned and died – a vengeance spirit kills a lecturer and a priest. Willow makes a case for his right to vengeance – Xander catches all the diseases the Indians died of. Spike takes refuge in Giles's apartment where the Scoobies are having a Thanksgiving meal; Angel arrives, and helps fight off the vengeful spirits, without Buffy knowing he is there. (See A1.8)

4.9   Something Blue *by Tracey Forbes*

Riley and Buffy date. Depressed, Willow casts a spell that enforces her will including her casual remarks. Amy is briefly deratted; Giles goes blind; Xander finds himself chased by demons; Buffy and Spike agree to marry. Willow is offered Anya's old job by D'Hoffryn, but declines, putting things right before demons overwhelm the gang.

4.10   Hush *written & directed by Joss Whedon*

Fairytale monsters, the Gentlemen, arrive in Sunnydale and steal everyone's voices as a cover for the harvesting of hearts. Willow meets Tara at a Wicca group and together they magically fight off a Gentlemen attack. Buffy and Riley separately trail the Gentlemen to their lair and destroy them; they then have to cope with their recognition of each other.

4.11   Doomed *by Marti Noxon & David Fury & Jane Espenson*

Buffy and Riley come to terms with each other's true identity. Three demons assemble tokens – a heart, some bones, a talisman stolen from Giles – to open the Hellmouth and bring the Apocalypse; Buffy, Riley and the gang stop them. A suicidal Spike is dragged along; he discovers he can kill demons and vampires which cheers him up.

4.12   A New Man *by Jane Espenson*

Feeling neglected, and patronized by Maggie Walsh, Giles goes for a drink with Ethan who warns him of Room 314, before changing him into a lumbering demon; only Spike can understand him and demands payment for help. Buffy, thinking the demon has killed Giles, attacks him in Ethan's room, but recognizes him in time. Ethan is interned.

4.13   The I in Team *by David Fury*

Buffy joins the Initiative, but irritates Maggie Walsh by asking questions about Room 314; when Buffy sleeps with Riley, Maggie is jealous. Willow, feeling neglected, spends the night with Tara. Spike is tagged by Forrest and goes to Giles for help; Giles makes him pay. Maggie sets up a demon ambush which Buffy survives, exposing Maggie to Riley. Maggie goes to Room 314 and is killed by her creation, Adam.

4.14   Goodbye Iowa *by Marti Noxon*

Riley discovers the gang's protection of Spike and becomes distrustful. Adam dissects a child. Riley becomes disorientated Maggie's 'vitamins' were something more. In room 314, Adam boasts to Buffy, Xander and Riley of his kinship with Riley, and then stabs Riley non-fatally. Tara sabotages a demon-seeking spell.

4.15   This Year's Girl *by Doug Petrie*

After dreams, Faith wakes from her coma; she confronts Buffy, but is hunted by the police. Watchers, warned by her nurse, come to town. Faith receives a videotape in which the Mayor offers her vengeance. She takes Joyce hostage; Buffy arrives and they fight. The Mayor's gadget switches their bodies; and Buffy-in-Faith is arrested.

4.16   Who Are You? *written & directed by Joss Whedon*

Faith-in-Buffy has a high time, taunting Spike, teasing Tara (whom she guesses is Willow's lover) and seducing Riley. She kills a vampire and is thanked; Riley's tenderness freaks her out. Buffy-in-Faith escapes execution by the Council and explains things to Giles. Adam's vampires, influenced by Adam, seize a church; Faith leaves an airport queue to save the congregation. Buffy helps her; they fight; Willow and Tara reverse the body-switch. Faith leaves town. (See A1.18)

4.17   Superstar *by Jane Espenson*

Suddenly Jonathan is a world-famous hero and Buffy his sidekick; everyone, male and female, is besotted with him. Buffy realizes something is wrong when Jonathan is weak against a demon that shares his tattoo; his world-changing spell created an evil demon for balance. When he and Buffy kill it, things return to normal. Jonathan helps Buffy forgive Riley for sleeping with Faith.

4.18   Where the Wild Things Are *by Tracey Forbes*

Buffy and Riley's lovemaking triggers and sustains poltergeist activity which causes sexual shame and general weirdness; the source of this is children disciplined when the house was an orphanage. Xander and Anya rouse Buffy and Riley before they die of exhaustion.

4.19   New Moon Rising *by Marti Noxon*

Oz returns, cured of lycanthropy, until he smells Willow on Tara and attacks her – and is captured and tortured by the Initiative. Willow comes out to Buffy. Adam asks Spike's help, promising removal of the chip. Riley is arrested for trying to free Oz; Buffy enters the Initiative, takes the new commander hostage and frees Riley and Oz. Oz and Willow talk, and he leaves town. Willow and Tara make up.

4.20   The Yoko Factor *by Doug Petrie*

Adam kills Forrest. On Adam's orders, Spike sows hostility between the Scoobies, playing on Giles's and Xander's sense of uselessness and Willow's fear of rejection. Buffy storms out. Angel comes to town and he and Riley fight; Angel and Buffy quarrel. Riley is summoned by Adam. The Initiative has captured so many demons its cells are full.

4.21 Primeval *by David Fury*

Buffy guesses Spike is working with Adam; she persuades the others to get over their differences. Adam tells Riley he has a chip which Adam controls — he will join Adam and Forrest as cyberdemonoids after a battle between demons and soldiers gives him spare parts. Buffy and the gang blend into a super-Buffy which defeats and kills Adam with help from Riley and Spike, whom Adam double-crossed. The Initiative is shut down.

4.22 Restless *written & directed by Joss Whedon*

Exhausted, Buffy, Willow, Giles and Xander fall asleep in front of videos. In dreams which reflect their insecurities, each is visited by a man with cheese and attacked by a mysterious being; Buffy learns from a guide with Tara's face that this is the First Slayer, who has been angered by the spell in 4.21, and that she has changes ahead. Buffy defeats the First Slayer.

BUFFY Season Five

5.1 Buffy vs. Dracula *by Marti Noxon*

Dracula arrives and seduces Buffy into letting him bite her; his mind tricks turn Xander into his bug-eating servant who delivers Buffy to him. Giles and Riley raid Dracula's castle and Giles is groped by his Brides. After tasting Dracula's blood, Buffy fights free and stakes him; he repeatedly re-forms. At home, Buffy has suddenly always had a sister, Dawn

5.2 Real Me *by David Fury*

Dawn writes in her diary how much she hates being Buffy's kid sister. Harmony's inept minions raid the Magic Shop for books on Slayers; Giles thinks about taking up the lease. Dawn is harangued by a maniac. Harmony attacks the Summers' house ineffectually. Dawn is taken hostage by a minion; Buffy stakes all the gang except Harmony.

5.3 The Replacement *by Jane Espenson*

The demon Toth shoots at Buffy with a magic rod, but hits Xander. Suddenly there are two Xanders, one suave and confident, the other dorky and clumsy; both think the other is a demon. In fact, both are aspects of Xander and need to survive; Willow reintegrates them. Xander and Anya get an apartment. Riley confides in a sympathetic Xander that he knows how lucky he is – but Buffy does not love him.

5.4   Out of My Mind *by Rebecca Kirshner*

Harmony takes refuge with Spike. Joyce is taken ill, momentarily not recognizing Dawn; Riley's heart is under strain from Maggie Walsh's enhancements; Spike and Harmony kidnap Riley's military surgeon to remove Spike's chip. He plays along; Buffy rescues him and he operates on Riley. Spike wakes from an erotic dream, realizing he loves Buffy.

5.5   No Place Like Home *by Doug Petrie*

Monks send a mystic key away before being slaughtered by evil, ditzy Glory. After finding a magic sphere, Buffy suspects evil magic is making Joyce ill and goes into a trance to seek it out. She discovers Dawn is not real. Glory, who sucks out people's minds, tortures a monk; Buffy rescues him after fighting the stronger Glory, but he dies, after telling Buffy that Dawn is the Key and all memories of her are false. Buffy decides that Dawn is her innocent sister even so.

5.6   Family *written & directed by Joss Whedon*

Buffy tells Giles about Dawn. Tara's redneck family arrive; her father claims she, like her mother, will turn demonic unless she abandons college and magic. Riley flirts with vampire Sandy. Tara casts a demon-obscuring spell which hinders the fight against demon assassins sent by Glory. The Scoobies tell Tara's father that they are her real family; Spike proves Tara's humanity by hitting her – it hurts him. Willow and Tara dance.

5.7   Fool for Love *by Doug Petrie*

Injured by a minor vampire and concerned about the deaths of Slayers, Buffy interrogates Spike about how he killed two. In flashbacks, we see ineffectual poet William turned by Drusilla, his self-invention as Spike and fights with Angel, his killing of a Slayer in China and of another in New York. Like them, Buffy will be killed by her own death wish. Buffy spurns his advances. Joyce is hospitalized; Spike, who has come to kill Buffy, comforts her.

5.8   Shadow *by David Fury*

Joyce has a brain tumour. Glory turns a cobra at the zoo into a hunter which tracks the Key and identifies it as Dawn; Buffy kills it before it gets to Glory.

Riley finds Spike in the Summers' house stealing Buffy's clothes; Riley lets Sandy bite him and then stakes her.

5.9 Listening to Fear *by Rebecca Rand Kirshner*

Ben summons a meteor-dwelling Queller which starts killing the madmen created by Glory's mind-suck; the tumour has made Joyce deranged – when she is allowed home for the night, the Queller follows her. Dawn fights it off; Buffy and Spike kill it. Joyce realizes the truth about Dawn, but, like Buffy, accepts her as her own. Joyce goes into surgery.

5.10 Into the Woods *written & directed by Marti Noxon*

The tumour is safely removed. Graham asks Riley to join a unit fighting demons in Belize. Spike tells Buffy that Riley uses vampire whores. Riley stakes Spike with a piece of plastic wood as a warning; they bond over drink and hopeless love for Buffy. Riley offers Buffy an ultimatum; Xander convinces her to ask Riley to stay, but she pauses to kill the vampire whores and misses his helicopter. Xander tells Anya he loves her.

5.11 Triangle *by Jane Espenson*

Left in charge when Giles consults the Watchers, Anya bickers with Willow about magic experiments, alienating Tara and Xander, and accidentally releasing a troll, once Anya's boyfriend whom she transformed. He wrecks the Bronze and pursues both women to the shop where he threatens to kill them. He is impressed by Xander's courage in fighting him and offers to spare one woman – Xander refuses to choose. Buffy fights the troll and Willow sends it away, leaving its hammer behind.

5.12 Checkpoint *by Jane Espenson & Doug Petrie*

A delegation from the Council arrives, insisting that Buffy pass tests and threatening Giles with deportation. They interview the Scoobies and Spike. Glory confronts Buffy in the Summers' home and threatens her family and friends. Buffy is attacked by the Knights of Byzantium, fanatics keen to destroy the Key. Buffy tells the Council that real power rests with her – they tell her that Glory is a god.

5.13 Blood Ties *by Steven S. DeKnight*

Buffy tells the other Scoobies about Dawn; Dawn guesses from their behaviour that something is going on. Spike helps her break into the Magic Shop where she reads Giles's diaries. Distraught, she cuts herself and burns her diaries; she goes to the hospital where she confides in Ben, who transforms into Glory. Buffy and the others arrive and fight Glory who is easily beating them when Willow teleports her five miles into the air.

5.14   Crush *by David Fury*

Spike persuades Harmony to impersonate Buffy for sex games; Dawn tells Buffy that Spike loves her. An LA train full of corpses arrives in Sunnydale. Buffy investigates; Spike tells her of his feelings. Drusilla tells Spike the chip no longer works and takes him to the Bronze, giving him a fresh corpse to drain. They capture Buffy, then Spike takes Drusilla prisoner, offering to stake her to prove his love for Buffy. Buffy rejects him; Harmony shoots him and leaves; Drusilla gives up on him. Buffy bars him from the Summers' house.

5.15   I Was Made to Love You *by Jane Espenson*

Mysterious April arrives looking for her boyfriend, Warren; she beats up Spike for chatting her up. Everyone realizes she is a robot built as Warren's girlfriend and abandoned when he found a real one, Katrina. Buffy saves his fiancée from April and then sits with April as her batteries run down. Spike orders a Buffybot from Warren. Buffy finds Joyce dead.

5.16   The Body *written & directed by Joss Whedon*

After a flashback to Joyce's last Christmas, Buffy calls an ambulance – Joyce is dead from a post-op aneurism. The Scoobies meet up to join her and Giles and Dawn at the hospital; Willow has a clothes crisis and Anya broods about mortality. Dawn goes to the mortuary where a vampire attacks her; Buffy saves her. They look at their dead mother.

5.17   Forever *written & directed by Marti Noxon*

Xander rebuffs Spike for bringing a wreath, which is unsigned. After Joyce's funeral, Angel consoles Buffy. Dawn asks Tara and Willow to raise Joyce; Tara tells her it is wrong, Willow leaves a book out so she can see the arguments. Dawn tries the spell – Spike takes her to sinister demon Doc, who sends them to fight a monster for its eggs. Dawn casts the spell and something rises; Buffy goes to welcome it and Dawn breaks the spell.

5.18   Intervention *by Jane Espenson*

Buffy goes to the desert with Giles to confront the First Slayer, who tells her that her gift is death. Spike takes delivery of the Buffybot, makes passionate love and goes out slaying with it; Xander and Anya are appalled. Glory's minions guess Spike is the Key and abduct him; Glory tortures him for the Key's identity. In the course of the rescue, the Buffybot is damaged; Buffy impersonates it to find out whether Spike broke and kisses him when she realizes he did not.

5.19   Tough Love *by Rebecca Rand Kirshner*

Willow and Tara quarrel; at a fair by herself, Tara is tortured and mind-sucked by Glory. After promising Buffy to do nothing rash, Willow does darkest magic to fight Glory, on whom she inflicts serious pain before starting to lose. Warned by Spike, Buffy arrives in time to help her escape; Glory follows them. Tara inadvertently reveals that Dawn is the Key.

5.20   Spiral *by Steven S. DeKnight*

Buffy and Dawn escape. The Scoobies and Spike leave town; on the road they are attacked by the Knights of Byzantium who wound Giles seriously. They warn that Glory's use of the Key will destroy the universe; they are prepared to kill an innocent child. Besieged in a service station behind a magic force-field, Buffy rings Ben to treat Giles; Ben turns into Glory and seizes Dawn. Buffy lapses into catatonia.

5.21   The Weight of the World *by Doug Petrie*

Willow takes charge of the retreat to town and sends Spike and Xander to interrogate Doc, whom they fight and seemingly kill; Spike eventually conveys to the others the link between Ben and Glory which mortals cannot remember. Glory prepares for a ritual in which she will bleed Dawn dry to use the Key. Dawn briefly escapes, but is betrayed by Ben to whom Glory promises continued existence. Willow enters Buffy's mind and talks her out of her despair over a moment when she thought of killing Dawn. After reading Doc's scrolls, Giles says that killing Dawn is the only way to save the world.

5.22   The Gift *written & directed by Joss Whedon*

Determined that Dawn not die, Buffy demands that other ways to beat Glory be found. At Anya's suggestion, they use the Buffybot, the troll's hammer, the monk's glowing sphere, a wrecking ball. Willow sucks Tara's sanity back out of Glory and the others help Buffy wear her down until she subsides back into Ben, whom Giles kills. Doc appears and starts Dawn bleeding; reality begins to crumble. Buffy realizes that Dawn's blood and hers are the same, and sacrifices herself to save her sister.

BUFFY Season Six

6.1   Bargaining Part One *by Marti Noxon*

The Scoobies have fought evil all summer using the Buffybot to hide Buffy's death from demons. A vampire damages it and reveals the truth to a demon motorcycle gang who raid Sunnydale. Giles leaves for England. Willow, Anya, Tara and Xander engage in a dark ritual to raise Buffy which is disrupted by the demon bikers. Buffy awakes in her grave.

6.2   Bargaining Part Two *by David Fury*

Buffy, deeply confused, claws her way out to find herself in a demon-haunted Sunnydale and thinks she is in Hell. The demons destroy the Buffybot; Buffy helps the Scoobies to fight the demons, but runs off confused. Dawn, who has been protected by Spike, follows Buffy to Glory's collapsing tower and prevents her from jumping again.

6.3   After Life *by Jane Espenson*

Spike and Dawn dress Buffy's wounds – Spike rebukes Xander for taking chances with magic. Each Scooby in turn is possessed by a spirit that has come back from death with Buffy and needs to kill her to stay in the world. Willow makes it solid so that Buffy can kill it. Buffy confides in Spike that Willow's spell dragged her out of Heaven.

6.4   Flooded *by Doug Petrie & Jane Espenson, directed by Doug Petrie*

A burst pipe reveals the bad state of Buffy's finances. Giles returns and rebukes Willow for using dark magic – she is angry with him. Warren, Jonathan and Andrew decide to pool their powers and become crime lords – they summon a demon to rob banks. Buffy, seeking a loan, fights it. Warren sends it to kill Buffy; she drowns it in the flooded basement.

6.5   Life Serial *by David Fury & Jane Espenson*

The trio research Buffy's weaknesses, disrupting her attempts at normalization – attendance at college by slowing her personal time; a building job by a demon attack; a job in the Magic Shop by endless repetition of a single sale until she satisfies a customer. A night on the town with Spike leads to her spotting their van and beating up a demon (actually Jonathan in disguise). Giles gives her a cheque to help with debt.

6.6 All the Way *by Steven S. DeKnight*

On Halloween, Dawn sneaks out to date cute boys and misbehave. The boys are actually vampires – an apparently sinister old man is killed by them. Buffy, Spike and Giles interrupt the attempted turning of Dawn – Dawn gets her first kiss from her vampire boyfriend and stakes him. Tara and Willow have a row about Willow's casual use of magic; Willow makes her forget it.

6.7 Once More With Feeling *written & directed by Joss Whedon*

Sunnydale becomes a musical – demon Sweet, who causes this, makes people dance themselves to death. Tara discovers Willow's spell and is furious; Giles decides he is protecting Buffy from reality and should leave. Dawn's theft of a talisman convinces Sweet that she summoned him and is destined to be his demon Queen. Buffy confronts him and nearly dances herself to death until prevented by Spike – in a song, she reveals she was in Heaven. Xander summoned Sweet – Sweet passes on abducting him. Buffy and Spike kiss.

6.8 Tabula Rasa *by Rebecca Rand Kirshner*

Willow's attempt to remove Buffy's memories of Heaven and Tara's of their rows accidentally deletes everyone's identities. Giles thinks he is Anya's fiancée and Spike's father; Spike thinks himself human, or at least good. Attacked by vampire minions of a loan shark over Spike's gambling debts, the group nonetheless fight effectively. The spell breaks; Tara leaves Willow; Giles departs; Spike and Buffy kiss again.

6.9 Smashed *by Drew Z. Greenberg*

The trio steal a diamond. Willow de-rats Amy; the two work mischief at the Bronze. Spike discovers he can hit Buffy painlessly – Warren checks the chip, which is still working. Spike draws the conclusion that Buffy is no longer quite human and attacks her. Their fight turns into violent sex that demolishes a derelict house.

6.10 Wrecked *by Marti Noxon*

Amy introduces Willow to Rack, a dealer in addictive magics. Out with Dawn for the evening, Willow goes to Rack and gets high, accidentally summoning a demon which chases her and Dawn; Willow steals and crashes a car and Dawn is injured. Willow decides she will give up magic entirely; Buffy decides she will break with Spike.

6.11   Gone *written & directed by David Fury*

Buffy's irregular lifestyle leads to visits from a social worker. The Troika build an invisibility ray and accidentally make Buffy disappear. She torments the social worker and teases Spike sexually. Anya and Xander discover the ray will cause Buffy to crumble. Willow tracks the trio, but is taken hostage; Buffy confronts them and Warren tries to kill her. Willow restores Buffy.

6.12   Doublemeat Palace *by Jane Espenson*

Buffy takes a job in a sinister hamburger joint whose employees keep disappearing; she assumes they have gone in the patties, but in fact these have no meat at all. Buffy and Spike make love. She and Willow defeat a demonic old woman who eats late-shift workers. Buffy is very bored, but has a job.

6.13   Dead Things *by Steven S. DeKnight*

Warren seduces ex-girlfriend Katrina with a compulsion ray; when she comes to and threatens prosecution, he kills her. Shocked, Jonathan and Andrew help him by summoning time distorting demons so that Buffy thinks herself responsible. She tries to turn herself in, beating up Spike when he tries to stop her, and upsetting Dawn. She remembers meeting Katrina and works it all out. She confides about her affair with Spike in Tara, who refuses to condemn her.

6.14   As You Were *by Doug Petrie*

Riley returns, happily married to a co-worker, in search of a demon eggs trader. He is appalled to discover Buffy working in the burger joint and sleeping with Spike, especially when it turns out Spike is the egg dealer. He destroys the eggs and leaves; Buffy breaks with Spike.

6.15   Older and Far Away *by Drew Z. Greenberg*

Buffy fights a demon which hides in its sword. Her birthday party starts and goes on for hour after hour as no one can leave – the demon escapes from the sword and causes mayhem until Buffy traps it again. Dawn's fears of abandonment have called Halfrek, a vengeance demon, who appears to gloat and is caught by her own spell, which she breaks.

6.16   Hell's Bells *by Rebecca Rand Kirshner*

At his wedding, Xander is visited by what claims to be his future self and shown how he becomes a bitter abusive drunk like his father. The man, a demonized victim of Anya's curses, is lying; Buffy defeats him. Nonetheless,

Xander is persuaded by his family's behaviour that he is doomed to become like them, and leaves. D'Hoffryn re-recruits Anya as a vengeance demon.

6.17 Normal Again *by Diego Gutierez*

Poisoned by one of the Troika's demons, Buffy drifts in and out of a reality in which she was not Chosen as Slayer, but went mad with delusions. Her psychiatrist convinces her she will only be sane if she destroys her imaginary friends and she leaves Willow, Xander and Dawn trussed where the demon can kill them. Just in time, she opts for her delusions, and saves them with help from Tara. The other reality's Joyce mourns as Buffy lapses into catatonia.

6.18 Entropy *by Drew Z. Greenberg*

Anya tries and fails to get someone to wish harm to Xander. She gets drunk with Spike and has revenge sex. Willow has tapped into the spy camera network of the Troika and she, Buffy and Xander witness this. Xander angrily confronts Spike who reveals Buffy and he had an affair; Xander is furious. Willow and Dawn also know. Tara returns to Willow.

6.19 Seeing Red *by Steven S. DeKnight*

The Troika kill a demon for spheres which make the bearer superstrong. Warren beats up Xander until prevented by Jonathan. Spike confronts Buffy in her bathroom and ends up attempting rape – he leaves Sunnydale. During a robbery, Warren beats up Buffy – until Jonathan tips her off to break the spheres. Warren escapes – the other two are arrested. Warren turns up in the morning and shoots Buffy – a ricochet kills Tara and Willow becomes magically, murderously angry.

6.20 Villains *by Marti Noxon*

As a dying Buffy is taken to hospital, Willow steals dark magic from the Magic Shop's books. She saves Buffy and tracks Warren, who decoys her with a robot. Spike arrives in Africa and confronts a demon. Willow tracks Warren into the forest, torments him with Katrina's ghost, tortures him with a bullet and then, as Buffy arrives too late, flays and burns him.

6.21 Two To Go *by Doug Petrie*

Buffy and Anya rescue Andrew and Jonathan from jail before Willow can kill them as Warren's accomplices. Willow absorbs Rack's magic and threatens Dawn. Willow teleports Buffy and Dawn to the Magic Shop where Anya temporarily prevents her using magic against others. Instead, Willow makes herself strong and beats Buffy and Anya while the others flee. She is felled by a magic bolt from Giles. Spike is tested with pain and combat.

6.22 Grave *by David Fury*

Buffy confides the season's events to Giles, who giggles. Bound, Willow enthralls Anya into freeing her and drains Giles of coven-given power. She shoots a fireball after Xander and the others; Buffy outruns it. Willow casts Buffy and Dawn into a pit to fight demons – Dawn impresses Buffy. Willow tries to end the world and its sadness – Xander talks her down, aided by the good magic Willow was tricked into stealing from Giles. Spike gets his soul back.

BUFFY Season Seven

7.1 Lessons *written & directed by Joss Whedon*

A girl is killed in Istanbul. Giles teaches Willow control in England. Buffy trains Dawn who starts at the new Sunnydale High, rebuilt by Xander's firm. Buffy meets trendy black young principal Robin Wood. Dawn and friends fall into the basement and are attacked by zombies, as is Buffy, whom the zombies blame for their deaths. Xander smashes a talisman and the zombies disappear. Wood gives Buffy a counselling job. Buffy meets Spike, who is tormented by apparitions of past dead villains and of Buffy.

7.2 Beneath You *by Doug Petrie*

Xander rescues Nancy from a giant worm who ate her dog. It turns out to be her ex, whom Anya cursed – Anya removes the spell. Willow has a vision of doom. Spike has helped, and first Anya then Buffy, realize he has his soul and is tormented to near madness. A girl is killed in Germany.

7.3 Same Time, Same Place *by Jane Espenson*

Willow returns – she and the others miss each other at Sunnydale airport. A flayed corpse is found; Buffy and Xander suspect Willow. A skin-eating demon paralyzes Dawn and then Willow, whom the others cannot see, though luckily Anya can. Buffy kills him and his victims unfreeze. Willow's fear of meeting her friends has worked a subconscious spell. Buffy helps Willow heal.

7.4 Help *by Rebecca Rand Kirshner*

Cassie's precognitive powers indicate her imminent death; she asks Buffy for help; Buffy has Dawn befriend her and saves her from demon-worshipping fellow pupils, helped by Spike. Cassie drops dead anyway.

7.5   Selfless *by Drew Goddard*

When C8 Swedish peasant Aud turns her unfaithful lover Olaf into a troll, D'Hoffryn recruits her as the vengeance demon Anyanka, who causes the 1905 Russian Revolution. She sings of her love for Xander. When she summons a spider and kills twelve students, Buffy decides she must die, in spite of Xander's pleas. Willow summons D'Hoffryn and Anyanka pleads for the lives of the students. He sets the price of a vengeance demon's life and she accepts – he kills her friend Halfrek to punish her.

7.6   Him *by Drew Z. Greenberg*

First Dawn falls for a quarter-back and then Buffy, Willow and Anya. Spike and Xander remove and destroy his magic jacket before Buffy can assassinate Principal Wood, Dawn can kill herself for love or Willow turn him into a girl. Anya robs banks.

7.7   Conversations With Dead People *by Jane Espenson & Drew Goddard*

Buffy fights, is analyzed by and slays Webs, a former student at Sunnydale High, and a psychologist, now a vampire. Willow is visited by Cassie's ghost and told to give up magic and kill herself if she wants Tara. Dawn fights a demon and sees Joyce who warns her against Buffy. Spike kills and sires a woman – Webs mentions that Spike sired him. Jonathan and Andrew return to Sunnydale – Warren's ghost orders Andrew to kill Jonathan on a Seal in the school basement.

7.8   Sleeper *by Jane Espenson & David Fury*

Spike realizes he has been killing and siring vampires when attacked by one; he drifts in and out of his old viciousness triggered by a double who sings a folk tune. Buffy is nearly trapped by him in a cellar full of his progeny but defeats them and him. She takes him captive. Giles is in mortal danger.

7.9   Never Leave Me *by Drew Goddard*

Andrew's murder of Jonathan was a failed ritual; Warren sends him out for blood and he is captured by Willow. Buffy realizes that Spike sees things and is triggered by a song – Spike tries to kill Andrew who tells the Scoobies all he knows. The house is attacked by Harbingers, servants of the First Evil, and Spike is abducted. Other Harbingers destroy the Watcher's Council. Harbingers torture Spike whose blood opens the Seal for a primordial Ubervamp.

7.10   Bring on the Night *by Marti Noxon & Doug Petrie*
Giles arrives in Sunnydale with three Potential Slayers, of whom the oldest, Kennedy, makes a play for Willow. Spike is tortured, a lot. Buffy meets and is defeated by the Ubervamp which kills a Potential who runs away and then beats Buffy again. She summons the Scoobies and Potentials and makes an inspirational speech.

7.11   Showtime *by David Fury*
Dead Potential, Eve, is impersonated by the First which spreads despondency. Buffy allows the Harbingers and the Ubervamp to chase her and the others from the house and then demonstrates how to kill it as an object lesson. She rescues Spike from the First's lair.

7.12   Potential *by Rebecca Rand Kirshner*
A spell to identify Potentials seems to indicate Dawn, who is ambivalent. Actually it indicates Amanda, her schoolmate, who exhibits Slayer-like abilities when the two of them are attacked in the school. Xander consoles Dawn with the virtues of ordinariness.

7.13   The Killer Inside Me *by Drew Z. Greenberg*
Kennedy kisses Willow, who turns into Warren, at first visually but gradually more totally. She confronts Amy, who denies knowing anything – in fact she has cursed Willow from envy, wanting her guilt to incur an appropriate punishment. Kennedy cures her with a kiss. Buffy takes Spike to the Initiative ruins when his chip malfunctions and scientists offer to replace or repair it. Xander, Anya, Dawn and Andrew prove that Giles is corporeal and so not the First.

7.14   First Date *by Jane Espenson*
Buffy goes on a date with Wood, who reveals he is the son of a Slayer. Willow and Kennedy smooch. Xander dates a demon who tries to use his blood to open the Seal and raise a new Ubevamp – he is rescued by his friends. The First appears to Wood as his mother, the New York Slayer (5.7), and confirms that Spike killed her.

7.15 Get It Done *written & directed by Doug Petrie*

Wood gives Buffy his mother's bag, which contains a shadow caster which pulls Buffy into a place where Shadow Men, ur-Watchers, offer to infuse her with more of the demonic energy that powers Slayers. She refuses and they give her a vision of an Ubervamp horde. Spike kills the demon that came in Buffy's place and Willow reopens the portal for her.

7.16 Storyteller *by Jane Espenson*

Andrew films a video journal of life with the Slayer and Potentials, irritating everyone. Xander and Anya have sex to make their breakup concrete. Sunnydale High goes into meltdown – Buffy, Spike, Wood and Andrew fight their way in and Buffy threatens to use Andrew's blood to close the Seal – as she guessed, his tears of repentance work.

7.17 Lies My Parents Told Me *by Drew Goddard*

1970s – young Wood sees Spike fight his mother. Giles tries magically to clear Spike's mind of the First's trigger. Wood persuades Giles that Spike is too great a risk and Giles keeps Buffy busy. Wood triggers Spike, then beats him – Spike remembers. The trigger was his dying mother's song – newly vamped, he turned her and staked her when she rejected him. He beats Wood; Buffy is angry with Giles. Willow goes to LA. (A4.15)

7.18 Dirty Girls *by Drew Goddard*

Potential Shannon is rescued by Caleb from Bringers – he mocks and stabs her. Taken to hospital by Faith and Willow, returned from LA, she tells Buffy that Caleb has something of hers. Wood sacks Buffy. Faith and Spike bond flirtatiously. Buffy tracks a Bringer to a winery, where superstrong Caleb defeats Buffy, Spike and Faith, kills Potential Molly and blinds Xander's left eye.

7.19 Empty Places *by Drew Z Greenberg*

The populace of Sunnydale leaves; Caleb beats Buffy – he and the First are manipulating her. Faith takes the Potentials to the Bronze where they are attacked by possessed police; Buffy, misunderstanding, beats Faith. Faith and Wood bond. Buffy decides to go back to the winery en masse – everyone refuses and the Potentials reject her leadership in favour of Faith. Buffy leaves.

7.20 Touched *by Rebecca Rand Kirshner*

After wrangling, Faith takes charge. Using Kennedy as bait, they trap a Harbinger and magically force speech from it, locating the First's armory. Spike confronts them all and is angry about Buffy. He and Buffy spend a chaste night; Willow has sex with Kennedy, Faith with Wood. Buffy goes to the vineyard and defeats Caleb by never letting him touch her. The armory contains a bomb.

7.21   End of Days *by Doug Petrie & Jane Espenson*

Underground, Buffy finds a mystic axe, the Scythe. Faith is injured; the Potentials are trapped by Ubervamps; Buffy arrives in time to save them. Andrew and Anya nurse the wounded and discuss his likely death; they bond. Buffy sends Dawn away with Xander, but Dawn overpowers him. Willow and Giles send Buffy to a pagan burial site where she meets a Guardian, one of the women who preceded the Watchers, whom Caleb kills. Buffy fights and kills him with help from Angel – they kiss while Spike watches, taunted by the First.

7.22   Chosen *written & directed by Joss Whedon*

Caleb revives and Buffy halves him. Angel gives her Lilah's file and talisman. (A4.22) She sends Angel away – he is needed in LA – and gives the talisman to Spike; she is too young, she says, to make permanent choices. The First taunts her that she will die alone, giving Buffy an idea. She has Willow cast a spell giving all Potentials full Slayer power and marches her army into the Hellmouth, where they hold the Ubervamps until Spike's talisman becomes a lens for sunlight, burning him and all Ubervamps. Anya and Amanda die; Sunnydale collapses; Buffy escapes with the others. Her future is now open.

ΛΠGEL Season One

A1.1   City of *by Joss Whedon & David Greenwalt*

Angel is killing vampires in LA and is approached by Doyle, a half-demon gifted by the Powers That Be with visions accompanied by blinding headaches. Angel needs human contact if he is to redeem himself. His first attempt to save a starlet pursued by vampire Hollywood magnate Russell fails; he ends up saving Russell's next victim – Cordelia, who is struggling in LA and decides to come and work for him. He kills Russell, affronting Russell's lawyer, Lindsey McDonald of Wolfram and Hart (W&H).

A1.2   Lonely Heart *by David Fury*

The trio make the round of bars, handing out fliers for Angel Investigations and get mixed up in a series of eviscerations, for which Angel finds himself suspected by cop Kate. A worm-like demon that burrows into people is using singles bars to pick up new victims; it takes a barman, who abducts Kate. She and Angel escape and burn it.

A1.3   In the Dark *by Doug Petrie*

Following 4.3, Oz arrives to give Angel the Ring of Amara. Spike pursues attempting to get it back; he abducts Angel and has him tortured by paedophile vampire Marcus. Cordelia, Oz and Doyle swap the ring for Angel; Marcus double-crosses Spike and steals the ring. Angel catches and kills him, and then smashes the ring as dangerous and contrary to the spirit of his redemption.

A1.4   I Fall to Pieces *by David Greenwalt*

Doyle's visions send Angel to Melissa, who is being stalked by control-freak Dr Meltzer – he stops her withdrawing money from her account by changing her PIN. He also has the ability to separate parts of his body and control them from a distance – Angel poses as a client and Meltzer tries to kill him. He attacks Melissa in Angel's apartment, and Angel kills him.

A1.5   Rm W/a Vu *by Jane Espenson*

Cordelia cannot bear her roach-infested flat; Angel cannot bear her staying with him. He agrees to help Doyle with a demon debt-collector if Doyle finds Cordelia a flat. The apartment is perfect, except for vengeful ghost Mrs Pearson, who dislikes young women and tries to drive Cordelia to suicide. Cordelia fights back and drives her out, allowing the ghost of Dennis, Mrs Pearson's murdered son, to stay

A1.6 Sense and Sensitivity *by Tim Minear*

Angel helps Kate arrest gangster Little Tony, a W&H client who complains about his treatment. Kate and the rest are obliged to take sensitivity training, which is magically enhanced to a point where they cannot function. Kate breaks down at her father Trevor's retirement party and insults him. Angel visits the warlock sensitivity trainer, but is tricked by him. In spite of the effects of the spell, Angel stops Tony killing Kate.

A1.7 The Bachelor Party *by Tracey Stern*

At the point where Doyle first discovered his half-demon nature, he was married to Harry; he became irresponsible and their marriage broke up. Harry has become a demonologist and is about to marry Richard, one of a tribe of demons who are almost entirely assimilated except for the custom of eating the brains of the first husbands of women who marry them. Angel rescues Doyle and Harry is furious with Richard. Doyle has a vision of Buffy in danger.

A1.8 I Will Remember You *by David Greenwalt & Jennine Renshaw*

After the events of 4.8, Buffy arrives to tell Angel off for coming to Sunnydale and avoiding her. He is attacked by a demon assassin and gets its blood in a scratch. Suddenly he is human – he and Buffy make passionate love and have a day of bliss. He pursues the demon and realizes he is too weak to be a champion any more – Buffy kills it for him. Angel does a deal with the Oracles, servants of the Powers, that time turn back – only he will remember.

A1.9 Hero *by Howard Gordon & Tim Minear*

Doyle's secret crime is that he failed to protect other Brakken demons from the Scourge – demon racists who kill half-breeds. The Scourge are on the rampage after a tribe of Lister demons; the Listers think Angel may be their promised saviour. He infiltrates the Scourge and discovers that they plan to use a device which burns all humans and humanness. Doyle, after discovering Cordelia is prepared to consider dating him, and kissing her, sacrifices himself to save everyone.

A1.10 Parting Gifts *by David Fury & Jennine Renshaw*

Cordelia has inherited Doyle's visions and headaches; Angel is hired by Barney, a demon who is being hunted. Wesley turns up, hunting a demon who kills other demons for magical body parts. This proves to be Barney, who abducts Cordelia for her seer's eyes, which he auctions. Angel and Wesley save her; she kills Barney.

A1.11 Somnambulist *by Tim Minear*

Angel has disturbing dreams of killings – Kate realizes he fits the profile, as do Cordelia and Wesley. They tie him to his bed, but the killings continue. The killer is Penn, a vampire whom Angel sired – Angel and Kate track him together and kill him, but the knowledge that Angel is a vampire turns Kate against him.

A1.12 Expecting *by Howard Gordon & Jennine Renshaw*

Cordelia's new friends, party girls centred around Sarina, introduce her to Wilson with whom she spends the night. Next morning, she is hugely pregnant, as are all of Sarina's circle, with multiple non-human foetuses of whom she becomes very protective. Angel and Wesley track down the giant Hacksall demon who used Wilson as his surrogate, and freeze it with liquid nitrogen. Cordelia smashes it to bits.

A1.13 She *by David Greenwalt & Marti Noxon*

A security guard at an ice plant is burned hideously; Angel tracks a mysterious woman, Jhiera, who proves to be a renegade princess from a demon dimension where men rule by clipping the spines in which female individuality rests. She is running an escape route and does not care who gets hurt in the process. Angel helps her against her male enemies but warns her against killing in his city.

A1.14 I've Got You Under My Skin *by Jennine Renshaw*

Strange goings on in the Anderson family are caused by possession of the boy Ryan by an Ethros demon. Wesley and Angel persuade the family to let them exorcize the child – which ultimately works, but the demon escapes. Angel tracks it, only to learn that the demon, whom he kills, wanted rescuing from the psychopath child. Ryan tries to kill his family, but Angel rescues them.

A1.15 The Prodigal *by Tim Minear*

Flashbacks show us Angel's poor relationship with his father, to whom he was a disappointment; killing his family did not help. He discovers that Trevor is corrupt, working with demon drug dealers; Trevor's vampire partners kill him. Even though he helps her avenge Trevor's death, Kate's bitterness against Angel becomes intense.

A1.16 The Ring *by Howard Gordon*

Angel is hired to protect Darin's gambler brother Jack; in fact, both brothers run a secret gladiatorial arena in which demons fight to the death. They enslave Angel, who refuses to fight; W&H lawyer Lilah offers to buy his contract, but he refuses. Wesley and Cordelia free the slaves.

A1.17 Eternity *by Tracey Stern*

Angel saves TV star Raven from her stalker; she hires him as bodyguard, but it turns out the whole thing is a publicity stunt cooked up because she is ageing. She cultivates Cordelia and discovers Angel is a vampire; she drugs his drink hoping to seduce him into turning her. He becomes, or thinks he becomes, Angelus; Wesley and Cordelia manage to subdue him.

A1.18 Five by Five *by Jim Kouf*

Faith arrives in LA, hospitalizes a pimp and takes his apartment; she goes wild in LA's clubs, in one of which she is picked up by Lilah and hired by W&H to kill Angel. She taunts him repeatedly, and eventually kidnaps Wesley, whom she tortures; Angel confronts her and she collapses – she took the contract because she wants Angel to fight back and kill her.

A1.19 Sanctuary *by Tim Minear & Joss Whedon*

Angel starts to rehabilitate Faith, interrupted by a demon assassin and then by Buffy, furious that he is helping Faith. The Watcher's Council hitmen turn up, and try to persuade Wesley to help them; he guesses that they plan to kill Faith and Angel and double-crosses them. Buffy helps Faith escape. Angel is arrested for harbouring her; Faith gives herself up to save him.

A1.20 War Zone *by Garry Campbell*

Angel helps millionaire David Nabbit, blackmailed over visits to a demon brothel. He meets Gunn, leader of street-kid vampire hunters, who are disinclined to trust him; vampires kidnap and turn Gunn's sister, whom Gunn stakes. Angel warns the vampires to leave Gunn and his friends alone.

A1.21 Blind Date *by Jennine Renshaw*

Lindsey is defending blind Vanessa, a mystic assassin who traded sight for power; when Lindsey discovers that her next hits are children, he has an attack of conscience and approaches Angel. They steal files and a mysterious scroll from W&H, and Angel fights and kills Vanessa. Once the children are safe, Lindsey makes his peace with his boss, Holland, and accepts a promotion.

A1.22 To Shanshu in LA *by David Greenwalt*

The scroll Angel stole contains prophesies of his coming death. Holland raises a demon priest, Vocah, who kills the Oracles, drives Cordelia mad with visions, steals back the scroll and blows up Angel's apartment, injuring Wesley. Angel disrupts a ritual, killing Vocah and slicing off Lindsey's hand when he tries to burn the scroll. Cordelia is restored and Wesley realizes that the scroll prophesies Angel's return to humanity. Meanwhile, it turns out that Vocah summoned Darla back from hell as W&H's new agent.

ΛΠGEL Season Two

A2.1 Judgement *teleplay by David Greenwalt, story by Joss Whedon & David Greenwalt*

Angel and the others are fighting evil out of Cordelia's apartment, and getting cocky. Angel misinterprets a vision and kills a demon who was in fact protecting a pregnant woman, and she refuses to trust him. He goes to the Host's karaoke bar, Caritas, and (humiliatingly) sings so that the Host can help him find her and become her champion in a trial by ordeal. Meanwhile, Lilah, Lindsey and Darla plot his downfall; Angel visits Faith in jail.

A2.2 Are You Now or Have You Ever Been? *by Tim Minear*

In A2.1, Angel visited a derelict hotel, the Hyperion; he sets Cordelia and Wesley to investigating its bloody history – they discover he lived there in the 50s. (1950s Angel befriends thief Judy who is passing for white; threatened with lynching, she betrays him. Angel gifts the hotel's staff and residents to the Thesulac paranoia demon that caused this.) He kills the demon and frees the aged Judy before moving into the hotel.

A2.3 First Impressions *by Shawn Ryan*

Gunn interrogates Jameel about Deevak a, powerful demon; Cordelia has visions of him in danger. Angel is befogged with dreams of Darla; failing to get hold of him or Wesley, Cordelia takes Angel's car to Gunn, which gets stolen. Their search for it brings them into confrontation with Jameel, who is Deevak; Angel arrives in time to help. Cordelia realizes the real danger to Gunn is Gunn. Angel's dreams of Darla turn out to be real visits from her.

A2.4   Untouched *by Mere Smith, directed by Joss Whedon*

Angel tries to help Bethany, who has killed two muggers with telekinetic powers; she grows suspicious of Lilah, who befriended her in order to recruit her as an assassin for W&H and moves into the hotel. Lilah sends Bethany's sexually abusive father to see her, hoping she will kill him and turn to evil; under Angel's influence, Bethany settles for sending him away.

A2.5   Dear Boy *written & directed by David Greenwalt*

Staking out an adulteress (who claims to be abducted by aliens whenever she wants a date), Angel catches sight of Darla – but she is human. She frames him by having killed the actor who is posing as her husband; Wesley persuades Kate that Darla is who Angel says she is. Angel abducts and confronts Darla, who begs him to come back to her.

A2.6   Guise Will Be Guise *by Jane Espenson*

Distraught over Darla, Angel goes to see a swami recommended by the Host; he gets good advice even though the man he talks to is actually an assassin. Bryce forcibly hires Angel to protect his daughter Virginia – what he gets is Wesley posing as Angel; in fact Bryce plans to sacrifice Virginia to his demon patron. With help from the others, Wesley rescues her.

A2.7   Darla *written & directed by Tim Minear*

In a companion to 5.1, we see Darla's past – her turning by the Master, her abandonment of the Master for Angelus, her slaughter of the gypsies who cursed Angelus, his brief return to her and her unpreparedness to accept any compromise on pure evil. Tortured by humanity and guilt, she seduces Lindsey and is threatened with execution by Holland; Angel rescues her and she asks him to turn her again. He refuses.

A2.8   The Shroud of Rahmon *by Jim Kouf*

Wesley is giving a statement to the police…Angel and Gunn go undercover to prevent the heist by human and demon criminals of a demon's shroud; it has the power to send people mad and affects everyone involved. Angel has to bite Kate and fake her death to save her from a homicidal demon; worryingly he enjoys it. He destroys the shroud.

A2.9 The Trial *teleplay by Tim Minear & Doug Petrie, story by David Greenwalt*

Darla is dying of the syphilis that killed her in 1609; she is desperate to be turned and Angel finds her cruising low-rent vampires. He takes her to Caritas and the Host suggests an ordeal whereby Angel puts himself in jeopardy three times to buy her a second chance. He succeeds, but is told she already had it. She accepts mortality – and is then forcibly turned by Drusilla.

A2.10 Reunion *by Tim Minear & Shawn Ryan*

Angel is too late to stop Darla rising as a vampire; she and Drusilla bond and go on a rampage. Angel realizes they intend to attack Holland and other W&H lawyers, but when he gets there, lets the massacre happen. Rebuked by Wesley, he sacks his team.

A2.11 Redefinition *by Mere Smith*

Wesley, Cordelia and Gunn go to Caritas and find they can fight without Angel. Darla and Drusilla are trying to recruit an army; Angel trails and kills their recruits. Lindsey and Lilah, survivors of Darla's massacre, are put in charge of the Angel problem and told he must be corrupted, not killed. Angel ruthlessly sets fire to Darla and Drusilla, who marginally survive.

A2.12 Blood Money *by Shawn Ryan & Mere Smith*

Anne, formerly Chanterelle and Lily, runs a homeless shelter which W&H fund as a charitable write-off. Angel tells her the money is tainted; Lindsey and Lilah hire Boone, an old demon enemy of Angel's. Angel sneaks a video into a benefit – actually it shows Wesley and Cordelia having fun. Boone steals the money and Angel fights him for it. Wesley and Gunn kill a fire-breathing demon.

A2.13 Happy Anniversary *by David Greenwalt*

The Host comes to Angel – a man sang karaoke the night before and the Host saw the world ending. The man is brilliant physicist Gene who plans to stop time in his room before his girlfriend can leave him, and is being used by Lubber demons to end the world; Angel and the Host stop this. Meanwhile, Wesley solves a magic country house murder.

A2.14 The Thin Dead Line *by Shawn Ryan & Jim Kouf*

Wesley and Cordelia take on a small girl infected with a demon third eye. Anne's centre and Gunn's friends are threatened by violent cops; Wesley is shot by them and the centre besieged. Meanwhile, Angel discovers that these are zombie cops – Kate helps him get into the precinct station and smash the local captain's voodoo statue just in time to save everyone at the centre. He visits Wesley in hospital – Cordelia sends him away.

A2.15 Reprise (Part 1 of 2) *by Tim Minear*

W&H expect a review from a demonic Senior Partner; both Angel and Darla plan to disrupt this – Angel plans to travel to Hell and attack the Partners. Virginia breaks with Wesley; Kate is sacked as a result of complaints from the captain in A2.14 and takes an overdose; Cordelia is ambushed by third-eye demons. Told by Holland's ghost that W&H rely on the evil of humanity, Angel despairs and, when he finds Darla at the hotel, has sex with her.

A2.16 Epiphany (Part 2 of 2) *by Tim Minear*

Discovering he still has his soul, Angel taunts Darla and sends her away; she despairs and leaves Lindsey's apartment. Angel saves Kate, allowed to enter her flat uninvited by the Powers. He saves Wesley, Gunn and Cordelia from third-eye demons who plan to impregnate them, in spite of being delayed by a fight with Lindsey. He offers to work for Wesley.

A2.17 Disharmony *by David Fury*

Wesley makes Angel grovel, a bit. Vampires are abducting humans and turning them, as part of a vampire self-motivation cult. Harmony arrives in town; she and Cordelia pick up where they left off, in spite of Cordelia's misapprehension that Harmony's interest in her is lesbian rather than vampiric. To everyone's irritation, Harmony decides to fight on the side of good, then betrays them to the cult, whom they slaughter. Harmony leaves town.

A2.18 Dead End *by David Greenwalt*

The time has come for W&H to decide which of Lindsey and Lilah gets killed, which promoted. Lindsey is given a transplanted hand, which starts scrawling messages; he investigates, as does Angel. W&H punish former employees by using them as an organ bank. Lindsey and Angel free those who can be freed and mercy kill others; Lindsey mocks his superiors and Lilah, and leaves town.

A2.19 Belonging *by Shawn Ryan*

A beast comes through a portal from the Host's world, as does his cousin, Landok; we learn that the camp Host comes from a species of barbarian warriors. Cordelia has a vision of a librarian, Fred, who disappeared five years ago; she has never been found. One of Gunn's old team is killed by vampires and Gunn feels responsible. Together Landok, Angel and Wesley track the beast and kill it; Landok is wounded and has to be sent home, using the book Fred had in Cordelia's dream to open the portal. Cordelia is sucked through.

A2.20 Over the Rainbow *by Mere Smith*

Cordelia is enslaved by demons in a medieval world. Gunn joins Angel, Wesley and the Host on a rescue mission. Cordelia has a vision and finds herself tortured by priests. Angel is happy to discover he can bear sunlight in this world – he and the others are arrested and taken to the Princess, who proves to be Cordelia.

A2.21 Through the Looking Glass *written & directed by Tim Minear*

The priests are part of W&H; they plan to make Cordelia have sex with the handsome dumb half-human Groosalug, in order to steal her visions, and then kill her. Wesley and Gunn escape and join the rebels; the Host and Angel rescue Fred from execution by the Host's relatives. Angel changes into a hideous demon that Fred manages to control. Cordelia decides to start freeing slaves and the priests put her in her place by beheading the Host.

A2.22 There's No Place Like Plrtz Glrb *written & directed by David Greenwalt*

The Host is not dead – he just has to be re-united with his body, and Cordelia, the Groosalug and Landok deal with this. Wesley and Gunn persuade the rebels not to execute them, and become their leaders. Boss priest Seth plans to explode the collars on all slaves – Cordelia beheads him. Angel challenges the Groosalug, changes into the beast, but manages to hold back. Cordelia passes up true love, ruling the world and passing the visions to the Groosalug, for her duty. Fred's formulae get them home – to find Willow waiting with bad news.

ΛΠGEL Season Three

A3.1 Heartthrob *written & directed by David Greenwalt*

Brooding in Sri Lanka, Angel fights demon monks. (C18 Angelus and Darla escape Holtz with young vampire lovers James and Elizabeth.) Rescuing her victims, Angel kills Elizabeth. James has his heart removed for a few hours of invulnerability to avenge her. He assumes Cordelia is Angel's love. Angel kills him and realizes he is over Buffy's death. Darla is pregnant.

A3.2 That Vision Thing *by Jeffrey Bell*

Cordelia's visions cause her claw marks, blisters and burning and lead Angel to parts of an interdimensional key. Fred and Lorne work out the visions have been tapped – by Lilah, who orders Angel to use the key and rescue evil Billy from torture by demon Skip. Angel does this, kills Lilah's psychic and threatens her. Cordelia's burns etc. heal.

A3.3 That Old Gang of Mine *by Tim Minear*

Various demons, evil and harmless alike, are butchered; Gunn has suspicions. Cordelia persuades Fred to be read by Lorne at Caritas. They walk into a massacre of demons by Gunn's old gang, who take them hostage so they can kill Angel – Cordelia has a security spell that prevents violence by demons removed, and Angel defeats them. Wesley warns Gunn of divided loyalties; Angel says he trusts Gunn to kill him if ever necessary.

A3.4 Carpe Noctem *by Scott Murphy*

Investigating dead young men, Angel is bodyswitched, as they were, by an old man. Lilah defeats rival Gavin by giving Angel paperwork to frustrate his legal harrassment. In Angel's body, the old man makes love to Lilah, then bites her. Angel's gang work out what has happened and restore him to his body. He goes to meet Buffy.

A3.5 Fredless *by Mere Smith*

Cordelia and Wesley mock Angel's Buffy obsession. Angel beheads a demon. Fred is perturbed when her parents arrive looking for her – their presence makes her Pylaea experiences real. She agrees to leave with them, then returns realizing the gang are about to be attacked by demon bugs whose young are in the demon head. The gang needs her scientific knowledge.

A3.6 Billy *by David Greenwalt*

Angel trains Cordelia in swordplay; Fred sees them as destined lovers. Billy has the power to inflict his own misogyny on men he touches – Gavin beats up Lilah and Cordelia momentarily bonds with her. Wesley and Gunn are infected – Gunn has Fred knock him out, but Wesley hunts her through the hotel. Cordelia and Angel track Billy to an airfield – Lilah kills him. Wesley is distraught over what he did when infected.

A3.7 Offspring *by David Greenwalt*

(C18 Darla rescues Angel from Holtz and the Roman Inquisition.) A prophesy indicates the coming of something terrible. Darla confronts Angel, father of her impossible child; she bites Cordelia. Angel traps her in an arcade where she is hunting children – about to stake her, he realizes her child has a human heartbeat. Holtz awakens in C21.

A3.8 Quickening *by Jeffrey Bell*

(C18 Angelus and Darla outwit Holtz, killing his family – he is recruited by demon Sahjhan.) W&H have bugged the hotel and plan to kidnap and dissect Darla. Vampire cultists attack Angel, Darla and the others in a hospital where they are looking at the child with an ultrasound. Holtz and Sahjhan's demon hirelings butcher W&H's team and capture Angel. Darla goes into labour.

A3.9 Lullaby *written & directed by Tim Minear*

(C18 Angelus and Darla turn Holtz's daughter, whom he exposes to sunlight.) Angel escapes Holtz. Darla's contractions continue without a birth; she realizes her child is dying and that its soul has made her love it. They hide in Caritas and Holtz destroys it. Darla stakes herself so the child will live. Holtz lets Angel walk away with his son – his vengeance will be crueller.

A3.10 Dad *by David H. Goodman*

The Hyperion is besieged by vampires, demon cultists and W&H. Angel leaves the others behind in order to escape with his child. This is a ruse to draw his enemies away and kill them with a bomb – he knows the hotel is bugged. He threatens Linwood, Lilah's boss. Meanwhile, Holtz poisons Sahjhan's minions and recruits Justine, whose sister vampires killed.

A3.11 Birthday *by Mere Smith*

A vision knocks Cordelia out of her body; she is visited by Skip who tells her the visions are killing her. The Powers have provided the life she was meant to have. Cordelia takes the deal – but as a sitcom star, she knows something is missing. She tracks the girl from the vision she half-remembers and meets a one-armed Wesley, Gunn and Angel, driven mad by visions and loneliness. She kisses him, restoring reality. To keep the visions, she accepts partial demonhood.

A3.12 Provider *by Scott Murphy*

Angel, obsessed with money for Connor's upbringing, takes on too many cases.

Wesley and Gunn get caught up in a domestic between a woman and her zombie victim/lover; Angel is defrauded by a man seeking vengeance on vampires who killed his lover; Fred is nearly beheaded by demon bugs who want her intellect. Angel learns his lesson. Holtz tests Justine's commitment with torture.

A3.13 Waiting in the Wings *written & directed by Joss Whedon*
Angel takes the gang to see a ballet company he saw years earlier – the performance is exactly the same. Fred and Gunn hold hands. Backstage, Angel and Cordelia are possessed by doomed lovers, Wesley by the company's jealous impresario who has kept them imprisoned in their performances. The gang strains his magic by fighting magic servants and Angel frees the dancers. Angel has feelings for Cordelia, who is distracted from him by the return of the Groosalug.

A3.14 Couplet *by Tim Minear & Jeffrey Bell*
Cordelia is concerned that sex with the Groosalug will deprive her of her visions and has Angel procure a magic prophylactic from a demon brothel to prevent this. Angel is sexually jealous of the demon prince and impressed by his prowess. Gunn and Fred, now a couple, are trapped by a tree demon that attracts prey by e-mail, and rescued by Angel and Groo, who give each other credit. Angel sends Cordelia and Groo on holiday. Wesley uncovers a worrying prophesy.

A3.15 Loyalty *by Mere Smith*
Concerned that Angel will harm Connor, Wesley talks to Holtz and to a possessed hamburger statue. Lilah conspires with Sahjahn. Holtz and Justine put Gunn and Fred in danger to observe their fighting skills. Angel acts strangely and the hamburger's prophesies seem to be coming true in the shape of accidents at the Hyperion.

A3.16 Sleep Tight *by David Greenwalt*
Holtz persuades Wesley that he should kidnap Connor. Angel's progressively irrational behaviour is traced by Fred to the spiking of his pigs' blood with Connor's by Lilah. Justine hijacks Connor from Wesley, slashing his throat. A three-way stand-off between Lilah, Angel and Holtz is interrupted by Sahjahn who threatens to plunge Earth into Hell dimension Quor-toth if Connor is not killed. Holtz seizes the child and plunges into Quor-toth.

A3.17 Forgiving *by Jeffrey Bell*
Angel, mad with grief, kidnaps Linwood and forces Lilah to take him to W&H's

White Room, where a mysterious, evil Little Girl tells him how to make Sahjhan solid. Gunn and Fred are taken to Sahjhan's lair by Justine and attacked by him; Sahjhan indicates the prophesies were forgeries. He needed to kill Connor, who is destined to kill him. Justine traps him in an urn. Gunn and Fred find Wesley before he dies; Angel goes to his hospital room and tries to kill him.

A3.18 Double or Nothing *by David H. Goodman*

At 17, Gunn mortgaged his soul. His love for Fred worries demon gambler Jenoff, who owns the mortgage and he decides to collect. Fred and Cordelia sever ties with Wesley. Angel confronts Jenoff and tries to gamble his soul for Gunn's; faced with losing, he suggests that Jenoff's various debtors help kill him, which they do. Gunn mortgaged his soul for his gang's truck. Fred forgives him.

A3.19 The Price *by David Fury*

A client comes to the hotel and is infested by a slug-like creature, which desiccates him to death. The hotel is invaded by slugs, one of which enters Fred and talks of fleeing a Destroyer. They have been drawn by Angel's dark magic. Wesley tells Gunn how to free Fred. Cordelia glows and deinfests the hotel. A monster comes through a portal, followed by a teenage Connor.

A3.20 A New World *written by Jeffrey Bell, directed by Tim Minear*

Connor attacks Angel, who fights him off. Connor flees into sunlit LA; he rescues a girl from gangsters; she proves to be an addict who overdoses. Angel rescues him from the gangsters and the police. Meanwhile, Connor's portal is finally closed after rendering Cordelia unconscious. Connor meets up with an aged Holtz who has followed him. Lilah offers Wesley a job and taunts him about betrayal.

A3.21 Benediction *written & directed by Tim Minear*

Holtz suggests Connor needs to spend time with Angel. Cordelia has a vision of a woman in danger from vampires – this proves to be Justine, whom Lilah has set up as a test of Wesley. Will he watch her die, or help? He hesitates – Angel and Connor rescue her. At the Hyperion, Connor insults Lorne and threatens Cordy for being demons – she glows and cleans his psyche. Holtz and Angel meet; Holtz renounces his claim on Connor – then has Justine stab him twice in the neck.

A3.22 Tomorrow *written & directed by David Greenwalt*
Connor, believing Angel killed Holtz, gets Angel to teach him his fighting tricks. Cordelia is told by Groo, Angel by Lorne, that they love each other; they arrange a meeting. Linwood organizes a kidnapping of Connor, which fails. Lilah and Wesley taunt each other, and end up in bed. Connor turns up at Angel's meeting point, stuns him and drops him into the sea in a coffin; Cordelia is prevented from arriving by Skip, who tells her she is a Higher Being and must ascend to Heaven.

AΠGEL Season Four

A4.1 Deep Down *by Steven S. DeKnight*
Angel dreams beneath the sea. Connor has prevented Fred and Gunn finding leads. Wesley is having sex with Lilah, who does not know he has Justine prisoner. Lilah kills Linwood and takes his job. Helped by Justine, Wesley rescues Angel and delivers him to the Hyperion. Angel confronts Connor, discovers Connor's ignorance of Cordelia's fate and expels him. Cordelia is bored in Heaven.

A4.2 Ground State *by Mere Smith*
Catburglar Gwen shoots electricity from her fingers and cannot be touched. She is hired to steal the Axis of Pythia, an artefact Angel needs to find Cordelia. She clashes with Angel's team, killing and resurrecting Gunn; Angel follows her – their fight starts his heart. Her employer tries a double-cross. Angel saves her. She gives him the Axis; he finds Cordelia is in Heaven. 'Get me out of here,' Cordelia rages unheard.

A4.3 The House Always Wins *by David Fury*
In Las Vegas, Lorne is the prisoner of a casino boss who blackmails him into pointing out potential high flyers who are tricked into gambling and losing their destinies. Angel plays and loses; Gunn and Fred rescue Lorne but are captured again. From Heaven, Cordelia nudges the slot machine Angel listlessly plays so he wins, creating a paradox. Lorne smashes the magic and returns to LA with the gang. They find an amnesiac Cordelia.

A4.4 Slouching Towards Bethlehem *by Jeffrey Bell*
Cordelia distrusts these people who claim to know her and tell her nothing, especially when she learns of Angel's vampirism. Lorne reads her before she

flees with Connor, finding apocalyptic visions. Lilah tricks Wesley, planning, on her cellphone in his apartment, a raid on Connor's hideout which is a feint to cover a raid on the Hyperion and the theft of Lorne's visions.

A4.5 Supersymmetry *by Elizabeth Craft & Sarah Fain*

Fred has written a physics article; her old professor Seidel asks her to present it, but she is attacked by extradimensional beasts on the platform. She realizes Seidel was to blame for her disappearances and those of other bright students. She sends him to Hell with a ritual provided by Wesley; Gunn breaks Seidel's neck to spare Fred the guilt she wanted. Estrangement ensues. Cordelia asks Angel, 'Were we in love?'.

A4.6 Spin the Bottle *written & directed by Joss Whedon*

Lorne tells how he made the mistake of magically restoring Cordelia's memories. The spell goes wrong, regressing all present, including Wesley, to 17; they work out they have amnesia and are locked in with a demon and a vampire. Panicy strife ensues, especially when Connor interferes. Eventually Lorne persuades Fred to let him complete the spell. Angel asks Cordelia, 'Were we in love?' – she says yes.

A4.7 Apocalypse, Nowish *by Steven S. DeKnight*

Cordelia tells Angel she loves him, but his past makes their love impossible. She leaves with Connor and is attacked by the Beast, which rises on the site of Darla's death. Angel and the others track it to a magical massacre, where it easily beats them before raining fire on LA. It taunts Angel, who witnesses Cordelia's eve-of-destruction seduction of Connor.

A4.8 Habeas Corpses *by Jeffrey Bell*

Rejected by Cordelia, Connor goes to W&H. Wesley breaks with Lilah. The Beast kills everyone in W&H except Connor, and Lilah, whom it wounds. Wesley rescues her and she tells him Connor is still inside. Angel and the others rescue him, fighting off the zombies W&H's employees have become before witnessing the Beast's slaughter of the Little Girl in the White Room.

A4.9 Long Day's Journey *by Mere Smith*

Gwen's new client is slaughtered by the Beast; like the Little Girl, it belonged to a mystical order. In spite of Angel's attempts to protect them, the Beast kills the three others, the last in Gwen's locked panic room, guarded by Angel and

Cordelia. The Beast uses the order's body parts to build a device that extinguishes LA's sun. Cordelia has a vision of the Beast talking to Angelus in C18. Wesley decides they need Angelus.

A4.10 Awakening *by Steven S. DeKnight & David Fury*

Wesley finds a shaman who starts a de-souling ritual, but proves to be the Beast's assassin. He commits suicide, but his tattooed corpse reveals a lost weapon's whereabouts. Angel, Cordelia, Wesley and Connor find it and re-bond. Angel and Connor kill the Beast; Angel and Cordelia have sex. The shaman announces completion of the ritual and Angelus laughs sardonically.

A4.11 Soulless *by Elizabeth Craft & Sarah Fain*

Angelus destructively mocks each of the gang, making Gunn jealous. Promised free access to Cordelia, he reveals that the Beast was taken out of the world by priestesses. They are in LA, but dead. Cordelia double-crosses Angelus. Angel's soul has been stolen.

A4.12 Calvary *by Jeffrey Bell, Steven S. DeKnight & Mere Smith*

Lilah hides in the Hyperion, bringing with her books from other dimensions that confirm Angelus's intuition that the Beast is a minion. Cordelia produces a spell to re-ensoul Angel; this appears to work but he insists on staying in the cage until Cordelia persuades him otherwise. The Beast gives its master a knife made of its bones. Angelus reveals himself once free; the gang chase him, but he doubles back and pursues Lilah. Cordelia stabs her with the Beast's knife.

A4.13 Salvage *by David Fury*

Believing Lilah to be Angelus's victim, Wesley beheads her corpse. Cordelia is the Beast's master. He tells Faith that Angelus is loose and she busts out of jail. Angelus hears of this and arranges for the Beast to fight her. While the Beast is distracted, Angelus kills it with its knife – and the sun comes out. Faith uses this to escape.

A4.14 Release *by Elizabeth Craft, Steven De Knight & Sarah Fain*

Angelus is telepathically threatened by Cordelia with re-ensoulment. Faith and Wesley track Angelus – Wesley tortures a woman addicted to the magic drug Orpheus for Angelus's whereabouts. They fight Angelus and lose; Angelus promises to turn Faith and bites her.

A4.15 Orpheus *by Mere Smith*

Angelus collapses; Faith had taken an overdose of a magic drug. In a coma, she finds herself in Angelus's dreams as he visits Angel's arrival in the USA and the lapse – draining a murder victim- which made him a bum. Angel fights and defeats him. Fred has summoned Willow, who breaks the soul flask at a distance and re-ensouls Angel. She flirts with Fred and leaves with Faith. Foiled, Cordelia reveals her pregnancy.

A4.16 Players *by Jeffrey Bell, Elizabeth Craft & Sarah Fain*

Gwen borrows Gunn for the rescue of a small girl from a Japanese tycoon; this is actually a robbery in which he is to be her patsy. Together, they steal an experimental device which enables Gwen to control her electric power and be touched; they make love. Meanwhile, Lorne undergoes a ritual to restore his powers – this is a scam to trick Cordelia into revealing herself as the villain.

A4.17 Inside Out *written & directed by Steven S. DeKnight*

Connor rescues Cordelia and they hide in a warehouse; she demands a virgin sacrifice to bring on her child's birth. Angel confronts and abducts Skip, who reveals that the Angel Investigations team have been pawns in a plot, especially Cordelia, possessed by her child. Wesley kills Skip. Darla appeals to Connor to spare the girl; Angel arrives too late. Cordelia gives birth to a fully grown woman and Angel and Connor fall to their knees.

A4.18 Shiny Happy People *by Elizabeth Craft & Sarah Fain*

Everyone worships the woman when they meet her and she takes the name Jasmine, sending them on an anti-demon crusade. Jasmine is wounded by an assassin; Fred scrubs her bloody shirt and suddenly sees Jasmine as a rotting corpse. She attacks Jasmine and then flees.

A4.19 The Magic Bullet *written & directed by Jeffrey Bell*

Jasmine sends Fred's former friends after her; Fred eludes them, seeking refuge in a bookshop, whose proprietor betrays her, as she planned. She shoots Jasmine, ensuring the bullet with her blood on it, strikes Angel. Angel and Fred flee together, and raid the Hyperion, freeing their friends from the glamour with the blood of the comatose Cordelia. Connor betrays them.

A4.20 Sacrifice *by Ben Edlund*

They escape into the sewers where they meet street-kids hiding from the darkness and as yet uninfected. They meet a monster, an insect from a world where Jasmine was worshipped and which she abandoned. One of the kids escapes outside and is enthralled. Connor arrives and captures the others for execution as Angel uses the monster's portal to enter its world.

A4.21 Peace Out *by David Fury*

Angel climbs up to a temple where he conquers the priest who will utter Jasmine's true name with its last breath. The AI gang escape. Jasmine is about to broadcast to, and convert, the world when Angel appears and forces her true face on her, breaking her glamour. She threatens universal annihilation and Connor, angry over her abduction of Cordelia, strikes her down. At the Hyperion, Angel finds the AI gang aghast at the reappearance of Lilah.

A4.22 Home *written & directed by Tim Minear*

Lilah offers Angel the use of W&H's LA office. Lorne and Fred get everything they want; something uncanny happens to Gunn in the White Room; Wesley tries and fails to free undead Lilah from her contract. Angel holds out, until Connor threatens to blow up Cordelia, the hostages and himself. Angel removes him from reality – Connor is now a son in a happy family. Lilah gives Angel the Sunnydale file and a talisman.